Arthur T. (Arthur Tappan) Pierson

Many Infallible Proofs

A Series of Chapters on the Evidences of Christianity

Arthur T. (Arthur Tappan) Pierson

Many Infallible Proofs
A Series of Chapters on the Evidences of Christianity

ISBN/EAN: 9783337163686

Printed in Europe, USA, Canada, Australia, Japan

Cover: Foto ©Lupo / pixelio.de

More available books at **www.hansebooks.com**

MANY

INFALLIBLE PROOFS.

A SERIES OF CHAPTERS

ON

THE EVIDENCES OF CHRISTIANITY,

OR,

The Written and Living Word of God.

BY

ARTHUR T. PIERSON, D. D.

"The writing which is written in the King's name, and sealed with the King's ring, may no man reverse."—*Esther viii: 8.*

CHICAGO:
F. H. REVELL, 148 AND 150 MADISON STREET.
Publisher of Evangelical Literature.

To
CHARLES BUNCHER, ESQ.,
of Detroit, Mich.,
to whose
intelligent sympathy, unselfish friendship,
and appreciative hearing, much of
the inspiration of my best
efforts, both with
tongue and
pen are
due,
I most gratefully inscribe
this volume.

CONTENTS.

INTRODUCTORY.
CHAPTER I.
WEIGHING THE PROOF, - - - - - - - 9

PART I.
THE VOLUME OF THE BOOK.
CHAPTER II.
THE PROPHETIC SEAL, - - - - - - 29
CHAPTER III.
THE PROPHECY OF THE RUIN OF JERUSALEM, - - 48
CHAPTER IV.
MIRACLES; ARE THEY POSSIBLE AND PROBABLE? - 79
CHAPTER V.
THE WITNESS OF THE BIBLE TO ITSELF; ITS SCIENTIFIC ACCURACY, - - - - - - - - 109
CHAPTER VI.
THE SCIENTIFIC PROOF OF THE WORD OF GOD, - - 127
CHAPTER VII.
THE MORAL BEAUTY OF THE BIBLE, - - - - 145
CHAPTER VIII.
THE MORAL SUBLIMITY OF GOD'S WORD, - - - 163

PART II.
THE DIVINE PERSON.
CHAPTER IX.
CHRIST IN THE OLD TESTAMENT, - - - - 185
CHAPTER X.
THE PERSON OF CHRIST, - - - - - - 215
CHAPTER XI.
THE MYSTERY OF THE GOD-MAN, - - - - 234
CHAPTER XII.
CHRIST, THE TEACHER FROM GOD, - - - - 265
CHAPTER XIII.
THE ORIGINALITY OF CHRIST'S TEACHING, - - 283
CHAPTER XIV.
THE POWER OF CHRIST'S TEACHING, - - - 297

INTRODUCTORY.

A WORD PRELIMINARY.

THE writer of these pages once found himself getting into the deep darkness of doubt. Beginning at the foundation, he searched for himself, till he found the proofs ample, that the Bible is the Book of God, and Christ the Son of God. It was like finding one's way out of a dense wood into the full light of day. Others are still in the dark, and these chapters are the blazed trees that mark the path by which one man got out of the forest; perhaps some one else may try the same route, with a like result.

ARTHUR T. PIERSON.

PHILADELPHIA, Pa., November, 1885.

CHAPTER I.

WEIGHING THE PROOFS.

The importance of the study of the Evidences of Christianity, which establish the claim of the Religion of Christ, as the one and only Divine Religion, cannot well be overrated, or overstated.

All knowledge is good, desirable in itself and desirable for the sake of the power which it adds to character; but especially is knowledge necessary, when it helps either to create or to confirm our faith in the great truths of our holy religion. The teachings of the Bible are at once so peculiar and so important, that it is one of our first duties and privileges to attain a certainty of conviction as to the divine origin of the Holy Scriptures, and the divine character and mission of Jesus Christ.

Such certainty ought to be attainable. If any human ruler should address to his subjects the most ordinary proclamation, touching their duties as citizens, those subjects have a right to claim good plain proofs that whoever may have written or composed that proclamation, it is by the King's authority, and that he is its proper author. No subject should be satisfied unless the grand royal signature and seal are found upon the decree; otherwise it might prove the device of some traitor or enemy to mislead and betray subjects, and even to overturn lawful rule.

If therefore God has given to mankind a revelation of His will upon matters of the first moment, there can be no doubt that it is in some plain, unmistakable way marked by His hand: it has on its very face God's signature and seal: there are many infallible proofs to satisfy honest doubt.

We need not fear to take strong ground and it is especially necessary in these days. Principal Fairbairn, in his recent address before the Union Seminary, remarked that an entire change has become necessary in conducting the defence of Christianity, owing to the change of ground on the part of its enemies. The Deism of the last Century conceded much, in admitting the claims of natural religion. Now everything is denied, and everything must be proved. But allowing this to be so, everything true must be capable of proof. God could not ask of us anything which is not right and reasonable; and it would be neither reasonable nor right to ask us to take it for granted that the Bible is God's own Book, simply because it says so, or somebody says so, or even because any number of people honestly believe it. God himself gave us reasoning powers to weigh evidence with, and he means that we shall test truth and falsehood, proving all things and holding fast the good.

There is a kind of doubt that is entirely right, and of that sort is the doubt of one who does not believe what he has no reason to believe, and what he has no proof of, as true. The mind is endowed with powers of investigation, reflection, reason, that we may carefully examine into evidence and so decide what is true and what is false. He speaks to our reason, who gave us our reason. He appeals to it even in his own Word. He bids us be ready always to give an answer to every one that asketh us a reason for the hope that is in us. Such an answer implies knowledge.

God himself, then, asks of us no blind faith. We should know what we believe and why we believe it. Nothing is to be accepted unless based on good evidence; to believe hastily may be to blindly embrace error and untruth. Equally certain is it, inasmuch as God gives the Bible for the guidance of all men, that the proofs that this is his Word will neither be hard to find nor hard to see; they will be plain, like the signature and seal on the royal proclamation, to be found and understood by the common average man.

This is a day of doubt. Scepticism is more than ever widespread. It is in our books, in the conversation of our friends, in the very air that we breathe. It is finding its way quietly into the very churches of Christ. We must be on our guard.

I. These proofs, if they are candidly examined, will cure all honest doubt. Much scepticism is born of an evil heart of unbelief, that departs from God on account of a perverse and wicked will opposed to God. Such doubts no amount of evidence will remove unless the heart is changed; such doubters would not be persuaded though one rose from the dead.

But all honest doubt will yield before the proofs of a fact or a truth; and so there is no excuse for doubting, where we have the means of knowing. It is wrong to be willingly ignorant. Whatever doubts then do not spring from a wicked heart and unwillingness to be convinced, will disappear when the proofs are seen and examined.

There have been many candid doubters, but never one who had carefully studied the Evidences of Christianity. Mr. Hume confessed himself the prince of sceptics, as Voltaire was the prince of scoffers, and dark indeed were those depths of doubt into which his speculations plunged him. He said of those speculations: "They have so wrought upon me and heated my brain that I am ready to reject all belief and reasoning, and can look upon no opinion even as more probable or likely than another." And yet, though pretending to great diligence in the search after truth, and using all his fine powers and culture to destroy faith in the Gospel, he confessed, as Dr. Johnson tells us, that he had never read even the New Testament with attention.

Whenever an honest doubter comes to me, I feel perfectly safe in calmly saying, to his face, "you have never studied the evidences, and it is likely never attentively examined the Bible." And that arrow never misses its mark.

Some five years since, I was brought into contact with a man, who took pride in his sceptical opinions and made a boast of not being misled by the credulity of Christians. I ventured to take the old arrow out of my quiver. I said, "you have never thoroughly studied the Bible, sir." He turned my arrow aside, saying very positively, "you are mistaken there; for I have been familiar with the Bible from my boyhood." And yet within ten minutes he had shown that he did not know the difference between *Job* and *Lot*, but thought it was Job that lived in Sodom and dwelt with his two daughters in the cave!

If there is one candid doubter living who has faithfully studied the Bible and the Evidences of Christianity, he has not yet been found. Before this course of argument is concluded, your attention will be called to two prominent Englishmen who agreed to assault Christianity; but in order to conduct the assault the more successfully and skilfully, they agreed also first to examine it thoroughly; but when they began honestly to search the scriptures, they could no longer doubt that the Bible was the Word of God, and so Gilbert West and Lord Lyttleton became converts and defenders of that same faith they were about to attack.

II. A careful study of the evidences makes intelligent believers.

A faith not firmly founded upon good evidence deserves not the name of faith, for the basis of all true faith or trust is belief which is the assent of the mind, or understanding, to truth supported by adequate proofs. Some things we believe on the evidences of the senses; other things, on the testimony of others; and yet other things, on the evidence of reason; in each case there is, at the bottom of belief, some form of evidence or proof. To seek to make broader and firmer the basis of knowledge upon which our faith rests, is to show respect for our own power to know, and respect for the Creator who honored us by conferring such noble powers.

If He had intended us to be mere sponges to be put asoak by our parents or teachers in some sort of tub, full of their notions of truth and duty, till we should take up all we could hold, He would have made us into sponges. But He did mean that we should have some better reason for our faith and hope than the fact that our parents had just such before us, and so He made us independent, reasoning beings, who naturally ask why a thing is so, and whether what we have been taught, is true.

We must not even be content to believe blindly, for blind belief makes bigots, that hold fast to their way of thinking, whether wrong or right, and will not bear with any who differ. All persecutions come in part from blind belief, sometimes of error, and sometimes of truth. Hence, to believe blindly makes us liable to believe wrongly, and so to prolong the reign of error. How many honest Mohammedans would there be, if every Mussulman should first take pains to find out whether there be any good grounds for being a follower of the false prophet? How many honest Romanists, if every man and woman, brought up in the Romish communion, should take time and trouble to examine all those questions which have to do with doctrine and practice? Error is always afraid of the light. Hence, the people are forbidden to read books that expose the errors of these false or corrupt religions, and especially is it esteemed a crime to read the Bible. The consequence of searching the Scriptures would be the ruin of false faiths.

You call yourself a Protestant; do you know any good reason why? Are you such because you were brought up to be, and is that all the answer you have to give for your faith and hope?

Then I ao not see how you can be sure you are not as wrong and as mistaken as any Mohammedan or pagan or papist whom you condemn.

Intelligent belief makes firm faith. St. Peter says that the things of the Bible which are hard to be understood, are by the unlearned and the unstable wrested to their own destruction. Who are the unlearned and unstable? Those who are unlearned are apt to be unstable, for that believer who has no intelligent reason for his belief cannot be stable; he cannot be sure that he may not some day lose his faith altogether.

The sponge absorbs easily, but it also gives out as easily under a little pressure. So do the human sponges. They take up whatever doctrine they chance to be dipped in, and are liable at any time when put under pressure, to give that up and in turn take in something exactly different; and so you will find unstable souls, so uncertain and changeable that they believe for the time almost anything that others about them do.

One period of life, especially, tests any believer. I call it the period of *transition*. Every young person, especially if engaged in reading and study, comes to a time when the powers of reason are growing fast, and habits of independent thought begin to start inquiry. The growing mind asks a reason for things; and so important is this spirit of inquiry, that all discovery and invention, and all human improvements are largely due to it. Luther and the Great Reformation would never have been linked in history, but for his earnest determination to know, by independent search, what is truth?

Suppose, now, that in this transition state between the intuitive and the rational periods of our development, one is without a knowledge of the evidences of Christianity. He begins to say of one thing after another which he may have been taught, "that is not true! I cannot any longer believe it." He begins to untie from one stake, but has no other to tie to; and so drifts away from all fastenings into a general doubt, if not denial, of all truth. Faith suffers wreck.

III. Such intelligent and firm faith helps us to a better service; it gives the tongue of the learned and fits us to speak a word in season to him that is weary.

The deeper our conviction and the firmer our persuasion of truth, the more intensely shall we be in earnest, and it is this grand quality of earnestness that convinces and persuades others. In fact, the earnestness, born of clear, deep and unchangeable conviction, is the most moving, melting force this side of God. It is a fire, to burn; a hammer, to break; a sword, to pierce. It becomes a contagious enthusiasm which is the mysterious secret of eloquence. Others see and feel when you know you are right and true, and they begin to say, "I am afraid I am not right."

There is, therefore, intense meaning in our Lord's words: "Every scribe, instructed into the kingdom of heaven, is like unto a householder that bringeth forth out of his treasure things new and old." The knowledge of divine things, that comes by faithful study and instruction, becomes to its possessor a *treasure* out of which he brings for the instruction of others, things new and old; and a thorough mastery of the evidences of

Christianity will accumulate an inexhaustible fund of facts and arguments, with which one can not be at a loss, when meeting the inquirer or the doubter.

It is true that many an ignorant disciple has been both firm in faith and rich in service. But, even he has studied one kind of evidences, and it is his knowledge of them that makes him strong. The evidences he has mastered are those which are understood by *experience* rather than *argument*. God has made it possible for even the most unlearned to know that the Bible is His Word, by finding it the power of God to their salvation and sanctification. There are simpleminded believers who know nothing of the proofs from prophecy and miracle, who do know that God is faithful to his promises, and see the miracle of the new heart and changed life actually wrought in themselves. Christ is a living Saviour by that most infallible proof—what He has done and is doing for them. He opened their blind eyes to see their sin and need, and his beauty and love; he cleansed the leprosy of their guilt, cured the palsy of their helplessness, and the fever of their raging passion, and cast out the demon from their hearts. Jerry McAuley, at whose burial thousands lately gathered, had, in his own conversion, as great an evidence of Christianity as though Christ's word had raised him from the dead! What less than the power of God could in a moment recover such a man from a life conspicuous for every crime, and not only set him free from the chains of his vices, but make him an apostle of grace to rescue other perishing souls!

But, notwithstanding it is possible to know by personal experience the truth of the gospel by its power, is there any reason why the other departments of evidence should not be studied? Is it not important to satisfy others? and is it not the peculiar quality of experimental knowledge that it cannot be understood except by ourselves?

Some experience misleads, and is not a safe guide or test of truth, until it is itself tested by the word of God. Mr. Wesley, in his day, found many who claimed to have such experience of grace as to be raised above all danger, even of sin; but he says that not one in thirty of these perfectionists held out or retained the blessing they claimed to have.

We should understand both kinds of evidence, whether from argument or experiment. Needless ignorance is not right, on matters so important. Are our convictions so firm that we should not be glad to have them take deeper root? Can not a human body stand on two legs better than on one? Let us seek to establish our own faith like the very cedar of Lebanon, and so help to make others the firmer, by guiding the honest inquirer to the light of truth.

For the sake, then, of all who are desirous to know the truth, let us "write the vision and make it plain upon the tablets." For the sake of making the disciple stronger and abler to do good work for Christ, taking the wise in their own craftiness, meeting the objections of the sceptic, who, however wise in science, is ignorant of scripture and its august claims; for the sake of creating or establishing faith, it is of the first importance carefully and candidly to study the evidences of Christianity.

It is but a small part of the broad territory, however, over which we shall be able to tread, in this little volume. Prophecy and miracle confirm the Word; Science and Revelation are co-witnesses to the same God; astronomy hints His eternity, immensity, infinity; natural philosophy tells of His omniscience, omnipotence, omnipresence; physiology suggests His wisdom and goodness; the beginnings of life, of consciousness, of intelligence and of conscience, are miracles which cannot be accounted for without Almighty power, and ought to make both Atheism and Pantheism alike impossible; while the heart of man and the history of man unite to witness to a need and a craving never filled except by Christ Jesus.

Yet, while these firm persuasions root themselves in the very fibers of our being, in dealing with those who find candid doubts and difficulties in the way of faith, we must not take too much as granted. Without assuming much, it behoves us to begin at the beginning, and feel our way, step by step, guarding every statement with scrupulous exactness, and testing arguments and proofs with impartiality and candor.

The writer feels deep sympathy with honest doubt, in which is found one mark of earnest search after truth, and of which is born all reasonable and intelligent faith. He has no wish to tilt the lance in the field of theological controversy, or take part in any war of words, or advocate any sectarian views, however popular. The Christian religion sets up the most august claim, yet it invites and challenges the severest and most rigid test of proof. Let us accept the challenge and apply the test.

Argument should be conducted calmly. Enthusiasm sometimes betrays into rash conclusions. There is a white heat of earnestness, that comes not of sound logic, but of mere sensibility and emotional ardor and fervor. Persuasion differs from conviction. Appeals to feeling often warp the judgment; the eloquence of burning speech sways the will and sometimes swings it to the side of error and wrong. Conviction is wrought of calm, cool reasoning: it waits upon sound argument and rests upon logical conclusions: after dispassionate address to the reason has produced conviction, we may arouse the sensibilities and mould the will into resolve. But, at the outset, the doubter needs to be met as a doubter, with clear analysis, exact statement and convincing proofs.

On what principles then should we study the Evidences of Christianity?

First of all, in a truly impartial and scientific spirit. Science is knowledge; it deals with what is, or may be, known; compels a clear comprehension of truths or facts; has little to do with ingenious theories. Sometimes a shrewd guess at truth is like a lamp, let down into the darkness, to see whether it will show us what is in the depths; but still a guess is a guess—a theory, a theory. And, as much harm has been done to our Christian faith, by infidels who take things for granted, it is well not to weaken our position by assuming even what is true.

We need not only to think on religious questions with scientific exactness and accuracy, but even to make careful statements. Daniel Webster declared that not one man in fifty states a fact exactly, without exaggeration or diminution; and Burke said that every word in a sentence is one of the feet on which it walks, and to lengthen or shorten which may change its course.

Second, we need also concentration of attention: in other words, to do with the mind what we do with a burning glass, gather the rays and focalize them upon one point. Without such concentration, no acquisition of knowledge or even application of mind is possible. If a subject repays study at all, it rewards the most conscientious concentration of all our mental faculties.

Third, we need also discrimination, to learn to distinguish things which differ, but which may seem alike, such as facts and inferences, facts and theories. Dr. Hopkins says, that men who are "most reliable in observing facts are often least so in drawing inferences." You may depend on the fact, but distrust the conclusions. Antecedents and causes are not the same. Chill antecedes fever, but does not cause it; so of blossom and fruit. There is risk of forging artificial links. It is alike unscientific, to join what belong apart, and to part what belong together.

Fourth, it is absurd to demand the same sort of evidence in *Ethics* as in *Mathematics*. The nature of evidence is adapted to its object. Mathematical evidence concerns quantity; Moral evidence concerns the relations between intelligent beings. You can prove, mathematically, that two and two make four; can you prove, *mathematically*, that food builds up and fever kills, or that honesty is a virtue. There are many truths capable of moral demonstration, that defy the mathematical, yet are none the less truths.

Fifth, we should cultivate scientific impartiality, not coming to the study of truth with a bias of prejudice, or a preconceived theory, to hinder impartial investigation and conclusions.

Robertson says, that critics inform Shakespeare with their own notions, and then find in his writings the sentiments they have put there, as Munchausen's wolf ate into his horse, and, was driven homeward in the horse's skin. The Romanist comes to the Bible with a theory, and warps its testimony to fit the crook of his dogma.

Sixth, we should avoid "begging the question," and therefore beware lest we assume things to be true, which are false, or false, which are true. Strauss, knowing that Christianity is based on miracles, and especially the miracle of Christ's resurrection, begins by assuming miracles to be impossible; and says, that "whatever Christ did, or was, he can have done nothing superhuman or supernatural." Thus he starts by begging the whole question at issue. To allow such an assumption, to begin with, compels us of course to reject Christianity as a divine religion. Its very basis would be fraud or at best a blunder.

A prominent pulpit orator says: "The trouble with Ingersoll, is this: he has selected the excrescences of human life, as it has grown in churches, and has represented the excrescences as the essence of religion. Suppose a physician, wishing to get up a museum, representing the human body in all ages and conditions, should collect idiots and lunatics, with wens and warts all over them. Suppose that the physician should gather them into a museum, and say: "There's humanity for you; what do you think of that?" That is what Ingersoll is doing in the religious world. He says scores of true things, that have been said before, but he doesn't know it. He is not widely read in theology. I'm afraid he doesn't read his Bible very much. What does he read it for? I'll tell you. The doves, flying over the landscape, see all that is sweet and peaceful, but when the buzzard and the vulture fly abroad, the first thing they see is a loathsome carcass, and, if it is anywhere in sight, they don't fail to see it. Ingersoll *sees what he is looking after.* He is a turkey buzzard!"

Seventh, much depends upon our mental and moral attitude, whether we are willing to be convinced, or deliberately take a position of hostility. Are we disposed to find harmony, or disagreement, between the Bible and universal truth? And if there be apparent discord, are we willing to wait patiently, until, as in stereoscopic pictures, we find the common focus, which brings harmony and unity?

Goethe says: "Whoever reproaches an author with obscurity, should first examine himself, to know if all is *clear within.* In the twilight a very plain writing is illegible."

Eighth, ridicule is not argument, and leads to no safe conclusion. It is easy to appear to overthrow truth by ridicule. Voltaire has been compared to a school-boy, exciting laughter by pencilling a moustache on some fine antique statuary. and Ingersoll sets up a man of straw, and then pelts it with ridicule; and unthinking people mistake the man of straw for a real image of the religion of Christ, and ridicule for argument. You might as well try to put out the stars with a watering-pot, or cannonade Gibraltar with pop guns and putty!

Ninth, perspicuity, both of thought and speech, is very needful. Obscurity may mislead even an honest man. To get hold of an idea clearly, and then put it in the plainest, fewest words, is a great triumph of brain and tongue. Some writers, as Whately says in his introduction to Bacon's essays, seem to think that it is a sign of a master mind, when thought glooms faintly out, like stars through a bank of fog. It is always possible, if one has a thought worth anything, to put it in plain words; and why not in good, homely Anglo-Saxon?

At the twentieth anniversary of the installation of Rev. Dr. Crosby, Rev. Dr. John Hall said happily: "A minister ought to be a student of the Bible, in the original languages in which it was written; but, he should be careful to preach in English, which his congregation can readily understand."

It is a sad fact that, so far as making themselves understood is concerned, some writers and speakers might as well be using an unknown tongue; they are, as Paul says, but as a barbarian to the hearer. It is very foolish to infer, when you cannot understand a man, that he is too wise and learned to be understood. Wisdom and learning are just what help a man to be understood.

Tenth, It is safe to distrust any argument that insults common sense. What is called "metaphysics" is often only a beclouding of a hearer's mind by subtleties that are meant to confuse and bewilder. A certain case at law turned on the resemblance between two car wheels, and Webster and Choate were the opposing counsel. To a common eye, the wheels looked as if made from the same model, but Choate, by a train of hair-splitting reasoning, and a profound discourse on the "fixation of points," tried to overwhelm the jury with metaphysics, and compel them to conclude, against the evidence of their eyes, that there was really hardly a shadow of essential resemblance. Webster rose to reply: "But, gentlemen of the jury," said he, as he opened wide his great black eyes, and stared at the big twin wheels before him, "there they are—look at 'em!" And as he thundered out these words, it was as though one of Jupiter's bolts had struck the earth. That one sentence and look shattered Choate's subtle argument to atoms, and the cunning sophistry, on the "fixation of points," dissolved as into air. I have great confidence in the strong common sense of an honest mind, feeling the utter worthlessness of an argument, even when unable to tell the reason why.

A christian physician, in a recent address before a class graduating from a medical college, remarked: "Doubtless some of you remember reading, that it was the contemplation of a statue of an illustrious member of our profession which led Coleridge to this strong utterance, as to the simian origin of the race: 'Look at that head of Cline, by Chantrey. Is that forehead, that nose, those temples, and that chin, akin to the monkey tribe? No, no! To a man of sensibility, no argument could disprove the bestial theory, so convincingly, as a quiet contemplation of that fine bust!'"

These are some of the principles upon which we purpose to examine, at least in outline, a few of the "many infallible proofs," that the Bible is the Word of God, and that Jesus Christ is the Son of God. And, if no one shall find any new light, the serene consciousness will, at least, be ours, that we have tried to help doubting souls.

PART I.

THE VOLUME OF THE BOOK.

CHAPTER II.

THE PROPHETIC SEAL.

Prophecy came not in old time by the will of man: but holy men of God spake *as they were* moved by the Holy Ghost. 11 Peter i: 21.

What grounds are there for holding the Christian religion to be of divine origin and supreme obligation? This is the question, around which all else clusters. The Bible is but the great *Book*, and Christ, the great *Person*, of the Christian religion.

Christian Evidences have, for convenience, been divided into "External" and "Internal." The *Internal* include the character of Christ himself and of the doctrine and morality taught by christianity, its adaptation to human wants, the unity and consistency of the Bible, and the marks of truth, purity and sincerity in its various writers. The *External*, or historical proofs, are such as are found in man's need of a revelation from God, and the corresponding presumption in its favor as a fact; the authenticity and credibility of scripture history, the argument from prophecy and miracle as sealing and sanctioning such revelation; the historical argument from the spread of the gospel in the face of opposition, and from the positive blessings it has conferred upon the individual and upon society. From these we shall select a few of the more prominent forms of proof, which best suit our present purpose, and the narrow space we have at disposal in a small volume.

Our examination naturally and properly starts with the External proofs, for Internal evidence largely concerns one's own experience, and cannot be appreciated, or in fact apprehended, without experiment. But, in order that one may be disposed to "taste and see," he must approach the subject from without. If the Gospel of Christ is God's golden milestone, let me from outside by some rational road find my way to it; then I can stand at the milestone itself and from that, as an inside point, take my survey.

If it can be shown that, starting from any proper point, "All roads lead to Rome,"—that the external evidences all converge in the gospel; that, for certain great facts and effects, no adequate cause can be found, except that God has authoritatively spoken to man in the Bible and through Christ Jesus; then how can we honestly evade or avoid the conclusion that Christianity is the divine religion and entitled to our homage and obedience?

Among these external evidences two are especially prominent: prophecy and miracle. Prophecy is a miracle of utterance. It prepares the way for coming events or persons, and attests them, in advance, as forming part of a divine plan, reaching through the ages. Prophecy and Providence are, therefore. twin sisters. There is no grander thought in this Bible than that, back of all these apparantly capricious, conflicting and accidental changes of human history, there is an infinite God, whose omniscience and omnipresence forbid that anything should escape his knowledge or evade his power, and whose goodness assures a benevolent design, even behind seeming disaster. How often do we look at human history and behold only one awful tragedy!

"Right forever on the scaffold, wrong forever on the throne!
Yet that scaffold sways the future, and behind the dim unknown,
Standeth God amid the shadows, keeping watch above his own."

Prophecy, unmistakably outlining events beforehand, shows that God is behind the curtain, and that his hand controls and shapes the history and destiny of men. The caprice is resolved into a consistent purpose; the conflict is only the apparent discord and disorder which are owing to our partial point of view; the accident becomes an incident in one grand, harmonious plan, where no chance can occur. We have a Providence, with its prevision and provision and presidence, directing and arranging, permitting and decreeing.

But prophecy does more than assure us of a Providence. It serves to outline the future, so that we have glimpses of coming glory and triumph for God and godliness. It brings the past and future into inseparable union with the present and spreads the grand scene before us in its unity. We are thus permitted to foretaste the future: the ancient Hebrew, by the glass of Messianic prophecy, beheld the Lamb of God taking away the sin of the world, and so the cross of Christ was borne backward through the ages, and the atonement was a present and accomplished fact to Abraham and David; and to us, to-day, the prophecies of the New Testament are the perspective glasses that bring nigh the

Delectable Mountains of a completed redemption, and make visible the towers of the celestial city!

Nothing therefore can be of more importance to a Bible student than a mastery of the prophetic Scriptures. Prophecies, already fulfilled, put the clear broad seal of God upon the Bible; prophecies unfulfilled, serve to inform our faith as to coming developments, and project us forward into the consummate wonders of the final day of victory.

Why does so much weight attach to the argument from prophecy? Christian evidence is like the holy city, which John saw, four sided, with gates opening toward every quarter: why then go in by one gate rather than others? We reply, there are indeed a score of paths by which the advocates of the inspiration of Scripture approach the heart of the theme; but the Scripture itself makes this the grand highway of proof. Hear the apostle Peter: "We have also a more sure word of prophecy, whereunto ye do well that ye take heed as unto a light that shineth in a dark place, until the day-dawn and the day star arise in your hearts; knowing this first, that no prophecy of the Scripture is of any private interpretation (invention or suggestion); for the prophecy came not in old time by the will of man, but holy men of God spake, moved by the Holy Ghost."

The Scriptures affirm that "the natural man receiveth not the things of the Spirit of God, neither can he know them because they are spiritually discerned." There are some sources of proof, whose force can be felt only by a converted man. But here is an evidence which needs for its examination only the reason of the natural man. He is in the darkness of doubt; he has not yet found, by faith, the personal and inward knowledge of God. Here is the very light which God gives him, to lead him to the rational conclusion that the Bible is the Word of God, and so prepare him for the higher guidance of faith. Accepting the will of God and the way of salvation, as here revealed, he is led up to those blessed mountain tops where the day star shines and the day dawn breaks in a flood of glory.

The Bible presents as foremost the proof from prophecy. Other arguments imply that we have examined this—other proofs branch out from this or fork from it; here is the foundation on which other arguments rest. If the Scriptures issue from the hand or mind of God, the seeker after truth asks for his royal signature and seal. And prophecy claims to be exactly this: the solemn seal of God's own hand upon the sacred scroll.*

This, then, is the mode chosen by God to make plain to man the fact that He has spoken. He says to loyal subjects in His great empire, "By this unfailing sign shall you know that a proclamation of my will is from my hand: through my chosen messengers, I will shew you things to come." And this may well be the gateway and highway to conviction, since it is so broad and straight and plain that none need err. Men have an instinctive conviction that when a future event is clearly and closely foretold, so that no guess, however shrewd, can account for it, and the event

---

* The appeal of God to fulfilled prophecy is found all through the Bible. Deut. xviii:21, 22; Isaiah xli:21 to 23; Jeremiah xxviii:9; 2 Peter i:19 to 21.

corresponds in every respect to the prophetic outline, it is a proof of the working of some power above nature. How natural that God should select this intuitive sense as the basis of his appeal! that he should say to men, "when I speak through a fellow-man, he shall speak words, or do works, plainly beyond the unaided natural power of man." Hence came both prophecy and miracle as the double witness to our holy religion. These two are closely akin. Prophecy is a miracle of utterance. Miracle is prophecy in action. Both imply supernatural power: one in words, the other in works; and hence both carry the sanction of God.

To establish one prophecy is to carry the whole fortress of the enemy by storm, for it settles the inspiration of the Word of God. To establish one prophecy of Christ is to settle not only his authority as a teacher, but his divinity, for it puts God's seal and sanction on Christ's witness concerning himself. Mark his own appeal to his prophecies: John xiv:29, "And now I have told you before it come to pass that when it is come to pass ye might believe."

The argument from prophecy must be a formidable one, since the foes of our faith have directed their biggest guns against it. Porphyry found such very startling correspondences between Daniel's predictions and historic events, that he saw no escape from conviction but in denying the authenticity of the prophecy, arguing that it was never written till events supplied the material. Paine did not venture to deny the authenticity of the prophecy, but simply denied that in any proper sense it was fulfilled. Between these two scoffers, however, we have both the authenticity and the fulfillment of prophecy admitted.

The death of the Lord Jesus Christ was so distinctly foretold in the fifty-third chapter of Isaiah, that Bolingbroke, in order to break the force of the argument from this prophecy, was forced to assert that Jesus brought on his own crucifixion by a series of preconcerted measures, merely to give the disciples who came after him the triumph of an appeal to the old prophecies! You see how grand must be the power of an argument, which compels infidels to invent such impossible theories to evade the force of its mighty appeal!

What is a prophecy? The primary idea of a prophet is not one who foretells, but one who "brings to light" or "makes manifest." A man might be a prophet, while yet not foretelling any future event. Elisha was simply an inspired teacher, unfolding the hidden things of God. The idea of foretelling is secondary: first, insight; second, foresight. Very naturally God, in giving to a man insight into His secret mysteries, might grant insight into that future which has to do with these mysteries; and such insight is foresight. Oftentimes a true insight into the present, implies a foresight of the future as the key to present problems.

Foresight was frequently granted to prophets, in order to furnish additional evidence of their divine mission and commission. But the prime element in the prophet is capacity to teach spiritual truth. This discrimination is important, for first, it leads us to look for evidence of the prophetic office and authority in the very nature of the truths he proclaims and teaches. In the character of his message is often higher proof of his divine calling than in miracle or prediction. This was preeminently true of Christ, the greatest of prophets. Secondly, this conception of the true criterion of a prophet will lead to rejection of any whose teachings are plainly unsound and unscriptural, even though he might work apparent wonders or predict future events. The Bible teaches us to find prophetic credentials, first of all, in this conformity of his moral and spiritual teaching to a divine pattern. There must be correspondence between his utterances and the Word of God and the moral sense of mankind. (Deut. xiii:3.)

In this law which demands, for prophetic character and utterance, consonance with the claim to inspiration, we find a grand factor in our argument. God asks that His word be held to be inspired, not only because prophetic writers have wrought miracles or spoken predictions, but because they spake as men would speak who were moved by the Holy Ghost. Their teachings present such conceptions of God and man and their mutual relations as accord with the intuitive convictions of man's moral being; the seal of God is upon the very quality of their utterances.

We are prepared to follow the logic of this position, and affirm that the prophetic office is essentially perpetual. It may not be needful that miracles be wrought or predictions spoken; but he is a true successor in the prophetic office who speaks according to the revealed word, and whose utterance God seals and sanctions by the power of the Holy Ghost.

For brevity's sake we confine our argument to that aspect of prophecy which concerns the future, and shall show how grand a confirmation of the claims of the word of God is found in the obvious foretelling of events. But first let us clearly understand that it is not commonly the object of prophetic prediction to inform us as to the details of the future; but rather, after an event is fulfilled, to shew that it all lay in the mind of God, and was part of his eternal plan.*

This may explain the necessary obscurity of prophecy. It presents a lock, for which only subsequent history can supply the key. If prophetic details were clearly announced, wicked men would be prompted, like Julian, to conspire to defeat the prediction; or disciples might be supposed to combine to bring about a seeming fulfilment, in order to authenticate the prophecy. When prophecy is fulfilled, it must be by no design of men—better still, if against their design, that it may be the more apparent that the fulfilment is wholly of God. For obviously, if fulfilled by intent of man, it might be resolved into a sort of mere collusion between prophet and those who, jealous for the reputation of the divine oracles, sought to bring about a correspondence with events. The general purpose of prophecy, then, concerns not the times in which it is spoken, since it is yet unverified; but, when fulfilled, it proves the God of prophecy and of Providence to be one. It shews us *Deus in Historia*, a divine administration in the world; and seals, as inspired and infallible, the teaching so attested.

---
* John ii:20-22, xii:16, xiv:29, xvi:4, xx:31; Luke xxiv:6-8, xviii:34.

A prophecy is not confirmed as a proof of revelation until fulfilled; and then it evidences God's hand, in proportion to the extent and accuracy of its predictions. A prophecy thus unlocked by events, opens a door that no man can shut, introducing us by a miracle of utterance to the very presence of Him to whom all the future is as the present, and compelling us to bow reverently to hear what He will speak.

What now are the canons by which a true prophecy is to be tested?

First, it must be such an unveiling of the future that no mere human foresight or wisdom or sagacity could have guessed it. Human beings sometimes exhibit remarkable foresight and forecast, where no supernatural element exists. A statesman might detect elements of corruption which lead him to predict the overthrow of some nation within a given time. Comparison of the records of a series of years enables a weather prophet to foretell storms. and even the comparative healthfulness of seasons. But back of this there lies simply an induction from facts and principles.

Secondly, the prediction must deal in details, sufficiently to exclude shrewd guesswork. General statements may be made with often a remarkable forecast of events; but every definite, specific detail or description adds to the improbability of its being an uninspired utterance, until the improbability becomes impossibility.

Thirdly, there must be such lapse of time, between prophecy and fulfilment, as precludes the agency of the prophet himself in effecting or affecting the result. Otherwise the author of the prediction might by secret, subtle means, bring about apparent accomplishment.

When prophecy is by such marks attested as genuine, its value as evidence is beyond words; and the argument it furnishes is one of growing force. The Christian faith supports its claim by a vast number of prophecies pertaining to different periods and persons. The argument from these prophecies began to be of use when the first prediction was fulfilled; and every successive event, which added a new feature to the profile, added strength and weight to the argument. Prophecy is thus at first a rill, receiving constantly tributary streams, till it grows to a river whose grand flood of evidence sweeps everything before it.

All through old testament times, the thousand hints of prophecy were fulfilling. Then Christ was born, and the most numerous and striking of all predictions met and mingled in Him, so that the apostles could boldly say, in support of the august claims of the gospel whose central figure he was: "To Him give all the prophets witness." No miracle, which he wrought, so unmistakably set on him the seal of God, as the convergence of the thousand lines of prophecy in him, as in one burning focal point of dazzling glory. Every sacrifice lit, from Abel's altar until the last passover of the passion week, pointed as with flaming fingers to Calvary's cross! Nay all the centuries moved as in solemn procession to lay their tributes upon Golgotha.

But that age of grand fulfilments was also the age of grander prophecies. And so the evidence goes on accumulating; the fulfilment of words, long since spoken, confronts us to-day. The histories of Assyrian lion, Medo-Persian bear, Greek leopard, and Roman complex "beast;" the existing facts of Tyre, Babylon, Egypt, Nineveh; the remarkable dispersion of the Jews, the most clannish of peoples, most attached to their own land, rich enough to buy every acre of Palestine with pearls, yet providentially kept out of it till the times of the Gentiles are fulfilled—all these, and a hundred fold more, furnish a colossal argument for the divine origin of the prophetic scriptures; and yet the power and weight of this argument are growing still. Miracles impressed the people who lived in the age of miracles, with a power which is comparatively lost on us by the distance of time. However conclusive the argument from miracles, it cannot impress us as it did those who witnessed the works. But the prophecies, fulfilled and fulfilling before our eyes, become a new miracle, more conclusive and impressive every year, and adapted to prove omsiscience as unmistakably as the miracles of two thousand years ago proved omnipotence. Scripture is seen by us as a colossal wheel, compassing all history with its gigantic and awful rim, and full of the eyes that tell of one who sees all things! You see the falsehood of the cavil which sneers at Christian faith, as resting on no better basis than the myths and marvels of eighteen hundred years ago. We have before our very eyes some of the most awe-inspiring proofs of our holy religion. Disciples, who saw his miracles and had evidence of the senses, left us their witness to Christ. But, of many prophecies, they had only the record, while we have the evidence of our very senses to their fulfil-

THE PROPHETIC SEAL. 41

ment. Some unbelievers say, "could we see a miracle we would believe." But he who can see prophecy fulfilled and not believe, is not to be persuaded by any other miracle. "If they hear not Moses and the prophets neither would they be persuaded though one rose from the dead."

The Christian religion is the only religion that has ever dared to rest its claim upon either miracle or prophecy, The appeal to such supernatural signs is so bold, that its audacity is one proof of its genuineness. The Old Testament, which even the most captious historical criticism concedes to have been in the hands of Jews at least 200 years B. C., draws a clear, minute and striking picture of future events, and calmly stakes, upon the result, all its claims to a divine origin. It challenges history, archæology, science, all the forms of human knowledge, to show one instance in which prediction has failed. This is divine boldness of appeal. There are false faiths, like Mohammedanism and Buddhism, that have tried to prop up their claims on pretended miracles, but even these have never ventured to frame prophecies.

Pagan religions claimed support from oracular responses, but what a vast gulf divides them from the oracles of God! They were trivial in import and purport, not worthy to be the responses of a divine being. The ends they served were often personal and selfish. The influence which secured them was unfit to move a god; it was sometimes greed of gain, or even servile fear, to which the appeal was made. They spoke because the voice of authority compelled, or the offer of gold persuaded. No poor or obscure man could arouse the sluggish divinity. The utterances of heathen oracles were never spontaneous, as though inspired by a divine fulness of matter, but were always reluctant, difficult to secure, rare and costly. When demanded, delay was required for preparation; and when the response was not verified, a thousand apologies were framed for the failure; there was on the part of the inquirer some omission or blunder; there was some mistake in the amanuensis who took down the response; or perhaps the Gods were not disposed to answer. And when the best responses were obtained they were ambiguous and equivocal. The most famous oracles were so disgraced by love of money that they became venal. The rich or powerful seldom found difficulty in obtaining favorable responses. Philip of Macedon by royal influence and gold thus bribed the oracle; and Demosthenes said, the Pythian goddess "Philipised."

A few examples may be given of the adroit ambiguity of the heathen oracles which justified Milton's famous line:

"Ambiguous, and with double sense deluding."

Before Maxentius left Rome to meet Constantine in that famous battle on the banks of the Tiber, he consulted the Sibylline books. "The guardians of these ancient oracles were as well versed in the arts of this world as they were ignorant of the secrets of fate; and they returned him a very prudent answer, which might adapt itself to the event, and secure their reputation, whatever should be the chance of arms:"

"*Illo die, hostem Romanorum esse periturum.*"
"On that day the enemy of Rome will perish."

Whoever proved the vanquished prince became of course the enemy of Rome. The defeat of Maxentius was overwhelming; he himself, attempting to escape back into the city over the Milvian bridge, was forced by the crowd into the river and drowned by the weight of his own armor.

The general characteristics of oracles were ambiguity, obscurity and convertibility, so that one answer would agree with several various and sometimes directly opposite events. To Pyrrhus:

"*Aio, te. Æacido, Romanos vincere posse.*"
"I declare thee, O Pyrrhus, the Romans to be able to conquer."

Herodotus tells us that Crœsus, the sovereign of Lydia, consulted the Delphic oracle as to whether he should proceed against the Persians; and this was the reply, as Cicero renders it:

"*Crœsus, Halym penetrans, magnam pervertet opum vim.*"
"By crossing Halys, Crœsus will destroy a mighty power."

He thought of course the kingdom would be that of Cyrus; it proved to be his own. A third time he consulted the oracle—anxious to be informed whether his power would ever suffer diminution. The Pythian answered:

"When o'er the Medes *a mule* shall sit on high,
O'er pebbly Hermus then soft Lydian fly!
Fly with all haste: for safety scorn thy fame,
Nor scruple to deserve a coward's name."

The catch was here: this "mule" was Cyrus, whose mixed parentage had caused this opprobrious epithet to be applied to him.

Compare Shakespeare—the witch's prophecy:
"The duke yet lives that Henry shall depose."

These were mere tricks—like the veritable sign, unpunctuated, over a barber's shop in London:
"What do you think
I'll shave for a penny and give you a drink"

Read as an exclamation, it encouraged applicants for a service that would cost nothing and pay them with a dram beside. But when such gratuitous service was applied for, the shrewd barber only repeated the words as a question.

What would be thought of the oracles of God if they descended to the puerilities of an ambiguous riddle, that might be read both ways, and so could not fail of accomplishment!

The extreme difficulty of framing a prophecy which shall prove accurate, may be seen in that familiar but crude rhyme known as "Mother Shipton's Prophecy." Some years ago it appeared as a pretended relic of a remote day, and claimed to have predicted the invention of steam as a motive power, diving suits, balloons, a three-fold revolution in France; the rise of D'Israeli, the Jew, as a figure in English politics, the erection of a crystal palace, etc. After its first appearance it was almost forgotten. Years later it reappeared, with a few very slight changes in the rhyme, such as to be scarcely noticed, and yet so including recent events as to make this "prophecy" seem more startling. At times in arguing with skeptics I was met by the statement that here was an old ignorant woman who lived four hundred years ago, and who had written an "uninspired prophecy which was of undoubted antiquity, and however rude in shape, containing several remarkable predictions." So for years I have been trying to unearth and expose what seemed to me a huge imposture, and having succeeded, here record the result. My first clue to the forgery was the discovery that at least three separate and different versions had been put before the people. The changes or variations were slight and sly, adroitly accommodating the pretended prophecy to the new developments of current history: till at last the whole thing has been traced to Charles Hindly, who acknowledges himself the author of this prophetic hoax, which was written in 1862 instead of 1448, and palmed off on a credulous public! It is one of the startling proofs of human perversity that the very people who will try to cast suspicion on prophecies two thousand years old, will, without straining, swallow a forgery that was first published twenty years ago, and not even look into its claims to antiquity!

The Christian religion challenges the severest test—fulfilled prediction. It is easier to counterfeit a miracle than a prophecy; and yet this method of confirmation, so certain to bring exposure to fraud, falsehood or impudent presumption, is the standard by which the Bible stands or falls; on this golden strand of prophecy all these divine precepts and promises are strung. Marvellous is their variety, extent and number, yet no prediction has ever failed; and if those whose set time has come have not failed, with what assurance may we look forward to the sure accomplishment of those prophetic words whose full time is not yet!

There was a certain sublimity about that act of the German astronomers who, at Aiken, S. C., left the stone, on which their meridian circle rested in observing the recent transit of Venus, to stand for the use of those who, in June, 2004, shall need to watch another transit. Think of it—the faith of science in the inflexible order of nature! One hundred and twenty years hence—three times, at least within that space a generation will have perished; thrones will have been emptied of occupant after occupant; empires will have passed away; changes, whose number and gravity are too great now to be conceived, will have taken place; nay, human history may have come to its great last crisis and the millennial march may have begun: but punctual to a second, without delay or failure, Venus will make her transit across the sun's disc. So, while scoffers sneer and doubters question, while empires vanish and nations perish, prophecy moves steadily onward, and nears its grand fulfilment. To a second of time and to the last minute jot or tittle of detail, the prophetic word shall be fulfilled.

The wise man will prepare for the sure future, get ready and keep ready for the coming crisis. Mr. Wiggins, in Canada, from study of the science of storms and storm centers, winds, their circuits, waves and tides, ventured to predict a great storm on this planet beginning March 9th, 1883. He made his prediction in September, 1882. He declared that it would start in the northern Pacific on the morning of March 9th, strike this continent from the south, sweep along the Atlantic coast on the afternoon of the 10th, traveling westward south of the 45th parallel, and returning from the Rocky Mountain range, cross the meridian of Ottawa, over the great Canadian lakes, at noon of the 11th. It was at best a shrewd guess on the basis of probabilities. Meteorology and kindred sciences are not sufficiently reduced to a system, to enable such predictions to be made with confidence. And yet notwithstanding the doubt that overhung the prophecy, wise men made prudent provisions against possible disaster—the plans of thousands were modified to meet the possible emergency and avoid damage; ships put off their day of sailing; excursions were deferred; exposed buildings were sheltered and strengthened, that if the storm should strike, it might find the people prepared. Such are the measures which human foresight and forecast suggest simply in order to be on the safe side! What shall be said of the folly, presumption, recklessness, that pay no heed to the prophetic warnings of the Word of God. That sure word of prophecy in clear terms foretells, beyond the certain day of death, a day when time shall be no longer; when earth shall be wrapped in a winding sheet of dissolving flames; when earth and sea shall give up their dead, and the great white throne shall flash upon the gaze of countless hosts of our humanity— when the books shall be opened, and the dead judged! Have you made ready for that day? In that storm whose thunders rend the earth and shake the sky—whose floods sweep away the last refuge of lies and sin—will your house stand, or fall forever!

CHAPTER III.

THE PROPHECY OF THE RUIN OF JERUSALEM.

"And now I have told you before it come to pass, that, when it is come to pass, ye might believe."—John xiv: 28.

One prophecy may be taken as a representative of all, viz., Christ's predictions as to the destruction of Jerusalem, and the dispersion of the Jews. Fairly and firmly settle this, that these words were literally or substantially spoken by Christ before his disappearance from among men; and we may safely risk the very fate of the Christian faith upon the issue. For, from this one passage of Scripture, with its parallel passages,* may be demonstrated and vindicated the existence of God, his moral government, his general and special providence, the divine inspiration of the Holy Scriptures, and the divine character and mission of Christ. Here, then, is the very field on which to meet candid doubt. But in order to a full and fair proof that history meets at every point the demands of the prophecy, and fills out the prophetic mould, it will be best to call in as witnesses only the professed opponents of Christianity, that it may not appear that the claims of Christ and the gospel rest on the partiality of friends.

Any fair examination of this matter compels us first to ask whether there be a reasonable cer-

---
*Matt. xxiv., Mark xiii., Luke xxi.

tainty that these prophetic words were spoken or written before the events occurred. This inquiry is at the very threshold of the whole investigation; to avoid it is to let everything else go unproven. A candid criticism can the less evade the issue, since it is forced upon us by the foes of the Christian religion. Porphyry, in the third century of the Christian era, made a desperate attack upon the Jewish and Christian Scriptures. Finding in the book of Daniel a prophecy that had been most minutely fulfilled, he first admitted with the utmost frankness that in every particular, history had verified the prophecy; and then adroitly turned his admission into a weapon of attack, arguing that a record so exact could be made only after the events: Daniel played the part of a historian in the mask of a prophet. If Porphyry was the first to suggest this easy escape from the argument of prophecy, he was not the last. Voltaire, in modern times, has, in the same way, admitted the wonderful coincidence between those prophecies of the ruin of Jerusalem and the wreck of the Jewish nation, and the actual facts; but dexterously argues that the pretended prophecy was never spoken or penned until after Jerusalem was destroyed.

As to Voltaire himself, any objection coming from such a source has very little weight. A man who could, in a letter to a friend, declare that "history is, after all, nothing but a parcel of tricks we play with the dead," and that, "as for the portraits of men in biography, they are, nearly all, the creations of fancy;" a man who, when asked where he found a certain startling "fact" with which he adorns one of his histories, replied, "It is a frolic of my imagination!" a man whose motto was, "Crush the wretch!" and yet who called on that same Christ in the dying hour; a man who, after leading the host of sceptics and scoffers, as the boldest of blasphemers, for sixty years, died in agony and remorse so terrible that even the Mareschal de Richelieu fled from his bedside, declaring that he could not bear so terrible a sight, and M. Tronchin affirmed that "the furies of Orestes could give but a faint idea of those of Voltaire;" a man, who said to his attending physician, "Doctor, I will give you half of what I am worth, if you will give me only six months' life," and who, when the doctor said, "Sir, you cannot live six weeks," shrieked, "Then I shall go to hell, and you will go with me!" and soon after expired; —such a man does not add much weight to his own objection. If a man does not feel the force of his own argument, others can scarcely be expected to give it much importance; and it is but too plain that Voltaire was not an honest sceptic, but a mocker, a jeerer, a sneerer—who, seldom himself in earnest, invented any objection which would serve his purpose. Yet, inasmuch as an objection may be entitled to weight independent of its author, we shall briefly examine as to the date of this prophecy.

If this charge of fraud could for a moment be separated from religion, and looked at with calm, cool judgment, without any bias of prejudice, its inherent absurdity would be very plain. To suppose this prophecy to be written after the event, is to suppose a deliberate imposture of gigantic proportions, palmed off on credulous dupes, in the sacred name of religion; a compound of hypocrisy, forgery and perjury, such as would disgrace even a monster like Nero. Think of it! A man in league with two others, like himself, lays a plot to prop up the claims of a mere pretender, by secretly preparing a description of an event already passed; and then by a series of lies, inducing men to accept it as a genuine prophecy! Could men, who could do that, have written the gospels? By the confession even of enemies of the religion of Christ, these records abound in the loftiest moral teaching, and the most sublime conceptions of God and duty. There must be some consistency between a man and his work; and the production of these gospel narratives by such abandoned liars, is inconceivable. To believe this requires more credulity than to accept the Christian religion with scarce a hearing of its claims. The supposition of intentional imposture in the production of the gospels must be abandoned as untenable; on its face it contradicts great established laws of human nature; and it supposes the whole body of believers to be imposed upon.

The Jews were very jealous of their sacred trust; considering it their chief advantage, that " unto them were committed the oracles of God." The greatest care was used in compiling the canon. The claim of a book to a place in the sacred collection was weighed with scrupulous nicety. Many books are to-day among the "Apocrypha," regarded worthy of being bound up with our Old Testament, so pure is their style, so exalted their tone; and yet rejected as unworthy to rank as inspired. How could Daniel's book have found a place in the canon? The Jews must have believed in its inspired character. Had it come forward to prefer its claim after its so-called prophecies were fulfilled, the claim would have been instantly rejected. If the book were offered to the Jewish church as inspired before the events which it foretold, it sustained its claim to prophetic character and divine authority.

Suppose something similar in our day. Let some pious scoundrel who aspires to rank as a prophet try the same mode of imposing on the public. Let him write out a minute pretended prediction of the War of the Rebellion, and attempt to make the world believe that he wrote it by divine foresight a quarter of a century before the war. How long would that pious fraud escape detection! A thousand things would combine to expose such a sham. Its author would have more chance of being cannonaded as a fool or a knave, than of being canonized as a saint. So many features must combine to put upon such a plot even the face of truth, that the detection of the scheme would be morally certain. Men would begin by asking what sort of a man is this, who claims prophetic character? Is he a true man, morally upright; is his word beyond a suspicion? Is he a sane man, mentally sound, and not misled by a delusion? Then if both his mental and moral character were found consistent with his claim, his prophecy would be subjected to microscopic scrutiny, whether it bears the internal marks of such inspired utterances; and even if this test were satisfactorily met, the author would still be required to produce evidence satisfactory to the common mind that his production was written in advance of the events. About matters of this sort we are not naturally credulous. The natural jealousy of human nature makes us slow to concede to others the high rank of prophetic character; and we are more likely to resist the proofs that God has chosen a certain man as a channel of special revelation, even when the proofs are ample, than to yield our homage to an unworthy candidate, by a hasty admission of his claims. Even if there were those who, within the church, conspired to give such false prophet a seat on the prophetic throne, their own character would awaken a suspicion of their partnership.

The exact year of the production of each of the four gospels cannot be fixed. But the most careful and scholarly modern criticism puts the date of St. Matthew's record at about 38 A. D., and his record of this prophecy is the fullest, as well as the first. Mark wrote A. D., 67 to 69. Luke A. D. 63. John A. D. 95. The siege of Jerusalem under Titus ended September 8, 70 A. D. The earliest record of this prophecy was therefore in writing more than thirty years before the event, and the later records from two to seven years before. John, the only one of the four who wrote after the event, is the only one *who makes no reference to the prophecy*, as though caution had been used not to give occasion for the charge that the event had given material for the prophecy.

But a more convincing proof is at hand. The first three centuries were centuries of both persecution and controversy. No weapon, whether sword or pen, that could be used against the cause of Christ, was left untried. Yet, although these prophecies are familiarly quoted by early

Christian writers, in support of Christianity, you must wait till the days of Porphyry, when the third century was in its sunset hours, before one writer even questions the genuineness of the prophecy! Controversy sifts, from the grain of fact, the chaff of fiction or fancy; beneath the eagle eye of searching investigation, prompted by hostility, even the corruptions or perversions of truth are discovered! Judge, then, whether a pretended prophecy, never heard of till after the event, would wait for three hundred years to be called in question; while even a reasonable doubt of its genuineness would have supplied its bitter foes with an irresistible weapon against the Christian religion! As well expect a mighty army, under skilled leaders, to hold a walled city in constant seige for three centnries, and not discover weak places where the walls are propped by rotten timbers! God permitted those three centuries of hottest hostility, with mighty foes arrayed against the gospel, in order to show us that the origin of Christianity was surrounded by no mists of uncertainty or delusion. Her enemies, both many and mighty, had to forge other weapons of attack beside the audacious charge of fraud.

Some of the most remarkable of these predictions are even yet in process of fulfillment. For eighteen hundred years since the fall of Jerusalem, the severe test of history has been applied to this prophecy. Christ, with the audacity of one who knew whereof he spake, challenged all the coming centuries to break his prophetic word; for his predictions reached far beyond the ruin of the regal city of David. But, as the procession of years, and even the more august centuries pass on, like military leaders lifting their plumed helmets in presence of a world's sovereign, the ages, in their turn, confess the divine character of the prophet, who, so long ago, drew the awful lines beyond which they even yet cannot pass. What shall we say, then, of the crucial test of Time!

In this prophecy may the correspondence be accounted for by accidental coincidence? To answer this proper doubt, consider the law of simple and compound probability. When a single prediction is made, about which there is but one feature, it may or it may not prove true; there is therefore one chance in two of its being fulfilled. For instance, suppose I say, there is going to be a very hot summer—it may be hot or it may be mild—the chance of fulfillment is represented by the fraction one-half. This is the law of simple probability. If I introduce a second particular, I get into the region of compound probability. For instance, suppose I say, without any scientific law at the bottom of my conjecture, that June fifteenth will be very hot. Here are two predictions; one is that there will be extreme heat; the other, that it will be on a certain day. Each prediction has a half chance of fulfillment; the compound probability is one-fourth, *i. e.*, there is one chance in four that both predictions will be verified. " A compound event has therefore a chance only in the product of its simple ratios." Every new feature added makes the fraction of probability smaller.

In this prophecy, there is no vague general prediction; but a startling array of minute particulars. Our Lord draws the portrait of the coming event in detail; time, place, persons, marked circumstances, all introducing peculiar features which leave no doubt as to our power to recognize the event, if it shall look like its portrait. We find some twenty-five distinct predictions, here, and, on the law of compound probability, the chance of their all meeting in one event, is as *one in nearly twenty millions*, i. e. the fraction that represents the chance of probability is one-half raised to its twenty-fourth power or about one twenty millionth chance!

And yet every one of those features met in the destruction of Jerusalem and never have combined in any other event! And in selecting examples, we omit all those features about whose exact meaning there is such doubt as to render them unsafe guides, in our investigation. We select only the plainer, bolder outlines which are so strikingly fulfilled as to leave no reasonable question of the correspondence.

One other remark should be made before we enter on the closer study of this particular prophecy. There seems to be in Christ's words a reference not only to the destruction of the city, but to the end of the world; and so closely are these two great events linked in these utterances that it is a matter of doubt to Bible students, where He ceases to speak of the lesser and begins to speak of the greater. But need this seriously embarrass us in studying this question? There is a law of prophetic perspective, which all those who scan the prophecies must understand. In a landscape, a near range of hills may strikingly resemble, in outline, a far more distant range of mountains; so that, although there is vast difference in their heights, and vast distance between their ranges, the same lines would define and describe them both. So in prophecy; one outline may describe an event. near at hand, and another of greater magnitude on the far horizon. Many words may have designedly a double meaning, referring immediately to some nearer occurrence, and remotely to some other of which that is a type; a reference here on a minor scale and there on a major scale. Or we may call this the law of prophetic shadows, a coming event being foreshadowed by another, the outlines of both corresponding as do shadows and substance.

But this is rather an argument for, than against, the divine inspiration of prophecy, since we have a double prediction, with a double verification. Surely if He speaks, to whom "one day is as a thousand years and a thousand years as one day," we need not be surprised to find him using one outline for events, between which there lies a chasm of a thousand years; since to him such vast ages seem but as a watch in the night, and all time is but an insignificant tick in the great clock of eternity!

One very marked proof of God's hand both in this prophecy and the history which fulfills it, is found in the very *authorities, who record the fulfillment*. The main account of the destruction of Jerusalem, it it had been written purposely to confirm the predictions of Christ, could not have been more exactly correspondent. Its author was the prince of the Jewish scholars of his day, and a Jewish general who, at first, stoutly resisted the Roman power, holding Iotapata, the stronghold of Galilee, for forty-seven days, against Vespasian; in 67 A. D., he was taken captive, and kept in bonds till Titus succeeded Vespasian in the control of the Jewish war. He was present at the siege of the city, and, after its downfall, went with Titus back to Rome, where he wrote his Annals; and Titus himself was so well pleased with the accuracy of his history that he gave it his formal approval and desired its publication. This historian was of course Josephus. He was certainly a competent witness, being very accomplished as a man, and, about the person of the Roman commander, having every chance for close observation and exact information. Who will venture to accuse a Jew, who lived and died one of the straitest of the Pharisees, of partiality for the crucified Nazarene or his prophecies? God chose an enemy of the Christian faith. to hand down to us a most minute record of the fulfillment of this most minute prophecy; so that the leading though unconscious witness to Christ's prophetic character, is one whose testimony cannot be impeached by either Jews or Pagans! Josephus traced no connection between the terrible events he recorded, and the words of the crucified Jesus; for he is constantly striving to find some reason for the fearful judgments which befell his land and nation.*

Who are the other authorities, to be cited in proof that our Lord's prophecy was exactly fulfilled? Tacitus, a Roman and Pagan historian; and Gibbon, the prince of sceptics, the English historian, who, even while writing to prove that the success of Christianity might be accounted

---

* Comp. Wars, 754, P. vi. v. iv. where he accounts for the ruin of the temple by the fact that the Jews had increased the area of its courts by taking in desecrated grounds, etc., etc.

for by natural and secondary causes, was, despite himself, compelled to record facts which prove Christ a true prophet. Frederick the Great, on one occasion said to one of his marshals, who was a devout believer, "Give me in one word, a proof of the truth of the Bible." "The Jews," was the laconic, unanswerable reply.

Harmonizing the gospels in one complete record, we find twenty-five distinct predictions, in connection with the ruin of the Jewish capital. We group them for convenience into classes.

I. Predictions as to pretenders to the character of Messiah. 1. They would be many; 2. Would draw people to the desert, and secret chambers; 3. Would deceive large numbers, etc.

Before this time there had been no such thing in Jewish history. After the crucifixion, false Messiahs multiplied, such as Simon Magus, the Samarian sorcerer; Dositheus, another Samaritan; Theudas, who promised to part the waters of Jordan like Elijah, and Josephus says, "by such speeches deceived many." The country was filled with imposters who deceived the people and persuaded them to follow into the wilderness, where they should see signs; a great multitude were led to the cloisters of the temple by false prophets."

II. Predictions of various signal calamities.

1. Wars. At the time when Christ spake, peace prevailed both among the Jews and nations round about. Even when Caligula's order to set up his statue in the temple provoked resistance, the Jews could not believe that war was imminent. And yet Josephus says "the country was soon filled with violence; disorders prevailed in Alex-

andria, Cesarea, Damascus, Tyre, Ptolemais and all over Syria." The Jews rebelled against Rome, Italy was in convulsions and within two years four Roman emperors suffered death.

2. Famine, pestilence, earthquake, etc. A famine of several years duration caused suffering in Judea, and there were famines in Italy, pestilences in Babylon, and only five years before the ruin of Jerusalem, in Rome. Earthquakes are recorded by Tacitus, Suetonius Philostratus; and Josephus gives account of them in Crete, Italy, Asia Minor, and one extraordinary, in Judea.

3. Fearful sights and great signs from heaven. Josephus affirms that just before the war, "a star resembling a sword stood over the city; and a comet for a whole year," that a great light shone round the altar; that the massive Eastern gate which it took twenty men to move, opened of its own accord; that chariots and troops were seen in the clouds at sunset; that there was an earthquake and a supernatural voice at Pentecost; that a man named Jesus persisted in crying, 'Woe to the city,' etc.

Tacitus records many prodigies that signaled the coming ruin. Armies appeared fighting in air; fire fell on the temples from the clouds; a loud voice proclaiming the removal of the gods from the temple, and a sound as of a departing host. About the reality and miraculous nature of these signs and sights and sounds, we cannot say; but it is enough that both Jew and Roman were impressed with them as real and miraculous.

III. Signs within the kingdom of God.

1. Persecution. Did not Saul make havoc of the church, before he was converted? Were not

Peter and John before councils and in prisons? Was not Paul brought before kings, and he and Silas scourged and put in stocks for their faith's sake? Yet what wonderful power was given, before adversaries, to Stephen, to Peter, to Paul. None of the apostles seem to have died a natural death but John. About six years before Jerusalem fell, there was at Rome a terrible conflagration of eight days, of which Nero was believed to be the author; and to turn the wrath of the people from himself he put the blame of it upon the Christians; thereupon began a persecution which even Pagan pages blush to record. Nero drove his chariot to the imperial gardens between rows of Christian martyrs wrapped in their burning sheets of flame.

2. Mutual betrayal. Tacitus says at first those who were seized confessed their sect, and then by their indication a great multitude were convicted.

3. The gospel to be preached everywhere as a witness. What a work to be done inside of forty years—with no printing press to publish the gospel, and no rapid modes of transit to make travel easy; and foreign tongues to be learned! And yet it was done. Pentecost, with its gathered representatives from all nations, hearing and then going back to herald the good news; with its miraculous gift of tongues, doubtless fitting those first preachers to preach in foreign languages; persecution, scattering the whole body of believers, and setting them at work everywhere making disciples; Peter going to the dispersed Jewish tribes eastward—Paul to the Gentile world westward—our Lord's words were again fulfilled.

Before the city fell, the gospel had been proclaimed in lesser Asia, Greece and Italy—north to Scythia, south to Ethiopia, east to Parthia and India, and west to Spain and Britain. Tacitus says that in the time of Nero's persecution, the religion of Christ had spread over Judea and even through the Roman Empire, and numbered so many followers that a vast multitude was apprehended and condemned to martyrdom.

IV. Signs pertaining to the city itself.

1. Jerusalem to be encompassed with armies.

2. The eagles were to gather as around a carcase. When the Roman army drew nigh and surrounded the city, above every floating standard rose the silver eagle. Banners distinguish an army—as its insignia; nations are known on sea and land by their flags. The Romans are through history so linked with this symbol that the Roman eagles are as celebrated as Rome herself. How fitting as an emblem! The eagle or vulture is marked by three things, "strength, swiftness, ferocity." How like vultures swooping down upon a carcase were the Roman hosts—so strong, so swift-moving, so ferociously cruel!

3. Destruction was to come as "lightning shineth from east to west." Now, it might have been expected, as the approach to Jerusalem was from the seacoast, that the Roman army would advance from west to east. Yet, as a fact, the approach was from Olivet, on the east, and toward the west; the lightning bolts of war which so soon shattered the fair capital first shot from war-clouds hovering on the eastern horizon, and their direction was westward.

4. "The abomination of desolation standing in the holy place" was a conspicuous token. Just what this means we may not decide, but only be-

cause these words have more than one possible fulfillment. St. Matthew's record may, by the abomination of desolation, mean what Luke does by the desolating Pagan army, with idolatrous eagle standards, betokening desolation or destruction, and standing on the holy ground—nay, hovering over the very sanctuary like unclean birds of prey. The Jews, holding every idol an "abomination," besought a Roman general when he was leading his army towards Arabia through Judea, to go some other way, lest, by the very passage of a Pagan host with Pagan emblems, the land be defiled. Some things favor the reference of these words to an army of zealots and assassins invited by the Jews to defend them against the Romans, and who literally stood in the temple courts and profaned them; or, again, some think the "abomination" means a statute of the emperor set up by Pilate, or of Titus set up by Hadrian, in the holy place.

5. A trench and an embankment were to be made around the city. Nothing seemed more improbable and useless. In all the previous sieges sustained by Jerusalem this had never been done. The situation of the city and the physical features of the country made it seem wasteful of time and strength. The valleys that wound about the city were a natural trench; the hills that round it rose were a natural embankment. Yet Titus, against the counsel of his chief men, actually built a wall and trench five miles in circumference around the doomed capital; and the Jewish historian describes the precise circuit.

6. Great tribulation was to mark the siege.

Hear Josephus: " No other city ever suffered such miseries, nor was ever a generation more fruitful in wickedness from the beginning of the world. It appears that the misfortunes of all men from the beginning of the world, if compared to these of the Jews, are not so considerable. The multitude who perished exceeded all the destructions that man or God ever brought on the world."

It was at the Passover, when the nation thronged its sacred capital. Nearly three millions are estimated to have been in the city. The famine was so severe that hunger drove men to eat sandal straps, leather girdles, straw. A mother brought to the maddened assassins who were ready to do any violence to get food, a half-devoured child, and bade them share with her the lamb she had made ready! As Titus saw the dead thrown over the walls into the valleys, by hundreds and by thousands, he lifted his hands to heaven to protest before God that all this was not his doing. Josephus reckons that 130,000 perished and 97,000 were sold into slavery.

7. The actual destruction of the city.

It was to be leveled to the ground.

Josephus tells us that three massive walls of great strength encompassed the city; and the garrison was ten times, in number, the beseigers. Think of laying such walls even with the ground! Yet, at the last, orders were given to " raze the very foundations," and nothing was left but three towers, and what little wall was needed, as a shelter to the Roman garrison, and as a specimen of the strength of the defences, which Roman power had laid low. The whole circumference was so thoroughly laid even with the ground that nothing was left to show it had been inhabited. Titus said: "We have certainly had God for our helper in this war. He has ejected the Jews out of these strongholds; for what could men or machines do toward throwing down such fortifications as these!" The hope of finding hid treasure moved the Roman army to tear up the very ground, till sewers and aqueducts were uncovered, and a plowshare was used to tear up the foundations of the temple, thus literally fulfilling the prophecy of Micah (750 B. C.) "Jerusalem shall be ploughed as an heap."

The temple was to be included in this awful destruction. The prophecy of its demolition is the first link in this chain of predictions. After our Lord uttered in the temple his lament over his people who would not be gathered under his wings, he said: "Behold your house is left unto you desolate!" and immediately departed from the devoted sanctuary. As they left it, his disciples, struck with the strange prophecy that such a house could ever become desolate, called his attention, "See what manner of stones and what buildings are here," *i. e.*, structures even then going on to completion. But he said, with more particular utterance, "There shall not be left here one stone upon another that shall not be thrown down."

This prediction was very unlikely of fulfillment.

(*a.*) The walls enclosed over nineteen acres; the east front rose to a height of one-sixth of a mile from the vale, and immense stones, some of them 65 feet by 8 by 10 wrought into its massive structure.

(*b.*) It was beautiful and sacred, a monument both of art and worship. It rose, like a mount of gold and snow. Its carved portals, alabaster porticoes, and golden sanctuary, won the most rapturous praises from even Pagans. If vandals and barbarians, in the sack of Athens and Rome, would spare the Parthenon and Pantheon, what might not be expected from the soldiers of the first and grandest of Empires! Would they not spare a structure which the proverb said, " If you had not seen, you had seen nothing beautiful."

(*c.*) It was built by Herod, a creature of Roman power and patronage, who was more loyal to the conquering nation than to those with whom he was connected, as himself a descendant of Isaac. And he was a deferential and obsequious Roman in spirit, who built cities to perpetuate Cæsar's name, and who tried to make Jerusalem a second Rome. To prostrate Herod's fane, was to lay one of Rome's very master-works in ruin.

(*d.*) And then Titus was mild, humane, cultured, a commander who would not be likely to favor it, who in fact forbade such wanton destruction. The temple was once put out by his orders, but fired again when his back was turned.

V. Christ's predictions, however, assured the safety of his disciples. " There shall not an hair of your head perish."

The fact is remarkable enough that in such universal slaughter not one disciple should perish; but more remarkable that it was after the besieging army should surround the city that they were to have opportunity to withdraw. What a strange signal for flight, when the hosts were already cutting off every escape! And yet this was Christ's token to his faithful followers that desolation was nigh, imminent. They should yet have chance to flee, if done with haste; there would be opportunity, but it would be short.

Hear again the Jewish annalist: " Cestius Gallus, after beginning siege, mysteriously withdrew, and without any reason in the world, and many embraced this opportunity to depart; a great multitude fled to the mountains." At this crisis, as we learn from church historians of the first century, all the followers of Christ took refuge in the mountains of Pella, beyond the Jordan, and there is no record of *one single Christian perishing in the siege!* As soon as the armies returned, the city was surrounded by a wall, and all hope of flight was now cut off.

VI. Prophecies respecting subsequent history.

1. The doom of the Jews; they should fall by the edge of the sword, and be led captive into all nations.

Even before the city fell, an immense number of deserters, falling into hands of the besiegers, were sold with their wives and children. Nearly 100,000 from Jerusalem alone, were sold into bondage. 6,000 choice young men from Tarichea were sent to Nero, and 30,000 from the same place sold beside. The tall and fine looking were borne to Rome to grace the triumphal entry of Titus: many sent to the public works in Egypt; many more distributed through the provinces into all nations, to be slain by gladiators or by wild beasts. And so it has been from that time until now. The sword is not yet sheathed, nor are the chains of their captivity broken.

2. The doom of the city: To "be trodden down by the Gentiles until the times of the Gentiles be fulfilled."

Here are three particulars: desolation, by the Gentiles, and continued until the Gentile world is brought to the knowledge of the gospel and the Jews are reclaimed.

To this day, the city has been trodden down by the Gentiles; and though the Jews have made desperate efforts to get control of their ancient capital they have never been re-established yet. About 64 years after their expulsion under Titus, the city was partly rebuilt by the Emperor Hadrian, and a Roman colony settled there. On pain of death Jews were forbidden to enter, forbidden even to look from a distance on the city. The suspicion that the holy place was to be defiled by idol images provoked them to revolt, but they were crushed with awful slaughter. Again, in the time of Constantine, they made a vain attempt to regain possession. At last they felt sure of success; for they had permission from Rome to rebuild. Julian, the apostate, bound to break down faith in this very prophecy, backing up Jewish zeal with Roman arms, wealth and power, undertook to restore the temple and ritual and plant round it a Jewish colony.

To show how strangely this project was frustrated, let us quote Gibbon.* "The vain and ambitious mind of Julian might aspire to restore the ancient glory of the temple of Jerusalem. As the Christians were firmly persuaded that a sentence of everlasting destruction had been pronounced against the whole fabric of the Mosaic

---
* II:436. 9.

law, the imperial sophist would have converted the success of his undertaking into a specious argument against the faith of prophecy, and the truth of revelation. He resolved to erect without delay on the commanding eminence of Moriah, a stately temple which might eclipse the splendor of the church of the Resurrection on the adjacent hill of Calvary; to establish an order of priests and to invite a numerous colony of Jews. At the call of their great deliverer, the Jews from all provinces of the empire assembled on the holy mountain of their fathers; and their insolent triumph alarmed and exasperated the Christian inhabitants of Jerusalem. The desire of rebuilding the temple has in every age been the ruling passion of the children of Israel. In this propitious moment the men forgot their avarice and the women their delicacy; spades and pickaxes of silver were provided by the vanity of the rich, and the rubbish was transported in mantles of silk and purple. Every purse was opened in liberal contributions, every hand claimed a share in the pious labor; and the commands of a great monarch were executed by the enthusiasm of a whole people.

But the Christians entertained a natural and pious expectation, that in this contest the honor of religion would be vindicated by some signal miracle. "An earthquake, a whirlwind and a fiery eruption which overturned and scattered the new foundations of the temple are attested, with some variations, by contemporaneous and respectable evidence. This public event is described by Ambrose, Bishop of Milan, in an epistle to the Emperor Theodosius; by the eloquent Chrysostom who might appeal to the memory of the elder part of his congregation at Antioch; and by Gregory Nazianzen, who published his account of the miracle before the expiration of the same year. The last of these writers boldly declared that this præternatural event was not disputed by the infidels, and this assertion strange as it may seem is confirmed by the unexceptionable testimony of Ammianus Marcellinus." This philosophic soldier records, that "whilst Alypius urged with vigor and diligence the execution of the work, horrible balls of fire, breaking out near the foundations, with frequent and reiterated attacks, rendered the place from time to time inaccessible to these scorched and blasted workmen; and the victorious element, continuing in this manner obstinately and absolutely bent, as it were, to drive them always to a distance, the undertaking was abandoned." "Such authority," adds Gibbon, "should satisfy a believing, and most astonish an incredulous mind." In a note, Gibbon attempts to explain all this by a long confinement, in the grounds beneath the temple ruins, of inflammable air, exploded by the torches of exploring workmen, etc.

Jerusalem has emphatically been trodden down of Gentiles. Not to speak of the destruction, when Pagan hosts trampled it under foot with the iron hoof of war, for sixty-four years it was occupied only by a Roman garrison. Hadrian's partial rebuilding was designed as desecration. He called it Ælia Capitolina (a name compounded of his own family title Ælius, and Capitolina, a name applied to Jupiter from his temple on Mt. Capitolinus). To Jupiter Capitolinus he consecrated the new city and built a temple to that Pagan God over the sepulchre of Christ. He set up a statue of Venus on Calvary—and the marble image of a swine—the peculiar abomination of the Jew, over the gate that opened toward Bethlehem.

The sacred site remained thus more than desolate, and known by its pagan name till Helena, the mother of Constantine, made a pilgrimage to it in 326. Justinian, in the sixth century, repaired and enriched its churches, founded convents, and built a church to the Virgin on Mt. Moriah. But all this, though acceptable to Pope-dom was profanation to the Jews: the city was still trodden down of Gentiles! In 610 A. D. it was stormed and greatly damaged by the Persians, who for a short time held it.

In 637, under Caliph Omar, the Saracens took possession, and for more than four centuries the Arabian, Turkish or Egyptian Mohammedans continued to tread down the doomed capital. In 1073, the Selzookian Turks took it, whose cruelties to Christian pilgrims provoked the first crusade; and July 15, 1099, the crusaders taking it by storm, made it the seat of a Christian kingdom, allowing only Christians there. In 1187 it was conquered by the Egyptian Sultan Saladin. For upwards of half a century it was like a toy tossed to and fro, between Christians and Turks, till 1244, since which date it has remained under Moslem sway, and the very fact of a mosque, crowned with a crescent, rising where the temple stood, is enough to show how profanely even Moriah is still trampled under foot of Gentiles.

We appeal to every candid mind, whether the

continued desolation of Jerusalem is not one of the historic marvels, we had almost said miracles. Consider the remarkable preservation of the Jewish nation—though scattered everywhere, still keeping their national traits and unity as a people, mingling but not mixing with other peoples —consider their religious tenacity and zeal for the ancient city and demolished temple—consider their great numbers and vast wealth, one family of Jews controlling enough capital to buy all Judea —consider that if any one thought and desire engrosses the Jewish mind it is to be re-established in the city of David—and can any human philosophy account for the fact that for eighteen centuries this desolation lasts!

VII. Our Lord's prediction limited the opening act of this drama of the ages to the lifetime of the generation then living.

The days of our years are three score years and ten, and it was seventy years after Jesus was born when Jerusalem was destroyed: or if we take thirty-five years as the average life time of a generation, it was just about so long after these words were spoken when their awful fulfillment began.

VIII. Christ foretold these as days of vengeance (Luke xxi: 22), *i. e.*, of avenging or retributive justice. All should be plainly the judgment of God upon the sin of Christ's rejection and crucifixion. An attentive student of history cannot but see God in history. There is at times such a striking, startling correspondence between the form of sin and the form and even time of its punishment, that men are constrained to say like Pharaoh's magicians: "*This is the*

FINGER OF GOD!" If the destruction of Jerusalem is to be recognized not as an ordinary calamity but a peculiar interposition of God, in just visitation of the crime committed by the Jews in crucifying his own Son, there will be some features about it which plainly exhibit its retributive character. How is it?

The Jews put Jesus to death at the passover; at the very season of that annual festival, thousands of them were put to death.

They clamored for the release of a robber and murderer that Jesus might be slain; they became the prey of robbers and murderers, in the siege.

They crucified Jesus, outside the walls; and outside the walls they suffered crucifixion in such multitudes that room was wanting for crosses, and crosses for bodies.

They mocked and derided their Messiah, even as he stood helpless before the tribunal or hung in agony on the cross; they were crucified in every conceivable posture, affixed to the crosses in modes so various that it was as though "done in jest."

They reckoned Christ, the faultless one, a malefactor, and their own dead bodies were flung over the walls like the despised carcases of criminals refused an honorable burial.

To convict Christ, they procured false witnesses, who perverted his prophecy of his own death and resurrection into a declaration of the destruction of their temple; and the perjured testimony proved unconsciously prophetic—the temple was destroyed. From Olivet, Christ uttered the sad prediction, and from Olivet moved the flock of 'eagles' to pounce on the carcase.

Pilate sat in the court of the castle of Antony to condemn Jesus to death; and from that very point was made the last and successful assault on the temple and city.

They intimidated Pilate by pretending great loyalty to Cæsar, whom they claimed as their only king; and under his imperial sway their nation was broken into fragments by the very hosts of Cæsar.

They rejected the true Messiah with his mighty works as well as words; and lent themselves as silly dupes to the control of Messianic pretenders and false prophets.

When Pilate declared Christ innocent and sought to release him, they assumed all responsibility, saying, 'his blood be on us and on our children,' and that very generation gave their blood for his. Never was there any imprecation more prophetic.

An individual may have his retribution beyond this life, for he lives beyond this life. A nation, however, is a temporal state, and its sins must be avenged, if at all, in this world. "Institutions are mortal: men immortal: the historical temporal judgment is of institutions and of organisms: the final judgment is of individuals, each one giving account of himself unto God."

Can any candid mind consider the crime of the Jews and the calamities that followed exactly in accord with prophetic predictions, and see in these marvellous correspondences no sign that God had their sin in mind in bringing on that very generation such pathetic but poetic retribution?

This wonderful witness to the divine inspiration of the gospels also attests the divine character of Christ, whose own words were: "And now I have told you before it come to pass that when it is come to pass ye may believe." He claimed Divine Sonship and Messiahship: and to verify his claim, uttered a prophecy so minute that no chance coincidence can explain it. How may we evade conviction?

As Porphyry did with Daniel—even so we may do with Christ, deny his prophetic character, make both the prophecy and the history the fair masks covering the most hideous and devilish plot ever devised to ensnare the credulity of men. We may, in other words, coolly and sneeringly say, "the prophecy was never written till Jerusalem was in ruins." But when men use such an argument as this in answer to such a mighty array of facts and truths, it must be because they feel their cause to be desperate. They violate all the common laws of historic criticism and evidence, for the sake of NOT being convinced. For no adequate motive or reason can be assigned for this wholesale and reckless denial of historical testimony, but a determination to oppose the Christian religion. Here is the argument, unmasked: "If this prophecy was recorded before the event, Jesus Christ must have been a genuine prophet. We are not willing to accept him as such. Therefore these words were not written until after the fall of Jerusalem!"

The same methods will make havoc of all history and all testimony, leaving us certain of nothing—all the facts of the past become the fancies of dreamers, or the fictions of liars. We are asked to escape the credulity of faith by running into the trap of more credulous doubt and denial—for the sake of disbelieving Christianity, to believe that men wrote the most pure and faultless records known, full of the sublimest moral teachings, and died rather than renounce their faith; and yet were only trying to get others to believe a crucified and dead traitor to be yet alive—slyly manufacturing prophecies of events already passed, in order to prop up his claims to divine honors!

When Mephistopheles, in Faust, is asked his name, he says he is the " spirit of negation " or denial! Nothing is easier than to deny what you cannot disprove; and proof, if it had on Mercury's talaria, or the seven-league boots of yore, never could overtake the spirit of negation. Suppose a case: an astronomer announces to-day that he has by means of a new instrument greatly superior to the telescope in power, found inhabitants in the moon. You deny it; pronounce it impossible, because there is no atmosphere in the moon, etc. But Prof. Watson or Peters has said so. You reply, " I don't believe it." It is proved to you that he said so. " I don't believe he is a thoroughly competent astronomer." It is proved that he is. " I don't believe that he is honest; he is fooling the scientific world; it's a hoax." It is proved to you that he is incapable of trickery. " Well, he is insane." It is proved he is sane. " Well, his new instrument fools him," etc. How long would it take for truth to come up to such reckless denial? Yet men affect surprise that believers do not run after all the various forms of denial which impeach the truth of the Bible! Infidelity begins this race by a stride so monstrous as to ask us to believe that a man that could write such a book as " Daniel " or the " gospels " could be a perjured hypocrite, and attempt to concoct a fraud, beside which Jo Smith's Mormon Bible is nothing.

This method of wholesale denial is one of the conspicuous weapons of modern scepticism. Nothing is easier than to discredit a fact or a truth; to confound denial with disproof, and to substitute unanswerable sneers or cavils for answerable arguments. We hold up such a prophecy, and side by side its corresponding fulfillment. A skeptic denies the fulfillment. If we prove the correspondence between prediction and event, he denies the prophecy; it was not written till after the event. We bring witnesses to show that the prediction preceded the event; he denies the truth or competency of the witnesses, claims they were mistaken; or, like Hume and Strauss, assumes miracles of knowledge or of power to be impossible, and asserts that no testimony can establish what is impossible! All argument becomes impossible with such antagonists. Bacon says: " I cannot reason with a man unless we can find a common footing in agreement on first principles."

We have promised our reader to deal with this theme calmly, as a surgeon in the dissecting-room uses the lancet and scalpel, with scientific steadiness of hand. Perhaps we have not done it, but it is because we cannot. The surgeon may be pardoned if his head is hot and his hand trembles as he uncovers the vital organs of his own child to discover disease, especially if it is a living child and not a dead body which he touches with the keen blade!

The gospel of Christ we cannot discuss without deep feeling. All we have, or hope, in this world and the next is bound up with it; he who touches, even with irreverence, this sacred faith, wounds us in the quick of our being; he who insults and assaults it, thrusts his steel into our very vitals. And it is a mystery that any man, whatever his own creed may be, can take delight in demolishing faith in others, and even ruthlessly blaspheming a name that is above every name to them. It is perhaps the mark of current infidelity that it makes its disciples malignant. Were one speaking to an audience of Musselmen, why shock them by insulting and blasphemous allusions to their Koran and Prophet? Let him rather calmly conduct them to a better sacred Book and sacred Person if he can. It is no sign that our faith is feeble or our faith weak, if, when a man publicly tears the Scriptures to tatters and spits in the face of the Christian's God, and bows in mock homage before the crucified One, we shrink and turn pale. The believer cannot be indifferent to anything which concerns Jesus of Nazareth.

We have pointed to the burning bush of prophecy with its many branches, wonderfully budding and blossoming into historic events. Well may we remove the shoes from our feet; the place where we stand is holy ground; that glory is the glory of God. If the reader sees no radiant light, let him ask himself whether he is WILLING TO SEE.

CHAPTER IV.

MIRACLES: ARE THEY POSSIBLE AND PROBABLE?

"Jesus of Nazareth, a man approved of God among you by miracles and wonders and signs, which God did by him in the midst of you, as ye yourselves also know."—Acts ii: 22.

What is a miracle? Definitions lie at the basis of all discussions, for they define or limit the ground which argument is to cover; they set bounds within which we both keep ourselves and hold our opponents. This is of as much consequence in debate as it would be in a contest between athletes to settle the rules of honorable championship.

Much importance attaches to a definition. Carelessly to accept a false premise may compel us to admit a false conclusion. A whole building is made unsafe by a treacherous foundation. If we begin with a wrong or faulty definition, we unsettle our whole argument.

If a miracle be defined as a " natural impossibility," how shall we meet those who, like Hume and Strauss, first assume miracles to be impossible, and then ask triumphantly whether any testimony can establish an impossibility? It is very plausible to start by assuming a miracle to be a violation of natural laws; next, assert the uniformity of those laws as a fact and a necessity to the very stability of the system of nature; next, to argue the absurdity and impossiblity of voluntary violations of those laws by the very Creator who fixed them as ruling forces; and so conclude that no testimony can establish a miracle.

A miracle, in a Scripture sense, is simply this: *A wonder and a sign.* Its sole use is this, that God appeals to it as a sign of His power. This is the reason why it must also be a wonder. Were there nothing in it that strikes the mind as out of the common course of nature, or beyond the power of man, it could not be used by God to produce the impression and conviction of His presence and power. It need not be on the grandest scale; it need not call God's power into its fullest exercise; that might be a waste. All that is necessary is that the act or occurrence shall be sufficiently wonderful to show that God's hand is in it, and its end is accomplished. So must it be wonderful, as out of the common course, that it may arrest attention.

A miracle must combine both these elements. It may be that you either mark a wonder which is not a sign, or a sign which is not a wonder; but neither is a miracle, because it does not meet both conditions. For example, sunshine is a wonder, and no familiarity with the daily mystery of the morning and the evening can take away the element of the marvelous. A vast globe, fifteen hundred thousand times the volume of the earth, gives to it life and heat and motion, at a distance of more than ninety millions of miles. If that bush in the desert of Horeb was wonderful, which burned with fire and was not consumed, what shall we say of a sphere of fire which six thousand years of unceasing combustion has not even reduced in size! Yet we do not call the sun a miracle, for God does not appeal to it as a special sign to confirm His word or show His power in connection with human agency. The rainbow is a sign, to which God appeals, as a token of his covenant with man that the flood of waters shall not again deluge the earth. Yet we do not call that a miracle, for it is not out of the common course of nature, and does not arrest the attention of men as showing a power above nature.

Let us then fix firmly in mind that when any occurrence is sufficiently out of the natural or usual order to indicate a sure interposition of a power above nature and above man; and when God points us to such an occurrence as a sign that He is speaking by man, we have both conditions necessary to a miracle. It must be above the power both of nature and of man. Nature represents blind, mechanical force, acting without intelligence. All nature's operations are marvelous, but not miraculous, for they move in the line of fixed laws. Man represents intelligent, intellectual force; all man's operations are marvelous, but not miraculous, for they move in the line of fixed laws—laws of mind as well as of matter. In order to a miracle, a marvel which shall show the power of God, there must be some proof of the intervention of an influence that is neither limited by the laws of matter nor by the laws of mind.

How will such proof or sign be likely to be furnished, if at all? There can be but one answer: There will be an interruption of those fixed laws which we have seen to guide the movements both of matter and mind. The objection urged against miracles, as an interruption of fixed laws, is not well taken. If there be a miracle at all, it *must invade the fixed order;* otherwise, however it might impress as curious or even marvelous, it would become no sign of a presence or power greater than those forces which obey the fixed order, and which we call mechanical, because, like the movements of a machine, they cannot act outside of fixed limits.

Suppose an ignorant and superstitious savage suddenly, as in sleep, transported to the very centres of the highest civilization! He stands beside a railroad track, and the iron horse rushes by. He looks with amazement at the rapid revolution of the driving-wheels, and the majestic movement of that symbol of mechanical omnipotence. He falls down to adore, but you arrest him. You tell him that is not a God; it is simply a machine; it moves according to a fixed law, and within the limits fixed by the rails, which also represent law. He cannot believe it. How shall you convince him? There is but one way. Show him that there is a power above the engine that can change its course; invade what appears to be a fixed order and a uniform law of its motion; and, if he have mind enough to appreciate your method of proof, he sees that the engine is a machine, and nothing more. You show him how, by the hand of the engineer, its motion is arrested; how, by the hand of the switch tender, its very track is changed at will; how, by the turn-table, its direction is changed; how, by quenching its fires, it can be made motionless and inert. Now, mark, you have given him a sign that some power greater than the engine is present, by interfering with its ordinary and uniform course. A very ignorant man knows that it is of the nature of a moving body to move on in one direction. When a moving body actually stops, backs, turns about—when all its ordinary movements are reversed, we conclude there is a power above the mechanical—and we call that power intelligence. If God gives us a similar sign of His presence, it must be in such a way as to show a power, not only superior to blind mechanism, but even to human intelligence; and that can be done only by some process which seems to reverse the ordinary laws both of matter and mind. We say, "seems to reverse," for it is not necessary that any law be either violated or suspended: let it only be plain that the divine engineer is guiding the engine, to convince me that he is present; and my need is met, though I may not understand the complex system of laws which has a place for the miracle.

Let us take note that, after all, in even a miracle there may in fact be no real invasion of the order of the universe. When the engine backs, wheels about, changes track, it as truly obeys law as when it moved on straightforward; there is, however, an intelligence guiding the machine, and bringing a new law to bear upon its motion. How do we know that a miracle invades or interrupts nature's fixed order? What if it be the engineer, the intelligence of the Creator, simply bringing a new set of laws to bear upon the universe?

When the secret things are revealed, we shall doubtless find that there are in this universe of matter and of mind *two planes* for the operation of law. One is the ordinary plane, the lower level, where everything moves in a uniform line and method; another, the extraordinary plane, the higher level, where the special intervention of the engineer introduces, for wise reasons, a new force not commonly in operation.

It may be safe to take still more positive positions than these. Every act, by which intelligence voluntarily interrupts the working of mechanical law, has in it the essence of the miraculous, on a smaller scale. For example, you throw a ball through the air. I put out my hand and catch it. It would have continued to fly, till another mechanical law which we call gravitation, bringing it to the earth, had arrested its motion; but a different agent has been brought to bear; a voluntary, intelligent force suddenly puts forth its energy and controls the working of a blind, mechanical force. There is no disorder introduced into creation, but there is a new power at work, which shows an intelligent agent.

What does God, in a miracle? Let us suppose it literally true that the sun stood still while Joshua fought the Amorites, and that this is not a poetic description, from "the book of Jasher," of a prolonging of daylight. The mechanical law would require the continued march of the sun through the heavens: but there comes in the voluntary, intelligent force to control the working of the blind and mechanical, and show the presence of the divine agency. Is not this occurrence like the other, but on a grander scale suited to prove the power of God?

Lazarus died and was buried. The operation of mechanical laws would bring decay; but a new force, voluntary and intelligent, controls the mechanical, and there is no decay. At the word of the Son of God the breath returns. Man cannot restore the dead; yet he can revive a body out of which breath has fled, where there is no pulse, and where even animal heat is scarce left, as in the recovery of one who has been drowned. The living embraces the lifeless, warmth goes from one body to the other, breath passes from one to the other. All this could not be accomplished by mere mechanical force. Leave that body to the operation of natural law, and there will be no breath nor pulse. But bring a voluntary, intelligent force to bear in time, and the decree of death, ordained by mechanical law, is reversed. We do not bring the resurrection of Lazarus down to the level of the resuscitation of one who, after apparent death from drowning, is brought to life. Our object is to show that, in our ordinary experience, the will of an intelligent being arrests and reverses the action of mechanical law, proving the presence of a superior agency, without any violation of the real order of nature. And may not a miracle simply be, on a scale suited to the grandeur of God's activity, the will of an infinite intelligence, arresting and reversing the action of mechanical law, proving the presence of a superior and supreme being.

Dr. William M. Taylor has happily illustrated the consistency of miracles with the uniformity of law by a reference to the Holly system of waterworks. The engine, which furnishes the pressure for the water supply, is so arranged that the demand regulates the supply. According to the rapidity of the discharge at the hydrant, is the rapidity with which the pumping engine works. Then, when a fire in the town subjects the apparatus to a very unusual tax, a signal in the engine room, acting automatically, causes the engineer to gear on some reserve power, always ready for use; and so, even in an emergency, there is provision for ample supply. And yet all this is a mere triumph of mechanics. Now let the ordinary working of the machinery represent the common course of nature: and the intelligent, personal intervention of the engineer, in an exigency, the personal interposition of the sovereign of the universe in the crises of affairs; and you have almost an analogy, refuting the objection on a scientific basis.

Lacordaire, in his conferences, finely satirizes this modern scientific doctrine of the helplessness of God. A woman cries out from the slums of Paris for light and help. God answers, "I would gladly help you but I cannot. I have established a fixed order of things and I have limited myself to its working. Prayer is of no use, you must submit to the fixed order."

If this view of miracles be sound and sensible it knocks away the prop from the main objection urged against miracles. Sceptical persons say: "I can't believe that God would first make laws for nature and set them in motion, and then go on and violate His own laws. What would be the use of making them, if He himself would break them or so easily suspend or set them aside?" We meet the objector on the very threshold, and honestly dispute his position. Is a miracle a violation of the laws of nature, or is it only such an interference with the established course of things, as infallibly shows us the presence and the action of a supernatural power?

I have a watch here—when wound up it runs straight forward until it needs winding. By a fixed law, in conformity with the very structure of the time piece, its hands move only in one direction, while they move at all. Yet, when I find that it is too fast I move the hands backward; I interrupt the usual movement, but I violate no law. The watch could not have turned back its own hands and corrected itself, but a superior intelligence interferes for a proper end. Have I suspended or violated any law? or have I simply brought a new law to bear which, though not in ordinary operation, is entirely consistent with the laws which govern the movements of the watch? As I examine more minutely into the structure of this delicate piece of mechanism, I observe a remarkable fact: the maker of this watch has *made provision for just such a reversal of that law*, by which both minute and hour hands move only forward. He has provided for a backward movement, when the intelligent owner chooses, without any interference with this exquisite arrangement: while I turn back the hands I disturb no wheel, and there is not even one tick the less: and yet, left to itself, the hands of that watch never could change their direction of movement. Who is competent to say that, when God reverses the hands on the great dial of nature, He has made no provision for such reversal?

II. If we may concede the possibility, may we not also, the probability of miracles?

These two questions are by no means the same, even in substance. Many things are possible that are not probable. God has power to do things, without number, which he never did and

never will do. He never acts without a reason.
He does not waste power by useless expenditure
of omnipotence. If, however, there is such a use
to be made of miracles as amply justifies the putting forth of such power we are prepared to find
them actually used.

In the natural world we find wonderful marks
of design. Wherever there is a socket there is a
ball to fit it and make the joint complete. If you
discover any apparent lack, something wanting
to render nature's arrangement and adjustment
perfect, further search will always reveal something else exactly adapted to supply the want.

Years ago, in the astronomical world, it was
found that certain changes are taking place which
threaten the very existence of the order of the
universe. For example: the orbits of the planets
are inclined to each other by an angle which does
not remain uniform. From the earliest ages the
inclination of the earth's equator to the ecliptic
has been decreasing, say about half a second a
year. Should this decrease continue, in about
85,000 years the equator and ecliptic would coin-
cide,—the order of nature would be entirely
changed, and the succession of seasons would give
place to one unchanging spring. But in fact, by
and by this decrease will reach its limit, and the
angle of inclination will then increase, and so the
seasons will keep revolving, and seed time and
harvest time shall not fail. God has provided a
compensation for what at first seemed a disturbing
cause, and as by the chronometer balance in a
model time-piece, regularity of movement is
insured, in the end. The action of this compen-
sating law may consume two hundred milleniums,

but this shows nothing more than the vast scale on which this machine is constructed.

So as to the changes in the angles under which the planetary orbits are inclined toward each other. Should these inclinations increase, the stability of the system would be impossible; order would give place to disorder, and the cosmos finally return to chaos.

Even such men as Humboldt have been misled into the prediction of a universal catastrophe. In his Cosmos he predicts the end of all things as surely coming, however remote from our day. The balance would be destroyed, wheels become dislodged, and the whole grand mechanism grind itself to atoms by its own collisions. Even astronomers and philosophers stood aghast at the prospect of such a final wreck and ruin. But the eyes of science continued to watch and search. And lo, it was found by Lagrange that these changes are like the movements of a pendulum which swings to the end of its arc and then swings back again, never once passing its proper and prescribed limits. How grand this conception! Think of a clockwork so magnificently vast and complicated that every tick of this pendulum represents millions of years! Yet what confidence it inspires in the Maker, when we find that, for every disturbing force, though, for periods too vast to be measured by time, it may seem to be driving the universe toward ruin, God has placed there another force or law to restore equilibrium and keep harmony!

So in the spiritual world we shall find no lack unsupplied. As surely as there is a need for miracles, the need will be met. Can we forsee that there would be need? Remember that a miracle is an occurrence so marked in its departure from the usual order of things as to be to men a sign of God's special power.

Let us suppose that we are all now living in the very year when Jesus Christ first appeared among men as a public teacher. The old Jewish church is corrupt and virtually dead. Even its beautiful forms of faith and worship are like the radiant skin of the serpent, when the living animal has cast it off and gone elsewhere; or like the " dead leaf retaining the form of its former self but performing none of its functions," a mere skeleton without the currents or even colors of life. Men grope in darkness and groan for light. The wise men of the East are waiting and watching for a star which may guide to the day dawn.

Let us suppose that God is purposing to give to men some clear and complete knowledge of His will. He might do it by a human teacher, like Plato; but how would mankind know that it is God who speaks? There have been many men who claimed to speak for God, and among them all we find it not easy to choose. All of them say something worth hearing, and perhaps something which is not unworthy to be a word from God; but even in the best of these teachers so much is at best uncertain, that it cannot be the utterance of Him who never makes a guess at truth or duty.

Now if God does speak to man, as to the grandest themes to which man can give heed, it is all important to hear and recognize God's voice, and know that it is God. Man has no right to be satisfied without proof that God has spoken; for he may be imposed upon and so misled into error and wrong doing. If anything is plain it is that I have a right reverently to ask for unmistakable evidence that the God of the universe is addressing me.

How shall He satisfy such honest doubt? By any method which shews that *it is He* who is actually revealing himself. If He shall choose to come down, as on Mount Sinai, and in a voice of thunder speak, till in terror we cry out, "Let not God speak to us lest we die!" we shall be satisfied that it is He. If He shall choose to appear, as to Moses, in a flame that burns a bush without consuming it, His whisper will be as convincing as the thunder was before; for we shall know that something more than a flame must be making that bush radiant and glorious. It is the fact of marked departure from the ordinary course of things, which arrests the mind and impresses it with the presence and power of God. There is an instinctive or intuitive conviction that where there is such a departure from the natural and usual order, God must be especially present and working. Nicodemus said to Christ, "We know that thou art a teacher come from God, for no man can do these miracles that thou doest except God be with him." There is the argument for miracles, and from miracles, in a nutshell. Where miracles are, we feel that God certainly is. And to meet this natural need of some clear proof that God speaks to us, it is probable that if He does speak through a man, that man will do such works as prove to all candid minds that he comes with the authority of God.

Miracles are simply God's signs that authority

comes with his messenger. When a minister or ambassador claims to represent the Court of St. James, the first inquiry is for his credentials. He may be a gentleman, scholar, statesman, hero—all this does not secure his reception as the representative of a foreign court. Nor should it. It is august business to stand in the stead of an empire that belts the world—on whose realm the sun never sets—whose beck makes the world tremble. When such ambassador meets our President and Cabinet in council, it is as though the British nation stood there in all the majesty of her greatness and power; and therefore we rightly require of such an ambassador credentials, so plain as to forbid a doubt of his mission and commission. Miracles are simply the credentials of God's special representatives, and their probability is established the moment we concede the grandeur of the occasion when the Lord of the universe declares His will, and the imperative necessity that we shall not mistake His true messengers.

This is the precise test which the word of God authorizes us to apply. Throughout these sublime pages there is but one uniform testimony on this subject. If any prophet arises, any religious teacher claiming to speak in behalf of God, this is the sign by which he is to be known: he shall, in his words or works, or both, shew that a power, beyond that of man, is moving in him and through him. What kind of words will answer these conditions? Not words of wisdom, only, however wise; for they would not prove that he who speaks is more than the wisest of men: not words of truth, only, for we cannot say how much truth a mere man may be able to discover and declare.

But, if this teacher shall *foretell future events;* if, like Elijah, he shall correctly prophesy a drought of three years, to begin and end only according to his word; men will say, this is more than human wisdom. Thus Samuel, even when a child, and after the prophetic fires had seemingly died out on the altars of Israel, was established as a prophet of the Lord—he declared, what no mere man could foresee or foretell, the sudden and terrible destruction of Eli's two sons: and when this awful word was fulfilled, all Israel said, the Lord is with him.

So may a teacher from God shew his credentials in his works, by *doing* anything which plainly shews a power above man. While the wonders which Moses wrought at Pharaoh's court were successfully imitated by the magicians, they carried but little weight; but when the rod was stretched forth and smote the dust of the earth so that it became lice in man and beast, and all the power of enchantment could not even imitate the miracle, even the magicians said unto Pharaoh, " *This is the finger of God!*"

III. If on any basis, we concede that miracles are *possible* and *probable*, they may certainly be most *naturally expected*, if the *Son of God* actually comes among men. The evidence will be on a scale correspondent with His dignity and majesty.

Now look at His miracles. The first of them was the changing of water into wine at Cana. Nature does that every season. By processes that are the wonder of all ages, and a mystery even to the learned, she gathers from air and earth the secret of their moisture, and by the marvelous action of roots and sap-ducts, distils it into the grape; then by the aid of air and light and heat and actinic ray, slowly changes the acid liquid into delicious nectar. By no artificial process has man been able to imitate the juice of the grape. He must wait on the vine, as his laboratory. When Jesus, by an instantaneous process, and without approaching the pots, changed water into grape juice, doing in a moment what nature does only in months, and doing it without her apparatus for distillation, He showed to those present that He knew nature's secrets and could, without her aid, work the same results; and so He showed himself the God of nature, and "manifested forth His glory." If you mark closely you will see in His recorded miracles a *progressive character*, and a gradual unfolding of His real self. The second miracle was one of healing and showed power over disease; the third, the miraculous draught, showed control over the animate creation; the fourth, the casting out of the devil, showed His power over demons; and so his miracles grow in importance, till the rising of the dead proves His control over death and decay.

Now, whatever may be said of miracles, as a sign that God spake by ordinary men, if ever a crisis justified them, it was when, last and best of all, God sent His only Son. We are justified in expecting that God's seal-ring will be on His finger. And, so, when John Baptist from his cell sent to ask him for signs of his Messiahship, He replied by referring to the grand scale on which he was wielding the power of God: "the blind see, the lame walk, the lepers are cleansed, the dead are raised up!" He wrought miracles, not to gratify curiosity; but to satisfy the reasonable demand for evidence that His power was divine. Did His miracles give certain proof of the presence and power of God? Let us see.

The famous clock in Strasburgh Cathedral has a mechanism so complicated, that it seems to the ignorant and superstitious almost a work of superhuman skill. The abused and offended maker, yet unpaid for his work, came one day and touched its secret springs, and it stopped. All the patience and ingenuity of a nation's mechanics and artizans failed to restore its disordered mechanism and set it in motion. Afterward, when his grievances were redressed, that maker came again, touched the inner springs and set it again in motion, and all its multiplied parts revolved again obedient to his will. When thus, by a touch, he suspended and restored those marvelous movements, he gave to any doubting mind proof that he was the maker—certainly the master, of that clock. And when Jesus of Nazareth brings to a stop the mechanism of nature, makes its mighty wheels turn back or in any way arrests its grand movement—more than all, when he can not only stop, but start again, the mysterious clock of human life, he gives to an honest mind overwhelming proof that God is with him. For a malignant power might arrest or destroy, but only He could reconstruct and restore!

IV. The argument for the *credibility of miracles* is grandly conclusive and magnificent in the scope of its horizon: in fact its very extent is embarrassing; but the main difficulty is that it must embrace in its wide range the entire question of the credibility of gospel history. If the writers of the New Testament are to be believed, then we are just so far on the road to believing their accounts of miraculous works. If their narrative is, for any reason, unworthy of credence, of course the credibility of the miracles which they record need not engage our attention. There is, however, a general question that can be examined without the extended argument on the credibility of the Scripture history, viz., is the account of a miracle, *in itself*, credible?

The foes of Christianity have wit and wisdom enough to see that they may as well give up the fight, unless they can break down the evidence of miracles. Let them allow that one miraculous work has been wrought, and there is a fatal breach in their wall of defense; for, if one miracle has been wrought, others may have been—if miraculous works, why not miraculous words? and so prophecy, as well as miracle, is conceded. And of what use to oppose a system of religion, buttressed up by both prophecy and miracle! No wonder the entire force of infidel argument, the whole mighty host, is massed and hurled against this giant fortress of our faith, and that every possible weapon of wit and wisdom, ignorance and learning, science and philosophy, sophistry and fallacy, is forged for this combined assault. Here is the Marathon, the Thermopylæ, the Waterloo, of the ages.

And what is their grand plan of attack? They boldly unite in this assertion: that no testimony can prove a miracle; they attempt to undermine and blow up the very foundation of all arguments for the credibility of miracles by claiming, as though it were a self-evident truth, that *a miracle is incredible.* This is a desperate measure, but it is becoming to a desperate cause.

Where a man voluntarily assumes a position like this, in order to make all argument impossible, there is no more hope of convincing him of the truth than of expanding or dilating the pupil of the eye by pouring more light upon it; bigotry, whether in believers or unbelievers, hates light, and grows narrower and more contracted as the light increases in intensity. But for the sake of candid minds, in danger of being misled by plausible sophistry, let us examine this infidel position.

Is there anything incredible in a miracle? Of course, if it be established at all, it must be by the evidence of the senses to immediate witnesses; and by their testimony to others who do not have the proof of the senses.

Are we to accept testimony on this subject? All questions of historic fact must be settled only by testimony: many matters of scientific fact are settled by testimony, for thousands who have no time, knowledge, opportunity for personal investigation; and yet we feel certain of historic facts and scientific discoveries.

Of course, if miracles wrought by Christ, and by prophets and apostles, are to be made credible to us, it can be by no other evidence than that of testimony. On what basis, then, rests the assertion that miracles are not credible? Are they not supported by testimony? Are there no witnesses? Are the witnesses not competent or trustworthy? If these were the ground of the attack, it would be easy to show how unsafe and unsound it is; for if on any subject, we have abundance of testimony and that of the most credible sort, it is with respect to miracles.

No other religion ever dared to make its appeal to miracles, and to rest its appeal on miracles! Where and when miraculous wonders have been claimed, it has not been as decisive signal tests, by which the claims of such religions should stand or fall. It is one thing to challenge an unbeliever to try a religion by its miracles, and quite another to ask a believer to accept them as part of a system in which he already believes. A man may not marry a woman because of her poverty or her fortune, or a wen on her neck, who will, if he first loves the woman, take her with poverty or wealth, and wen beside.

When a religion approacnes a man and boldly says: " God bears me witness, both with signs and wonders, and with divers miracles," it meets him with a challenge; it bids him dispute its claims if he dare, by first disproving its signs if he can. But when a man has already become a disciple, for example, of Mohammed, he is disposed to receive his miracles as genuine without any witness but his word; and so the religious system instead of being based on these miracles as its proof, rather becomes the basis which supplies them with proof. But Christianity *starts* by bidding us apply these severe tests. If we can even disprove one miracle, the resurrection of Christ, St. Paul confesses that the whole structure falls; " our preaching is vain; your faith is vain."

The grandeur of this bold challenge to try the Christian faith by the test of miracles, needs to be appreciated.

Mohammed did not claim miraculous powers,

though, centuries after, they were claimed for him; and such marvels as he did impose on the credulity of his followers, he took good pains not to make dependent on any other testimony than his own. But see how audacious the challenge of our Lord: " If I had not done among them the works which none other man did they had not had sin!" And none of these things were done " in a corner," but openly, in temple courts, on public streets, by lake shores, before thousands.

Mohammed might tell of Gabriel's night visits and his own night journey; of the celestial delivery of the divine book, in fragments, till the Mohammedan bible was complete; but who was there to prove or disprove his testimony? But Christ moved, during at least three years, among men publicly, and every step marked by words and works such as never before or since challenged the faith of man. These miracles could not be ascribed to natural causes; they were such as admitted of the test of the senses; they were so public as to command universal attention; and they were of such various character as precludes the notion of deception or delusion. Their number, the instantaneous and complete character of the cures he wrought, and the absence of one failure in the attempt even to raise the dead, put infinite distance between these miracles and the pretended wonders of this or any other age, where those who claimed to have been cured, at sight or touch of sacred relics, were the few exceptions to hundreds of disappointed applicants for healing virtue.

No confirmation of the miracle of scripture is more remarkable than the silence of enemies; nay, we have more than silence—confession of the fact that they were wrought. Let us remember that, from the beginning, the founder of this great religion was the focal centre of all the intensity of human hate. All eyes turned to him and subjected him to microscopic scrutiny.

Forgeries of any kind, though as well done as the poems that Chatterton feigned to have found in old St. Mary's, are sure of detection sooner or later. No forgery is so difficult as that of miracles, especially when publicly wrought, under the scrutiny of keen-eyed foes. Yet, though there was every motive for overthrowing them if possible, and although they were constantly appealed to as known facts, they went unchallenged! In days of persecution, thousands suffered torture and death, where, to have confessed the miracles of our Lord to have been impostures, would have been deliverance,—and yet no disciple ever made a confession such as this!

Most remarkable of all, even the Jewish Rabbis, in the Talmud, acknowledge these miracles, but pretend they were wrought by magic or by the use of a secret charm which Jesus stole out of the temple. Celsus, learned and able as he was among the assailants of Christianity, both allows the facts of the gospel history and concedes that Christ wrought miracles, but ascribes them to magical arts learned in Egypt. Hierocles, the persecutor, does not deny these miracles, though he ridicules the idea of worshipping Christ. Julian, the apostate, confesses that Christ cured the lame and blind, and cast out demons, but thinks these works did not make him worthy of such fame.

Modern foes of Christianity do not venture often to attack our faith from this quarter; it is too well defended. No, they put on the air of gracious, condescending concession: they allow the testimony to be honest and ample, but mistaken. Mr. Hume's fertile and ingenious mind suggests a short path by which to escape the necessity of faith: "deny that any testimony can prove a miracle," and it is done! And the modern sceptic is tempted to ask with Isaac, when Jacob got ready his venison so soon by making a tame lamb from the fold answer for a wild deer from the fields, "how hast thou found it so quickly, my son!"

It must be confessed that Hume's argument is very plausible and subtle. "Nature's laws are uniform; miracles imply a violation of that uniformity —it is easier to believe a hundred men honest but mistaken than to believe one such absurdity to be possible!" No room remains for the exposure of the sophistry of Hume's argument. Already it has been partly answered by showing that a miracle is not a violation of natural laws. But a few suggestions may be added.

One of the hinges of Hume's argument is this, that a miracle is contrary to experience. Of course if miracles were not contrary to our common experience they could have no power as a sign of divine interposition. But were they contrary to the experience of those who witnessed them? If I am to believe nothing that is contrary to my experience, the door is shut to all grand discoveries, and corrections of erroneous opinion. The savage in equatorial Africa is justified in denying that water is ever solid so that its surface will sustain many tons, for it is contrary to his experience: and if he sees the magnet lift and hold a heavy weight without hands or visible means, or a balloon inflated with hydrogen gas dart upward with heavy ballast in the basket, he is justified in disbelieving his own senses, for his experience of the uniformity of nature's laws is, that what is heavy falls to the earth. And here is a suspension of the laws of gravity.

This objection argues absurdity: for it renders incredible all exceptions to the otherwise uniform experience of men. This is unfair. On a basis of simple science, when any new fact contradicts our hitherto uniform experience, instead of denying the fact, we make our science broader, and look for some new law or force, unknown or not understood before. Just this, God means we shall do when we behold a miracle: stop and ask what new force is at work, which is not found in the ordinary uniform operation of mechanical laws: and what means this intervention of a superior hand to control and reverse nature's ordinary movement.

Hume's argument will have little weight with those who understand Mr. Hume, and see how he was forced by his own philosophy to this position. One of his unfortunate admirers acknowledged that the disposition to doubt everything was so interwoven with his whole character, that he seemed to be uncertain even of his own existence. He was the modern Pyrrho, and not an unworthy successor of that ancient doubter who was not sure of anything—who did not know anything, and was not sure he did not know— who doubted whether even the world itself were not an illusion, and whose friends accompanied him in his walks lest he should doubt the reality of a precipice and so walk off its edge to his own ruin.

Hume's arguments failed to satisfy his own mind. Hear his own words speaking of his speculations: "They have so wrought upon me and heated my brain that I am ready to reject all belief and reasoning, and can look upon no opinion even as more probable or likely than another. Where am I or what? From what causes do I derive my existence, and to what condition shall I return? Whose favor shall I court, and whose anger must I dread? What beings surround me, and on whom have I any influence, and who have any influence on me? I am confounded with all these questions, and begin to fancy myself in the most deplorable condition imaginable, environed with the deepest darkness and utterly deprived of the use of every member and faculty."

It partly refutes Hume's view of miracles to show how he came to hold it. His theology compelled his scepticism; his denial of miracles was necessary unless he gave up his philosophy. To one who believes in a personal God, who may for good reasons interfere with nature's ordinary processes, miracles are not incredible; but an Atheist, Pantheist or Deist *must* deny the possibility of miracles. For if, behind and above nature, there be no intelligent, divine, controlling hand, the very existence of the universe depends on the absolute uniformity of nature's laws and processes. Mr. Hume was a Deist. He traced the various effects of nature to a uniform series of causes: no interruption could be supposed to occur, for there would be nothing to restore order and harmony. It is well to have provision for that extra pressure in the water works, if there be an intelligent person there, to determine when to gear on the spare machinery, and to disconnect it when the need of it ceases: but, if the machine should have no brain behind it, it would not do to allow such extra pressure, for the machine cannot restore itself to its ordinary and uniform working—and to have fourfold pressure when the hydrants are closed would destroy both machinery and distributing pipes. For Hume to admit miracles would be to admit a personal God—back of a nature's enginery, an engineer whose power and intelligence first fixed the uniformity of nature's ordinary workings, and who if he chooses to bring some new force to bear, can disconnect it when his purpose is answered. Hume's argument against miracles was not simply the result of candid reasoning, but a manufactured theory invented to fit into his deistical philosophy.

I am prepared to prove that his dishonesty in the matter lies even deeper, in a deliberate determination to oppose the claims of the religion of Christ. I quote his own words, that it may be seen how he contradicts himself. After boldly saying that "a miracle supported by any human testimony is more properly a subject of derision than of argument," he says, "I own that there may possibly be miracles of such a kind as to admit of proof from human testimony;" and then imagines a case of miracle, so attested by competent witness that philosophers ought to receive it as certain. And then mark how he sneaks out as by a trap door, lest he be caught in his own admissions. "But should this miracle be ascribed to a new system of religion, men in all ages have been so imposed on by ridiculous stories of that kind that this very circumstance would be a full proof of the cheat!"

Verily, a Daniel come to judgment! Here is a learned man, a prince among sceptics, who says in one breath that "no kind of testimony for any kind of miracle can possibly amount to a probability, much less to a proof:" then, in another breath, concedes that "there may be miracles of such a kind as to admit of proof from human testimony, and be received by philosophers as certain;" and, yet in another breath, hastens to say that if such miracle be used as a sign of a divine religion we must again reject it!

The jewel of consistency evidently burns very dimly in the diadem of this deist: a miracle cannot possibly be credible, yet it may be credible; and again even a credible miracle may be also incredible! The fact is Mr. Hume was bound to overthrow Christianity, and he would hesitate at no violation of logical consistency. or moral candor, to avoid giving the religion of the Bible a show of support. If one should descend to such unfairness in dealing with religious doubts and difficulties, he would be met, and deserve to be, by a pelting hail of hisses.

Let one guard be put about what has been said, to prevent perversion. Some, in arguing for the truth of Revelation, start by proving miracles to be credible, and inferring the doctrine to be divine because so sanctioned. But this is by no means the whole truth. Our Lord himself did not seek to force a faith or even conviction upon the minds of men whose hearts were hostile to Him and his work. If a man, by his bondage to his philosophy, or to an accusing conscience, or to selfish interests, is predisposed and determined not to see that Christianity is of God, no amount of evidence will convince him. Sight does not reach a shut eye, which is for all purposes of seeing, a blind eye. The heart makes the theology.

If a man comes to the Bible with open eye he will find two influences operating together to produce conviction. First he will find such truth and such a person there as dispose him to expect divine credentials: and then he will find divine credentials disposing him to believe the truths and the person to be all that they claim, essentially divine; the written word and the living word of God. And many an examiner of Scripture scarce knows which way conviction first takes hold of his mind, that Christ must be a divine being; whether from his teaching and life; or because His wonderful works reveal His divinity. You stand in sunlight and you are at the same moment dazzled by its brightness and thrilled by its warmth. Whether you were conscious of light or heat first, you scarce know. You approach the Bible; there breaks upon you a sense that you are walking in light: if there be truth anywhere it is here. You find a record of miraculous signs, confirming the teachings of the book of God. Whether the signs lead you to look at the truth, or the truth leads you to expect the signs, you cannot tell.

"It becomes easier to believe in the miracles, because of our personal faith in Him as a being of whom such extraordinary deeds might be reasonably expected, than to believe in Him primarily on the ground of His having exercised miraculous powers." Some have been drawn to the cradle of this wonderful child by seeing His star in the east, and being prepared to find the holy One, by the signs that herald him. Others first found Him at the cross, and, when the precious drops fell on them with cleansing, healing power, could well believe the story of the magi.

We have no hope of convincing a sceptic simply by miracles. But, if in a candid spirit any man will search the Scriptures, he shall find that they testify of Christ, that Christ is a witness unto Himself. There have been those who, like Gilbert West and Lyttleton, have started to lay hands on Him as an impostor, but who approaching Him through the paths of Scripture study have, when their eyes rested full on His blessed person, seen the divinity flash forth even through the veil of humanity, and, like the soldiers in the garden, have gone backward and fallen to the ground. They started to oppose: they stopped to espouse and embrace.

Every study of the Bible is a study of the evidences of Christianity. The Bible is itself the greatest miracle of all, and the Son of God more wonderful than any of the wonders that confirm His claims. The believer feels this in every fibre of his being. Rob me of miracles and of prophecy: you have not robbed me of Him. Before Him I bow, because of what He is. The morning star pales and fades at sunrise. There is a glory, in the presence of which all else is dim.

And if you will come and stand in the radiance of that presence, with eye unveiled by wilful hostility to light, and wait there until you are bathed in the glory, filled and thrilled by the love and life that come in the same beam with the light, you shall need no starry miracles to herald the morning, and assure you that He, who can impart to you the knowledge of God and the peace of God, can be no other than the Sun of Righteousness!

CHAPTER V.

THE WITNESS OF THE BIBLE TO ITSELF — ITS SCIENTIFIC ACCURACY.

"Forever, O Lord, thy word is settled in heaven."—PSALM CXIX : 89.

This sublime assertion of the eternal stability of the Word of God is "Luther's text." He had it written in charcoal on the walls of his chamber, and wrought in embroidery on the dress of his servants. Earthly changes reach not the heavenly sphere; and there the Word of God is settled, far beyond the reach of disturbing causes. Even progressive Modern Science, which has unsettled the notions of centuries, is unable to prove the testimony of God's Word to be false.

The Bible is a very remarkable book, from whatever source it has come. One of the princes of men, the light of the fourth century, whose oratory gave him the name of Chrysostom, "the golden mouth," and whose virtues made him the admiration and terror of the corrupt court of Eudoxia—such a man, himself one of the foremost scholars of his day, has given to the Bible its very name, "*O Biblos*"—the Book!

In every work we see the workman—his skill in handling tools, his inventive genius in planning, his taste in arranging and adorning. The artist breathes in his canvas and speaks in the marble. If there be a work of God, we expect it to express and exhibit him. You go to St. Peter's Cathedral; you stand beneath that vast dome, prepared to feel a sense of awe at the grand proportions and exquisite decorations—for Michael Angelo designed and adorned it. And when, in the hush of midnight, you look up into the dome of heaven and see thousands of lamps that burn for whole milleniums unconsumed, and shine at a distance beyond calculation—when you remember that that streaming banner of light, the "Milky Way," is myriads of stars, in close ranks, like countless warriors, so that you see only the lines of light flashing from their silver helmets, you are prepared to believe that God planned that concave, and wrote his own name on it in letters of light. "The heavens declare the glory of God, and the firmament sheweth his handiwork."

So, if this book be the Word of God, we shall find in it proof and mark of a divine mind and hand. There will be a grandeur in the sweep and span of its teachings which reminds of the arch of the firmament—a glory about its facts and truths which suggests the radiance of suns and stars; there will be that which is too high for our attainment, and too broad for our measurement. God will compel us to say, "Hath not my hand made all these things!" The Bible asks you to try it by this test: Does it bear marks of a more than human mind? If there be nothing in it inconsistent with a merely human origin, it is idolatry to call it the Word of God—to treat it as of divine origin, and yield it divine honors. But if there be here such a gigantic structure of truth as that not even a race of Titans could have built it; if its basis is laid deeper than man ever dug, and its pinnacles rise higher than man ever reached, how are we to escape the conclusion and conviction that its author and maker is God?

The Bible has always been the focal point of all controversy; for it is the very key of the whole system of Christianity. To carry this by storm, or undermine it, is to take Christianity at its centre; and the outposts follow the fortunes of the main defenses. Of late, the form of attack and the tone of assault have changed. Infidelity is rarely insulting, contemptuous. It is rather plausible, patronizing. It used to pound the Bible with denunciations; now it pats the Bible and says, "Really a very fine book, but by no means faultless!" Dr. Pressense says of Renan: "He very skilfully undermines Christianity while profuse in its praise; he buries it in flowers. He comes to the tomb of the Saviour not to weep and worship like the women of the gospel, but to stifle with perfumes and spices any lingering spark of life in the religion of Jesus. He does not deal a blow with a sharp sword; no, he embalms. But the result is the same as though he made a violent attack."

Modern scepticism, with the lofty air of profound learning and philosophic doubt, approaches the Divine Word. Under pretense of a careful, conscientious, impartial investigation, as though reluctant not to believe that the Bible is all it claims to be, it applies its strictly scientific tests, and, like a physician who feels a feeble pulse, sounds a decayed lung, or tests a diseased heart, turns away with a sigh of disappointment and an ominous shake of the head. And yet the more we see of scientific and philosophic scepticism, the more we are satisfied that, like Lord Nelson, it covers the only sound eye, and declares it can't see with the blind one. Underneath all this assumption of judicial coolness and fairness we detect voluntary suppression of the truth, partial pleading, desperate corruptions of the doctrines and perversions of the facts of Scripture, and the same hot hate of the religion of the Bible, the same passion to overthrow it, the same resolute hostility to everything supernatural, as in the bolder and more defiant forms of attack. You may find this plausible scepticism in the sanctum of the editor, the silver tongue of the orator, the chair of the university professor, and even the pulpit of the nominal preacher. The Bible is, by the confession even of sceptics, the best of books, and, on the whole, most marked by all that gives permanent value; but they would have us believe that it is scarcely abreast with our advanced age, and that its claim to infallibility is absurd.

But the Bible accepts no patronage, no hesitating homage, no qualified encomium. Submit the Word of God to any and every test which is possible and proper—intellectual, moral, philosophical, ethical, literary, or scientific. If, on any rational ground, it does not stand the test, it must fall; if it has no granite buttresses, it is folly to attempt to support its tremendous claims to divine authority by any rotten props of our own.

Of all tests, *the scientific* is the most unpromising; for here, if at any point, we may expect to find the Bible weak, exposed to successful assault. That is a grand fort which has no angle which its guns do not fully command. Even firm friends of the Bible show some little apprehension when we talk of applying scientific tests; when science comes, as with crucible and lancet, to try its severe processes on the Word. But even at this weakest point, God's Word is too strong for the combined strength of all its foes. From this angle, as well as every other, its guns command the approach and make a clean sweep; and every candid doubter may find abundant proof, even on the scientific side, that a more than human mind has produced the Bible. It is a Gibraltar, and they who attack it, like the waves that sweep against that giant rock in the Mediterranean seas, do not break or even shake it, but only cleave themselves asunder!

The argument from the side of science is the more conclusive because the Bible is not, and cannot be, in the nature of the case, a scientific book. In history, any matter of science touched upon would be only casual, and whatever scientific errors or inadvertencies might occur would not impair its value as a narrative of facts. So a treatise on mathematics would not be the less trustworthy as a guide in working out difficult problems, simply because there might be words misspelled, or inaccurate statements about geography. Every book is judged by its main purpose; all else is incidental.

The object of the Bible is not to teach science, but moral and spiritual truth. Scientific facts and truths may be discovered by the intellect and industry of man; and hence no revelation of them is needed. But our origin and destiny, our relations to God, the way of peace and purity, the link between the here and the hereafter—the highest wisdom of man has only guessed at these things; and here comes the need that God shall speak.

We are therefore to judge the Word of God by its professed purpose, and if, in the unfolding of moral and religious truth, scientific errors or inaccuracies appear, which have no relation to spiritual truth, they may not make the Bible unworthy of acceptance as a guide to the knowledge and practice of duty. Lord Bacon, from a strictly philosophical point of view, has said that the "scope or purpose of the Spirit of God is not to express matters of nature in Scripture, otherwise than in passage, for application to man's capacity and to matters moral and divine." It was no part of the design or mission of inspired writers to tell us scientific truth. Hence it was natural that, in referring to the Kingdom of Nature, they should use the language of appearance, as we do now at an age of the world far more advanced in scientific knowledge. We know that the sun is the centre of the solar system, and that the earth moves around it; yet we talk of the sun as rising in the east, setting in the west, and revolving about the earth. We speak of the dew as descending from the heaven, as though distilled in the far depths of space, while in fact the atmosphere gives up its vapor at the touch of a colder surface, as an ice-pitcher collects and condenses the moisture from the air. When, therefore, sacred writers use forms of speech which fit appearances, not realities, and accord with popular impressions, rather than scientific discoveries, "the absence of scientific accuracy by no means involves any real discrepancy or contradiction."

Had the language of Scripture been scientific,

instead of popular, it would have been a blemish and a hindrance, because it would have arrested attention and diverted it from the grander truths that the Bible was meant to unfold, and created controversies on matters of little consequence. Suppose, for instance, that in the opening chapters of Genesis, Moses had accurately announced, in plain terms, all the discoveries of modern geology and astronomy; had given this globe a great age, even prior to the creation of man; had made the six days of creation six periods of vast length; had described the vast vegetation of the carboniferous age, and the marvellous process by which it was converted into coal; had told men of the original chemical or "cosmical" light and heat that preceded the appearance of the sun—of the mighty monsters that sported in the waters and roamed on the land; had recorded the tremendous convulsions that rocked the earth as on the bosom of a vast crater—what would have been the effect?

First, scientific discovery would have been announced prematurely, before mankind was fitted to understand or use it. Secondly, God would have been contradicting himself by communicating directly to man knowledge which He had decreed man shall dig out for himself. Thirdly, men would have forgotten the more important spiritual truths, that are the main matters of revelation, in discussions of subordinate questions, for which the race was not yet ready. Fourthly, the effect would be to discredit the whole revelation—to make Moses appear either as a madman or a dreamer, and thus to defeat the grand end for which the Inspired Word was given! And yet, if the Bible is God's Truth, it ought not, even by the way, to affirm what is actually untrue. We cannot imagine the infinite God as telling man the grandest truths on spiritual themes and surrounding them with many little falsehoods, simply because man was not mature enough to understand the full facts.

Was there any way by which all desirable ends should be met? One only suggests itself. God might lead inspired men to use such language, that, without revealing scientific facts in advance, it might accurately accommodate itself to them, when discovered. The language might be so elastic and flexible as to contract itself to the narrowness of ignorance, and yet expand itself to the dimensions of knowledge, like the rubber bandage, so invaluable in modern surgery, which stretches about an inflamed and swollen limb, yet shrinks as the swelling abates. If there be terms or phrases which, without suggesting puzzling enigmas, shall yet contain within themselves ample space for all the demands of growing human knowledge; if the Bible may, from imperfect human language, select terms which may hold hidden truths, till ages to come shall disclose the inner meaning,—this would seem to be the best solution of this difficult problem. And when we come to compare the language of the Bible with modern science, we find just this to be the fact.

I. Take, for example, *astronomy*. How bitter has been the battle between undevout astronomers and the Word of God!

We are told that the Bible term, "firmament," is an ancient blunder, crystallized. Modern science, taking a dignified stand, says: "Ye have heard it hath been said by them of old time, there

SCIENTIFIC ACCURACY OF THE BIBLE. 117

is a solid sphere above us which revolves with its starry lamps; but I say unto you that this is an old notion of ignorance, for there is nothing but vast space filled with ether above us, and stars are suns varying by infinite distances, and the earth turns on its axis."

But look closer at this word "firmament." While Mr. Goodwin declares it "irreconcilable with modern astronomy," and timid apologists venture to suggest that Moses simply made a mistake, or may be pardoned for speaking after the manner of men, we find that the original term *rakiya* means that which is spread out, or overspreads—an "*expanse.*" Now, read the word expanse where firmament occurs, and there is not only no contradiction as to the facts of astronomy, but perfect harmony. If Moses had been Mitchell, he could not have chosen a better word to express the appearance, and yet accommodate the reality. He actually anticipated science. And this is one of the "Mistakes of Moses."

Another error of them of old time was that of the revolution of the heavenly bodies around the earth; and after Copernicus, Kepler and Galileo taught the true law of the solar system, men raised an outcry against the Bible. And yet the Bible is found to be entirely consistent with the discoveries of science, that the earth is not flat, but a sphere, and that it moves with perfect uniformity on its axis.

Take such expressions as these: Job xxvi:7—He hangeth the earth upon nothing. Job xxxviii:8—Who shut up the sea with doors when it rushed forth and came out of the womb; when I made the cloud its garment, and thick darkness its swaddling-band? and established my decree upon it, and set bars and doors, and said hitherto shalt thou come, but no further, etc. Job xxviii:12— Hast thou commanded the morning since thy days, and caused the dayspring to know his place?

How beautifully this language adapts itself to the scientific facts not then known—that a relation is established between land and sea, by which the waters cannot overwhelm the earth; that this globe is not supported on any other solid substance, as the Pagan mythologies even now teach, but held in place by invisible forces of gravitation; that the revolution of the earth upon its axis is so absolutely regular that, as LaPlace says, it has not for two thousand years varied the one-hundredth part of a second; so that the dayspring never fails or lingers in the eastern sky.

Jeremiah xxxiii:22—"The host of heaven cannot be numbered, neither the sand of the sea measured."

The fact of the vast host of stars is a fact of modern discovery. Hipparchus, about a century and a half before Christ, gave the number of stars as 1,022, and Ptolemy, in the beginning of the second century of the Christian era, could find but 1,026. We may on a clear night, with the unaided eye, see only 1,160, or, if we could survey the whole celestial sphere, about 3,000. But when the telescope began to be pointed to the heavens, less than three centuries ago, by Galileo, then for the first time men began to know that Jeremiah was right when he made the stars as countless as the sand on the sea-shore. When Lord Rosse's instrument turned its great mirror to the sky, lo, the number of visible stars increased to nearly 400,000,000! and Herschel compares the multitude of them to glittering dust scattered on the black background of the heavens. When John Herschel, at the foot of the dark continent, resolves the nebulæ into suns, and Lord Rosse, as with the eye of a Titan, finds in the cloudy scarf about Orion "a gorgeous bed of stars," and the very milky way itself proves to be simply a grand procession of stars absolutely without number,—how true is the exclamation of Jeremiah, 600 years before Christ, 2,200 years before Galileo: "The host of heaven cannot be numbered!" Who taught Jeremiah astronomy?

II. When the modern science of *Geology* began to unwrap the earth's coverings and read the records of the rocks, timid faith grew pale and trembled for the Word of God. A vast age was revealed for our globe, and what must we do with the "Mistakes of Moses?" How came these fossils or organic remains in the rocks? and in such quantities that coral reefs represent countless millions of zoöphytes, and mountain masses are composed of shells not larger than a grain of sand? The Tuscan hills are built of chambered shells so small that one ounce of stone contains over 10,-000; and the dust that falls from the chalk at the blackboard under the microscope proves to be fossils! And what enormous periods were required for living creatures to build such masses as these!

Some attempted to account for the deposit of these fossils by the convulsions attending the deluge; others suggested that God built the world out of fossils, in which life had never dwelt, so that the rocks, after all, really lie to us. Others have been ready to thunder anathemas against science, because they could not reconcile it with Scripture, after the fashion of the Brahmin who, when the microscope showed him the folly of his pagan notions and practices, rid himself of his doubts by dashing the microscope into fragments! But surely the Bible cannot need such methods of defense. If truth be divided against itself, how, then, shall his kingdom stand?

The correspondence between the Mosaic account of creation and the most advanced discoveries of science proves that only He who built the world built the Book. Note a few instances:

1. The order of creation.

Geology teaches a watery waste, whose dense vapors shut out light: Moses affirms that, at first, the earth was formless and void, and darkness was upon the face of the deep. Geology makes life to precede light, and the life develops beneath the deep: Moses presents the creative spirit as brooding over that great deep, before God said "Let light be." Geology makes the atmosphere to form an expanse by lifting watery vapors into clouds, and so separating the fountains of waters above from those below: Moses affirms the same. Geology tells us that continents next lifted themselves from beneath the great deep, and bore vegetation: Moses also declares that the dry land appeared, and brought forth grass, herb, and the tree, exactly correspondent to the three orders of primeval vegetation! Geology then asserts that the heavens became cleared of cloud and the sun and moon and stars appeared: Moses does not say that God *created* all these heavenly bodies on the fourth creative day, but that they then began to serve to divide day from night and to become signs for seasons, days and years! Geology then shows us sea monsters, reptiles and winged creatures: Moses likewise reveals the waters bringing forth moving and creeping creatures and fowl flying in the expanse. Geology unfolds next, the race of quadruped mammals—and so Moses makes cattle and beast of the earth to follow, in the same order and on the sixth day of creation. Geology brings man on the scene last of all, and so does Moses. Geology makes the first light and heat not solar but chemical or "cosmical." Moses makes light to precede the first appearance of the sun, by the space of three creative days!

2. Look at the order of animal creation! Geology and comparative anatomy combine to teach that the order of creation was from lower to higher. Fish, proportion of brain to spinal cord; 2 to 1. Reptiles 2½ to 1. Birds, 3 to 1. Mammals 4 to 1. Man 33 to 1. Now this is exactly the order of Moses. Who told Moses, what modern comparative anatomy has discovered, that fish and reptile come below birds?

And these are some more of the "Mistakes of Moses!" Here is a record of creation, produced fifteen or twenty centuries before science unveiled these modern facts and truths; and yet there is not one scientific blunder or error, and the coincidences and correspondences are so many and so marked, that a modern scientist has confessed, that if one should sketch briefly the celestial mechanism of LaPlace, the Cosmos of Humboldt and the latest system of geology, no simpler and sublimer words could be found than those of Moses!

3. Again geology shows us that the vast plants of the great coal age are such as never grew in sunlight but in long continued shade; they are such as must have fed upon an atmosphere full of vapor—and their wood is not hardened as it would have been under sunshine. Who taught Moses to put the growth of that earliest vegetation in the period preceding the first appearance of the sun in the sky!

4. Geology teaches six periods of creation, extending through ages. Moses appears to teach six days of 24 hours each. But again on examining closely, we find the Hebrew word, *Yom*, means *a period of time*, and is often used of indefinite periods or seasons! In the first chapter of Genesis, sceptics triumphantly say, it makes creative periods to be measured by 24 hours; and yet in Gen. II: 4, it is used of the whole time occupied in creation! In Psalm xcv: 8, "in the day of temptation," it means forty years. We use the English word with the same looseness of application—a "polar day" means six months—the day of grace, the period of probation. Origen and Augustine, long before science suggested that day might mean a period, maintained that the Hebrew word was indefinite; and when the Bible declares that "one day is with the Lord as a thousand years," it gives a clew and key to its own interpretation.

Again you will notice that of these creative days Moses said "and the evening and the morning were the first day." If the solar day is meant, why begin with the evening? the solar day obviously begins with sunrise. To account for this curious feature in the Mosiac record by the fact

SCIENTIFIC ACCURACY OF THE BIBLE. 123

that the Jews reckoned their day from sunset to sunset, is to reason in a circle, for it was from this first chapter of Genesis that such an unnatural mode of reckoning proceeded. Now when we turn to geology and find that each creative period began in an evening and developed into a morning—light developing out of darkness and order out of confusion—we see why Moses was guided to make each day to begin with evening.

5. The Deluge, as recorded in the days of Noah, has been thought to be irreconcilable with modern science. The grand point where objections center is that of the universal character of the flood. As the human race then occupied but a small part of the globe, to submerge the whole, so that even the loftiest mountains should be more than covered seems a needless waste of divine energy; especially as it may well be doubted whether the entire atmosphere, condensed into rain, would suffice to lift the seas to such a height; and there are believed to be many evidences, in certain parts of the earth, that no universal flood has prevailed within the last 6,000 years.

To these objections it is only necessary to reply that the moment the Bible record is interpreted with reference to the inhabited world, all difficulties vanish. Such phrases as "the whole earth," "under the whole heaven," etc., are frequently used in Scripture of so much of the earth as was peopled; or even of Palestine, and the lands lying about it. Terms of a universal character are to be interpreted not literally, but by the design and end of the writer. When we are told that "all countries came into Egypt to buy corn"—what do we understand? Are we to suppose that, if there were inhabitants in Britain, they journed to Egypt for grain? It would take about as much time, in those days, to get there and back, as it would to secure a new harvest. But if we understand that Egypt became a granary—a house of bread, to all the district, over which the famine prevailed, the record is plain.

Now, in the account of the deluge, Moses is writing of God's awful judgment upon the sin of the race. His judgment fell upon the earth, for man's sake and only so much of the earth as was the scene of man's sin, was necessarily concerned. If then we understand the whole earth to refer to the entire *inhabited surface*, the flood is still relatively universal, *i. e.*, universal as to mankind; and the usage of similar terms in other parts of Scripture justifies such interpretation! Hugh Miller has shown that all the phenomena of the flood might be produced by the gradual sinking and rising again of that part of the earth's surface known as the cradle of the race; and this would produce the very effects, so graphically described by Noah, "breaking up of the fountains of the great deep and the returning of the waters from off the earth." It ought to be added that tradition even among the Pagans confirms the fact of the flood and the resting of the ark on Ararat.

Haywood W. Guion of North Carolina has suggested a theory of the Deluge, which both harmonizes all the discoveries of science with the record in Genesis, and may yet displace all previous conceptions of the subject. He takes literally the statement of St. Peter, "the world that then was, being overflowed with water, perished."

In Genesis we read—"let the waters under the heaven be gathered together unto one place and let the dry land appear." In both passages there is no hint of more than one continent or more than one sea. The dry land or earth seems to be by itself in one grand elevation above sea level, and the waters gathered in one place. This would imply, as any scientist knows, certain peculiar conditions. This solitary continent, rising in one mass from the midst of one sea that surrounds it, would present no great inequalities of surface, though there might be elevations that, compared with the rest, would be hills or even mountains; there would be a great uniformity of climate and temperature, no rains or clouds, but heavy mists constantly keeping the earth moist; and consequently vast vegetable growths, very luxuriant and abundant, making animal food unnecessary either for man or beast—there would be a paradise of verdure, and one perennial spring. This Mr. Guion holds was the case. At the time of the deluge this huge dome, that rose out of the water, was shattered by volcanic explosions and a great earthquake, and its grand roof fell in and became the bed of what is now the Pacific ocean, while its shattered and irregular rim was tilted up into the great mountain ranges, that line the eastern boundaries of the Pacific; and the bed of this original ocean was lifted into the continents of our eastern and western hemispheres, while the sea rushed into the new bed formed by the submersion of the original continent. This would give us in the new order of things great mountain ranges, with marked inequalities of climate and temperature—and all the phenomena of the changing seasons, winds, clouds, storms of rain and snow; and consequently the first rainbow. Animals inhabiting barren districts would be driven to devour animals weaker than they, and animal food would become necessary to man. This theory makes the whole original world to be submerged and all the high hills covered. The gigantic animals of that primeval continent engulphed in the foaming waters and afterward buried beneath the superficial mass of shifting soil, would furnish the remarkable remains found in so many places, shewing that the creatures they represent were overtaken in some universal catastrophe.

Mr. Tullidge says: that "with the advance of discovery, the opposition, supposed to exist between Revelation and Geology, has disappeared; and of the eighty theories which the French Institute counted in 1806, as hostile to the Bible, not one now stands." Not only so; but among the mightiest advocates of God's Word are many of the masters who have explored his works. Their united testimony is, that we have no occasion to fear for the Bible notwithstanding the oppositions of science falsely so called. For "Heaven and earth shall pass away, but My Word shall not pass away."

CHAPTER VI.

THE SCIENTIFIC TRUTH OF THE WORD OF GOD.

"Thy word is true from the beginning."— PSALM CXIX: 160.

That is, "from the first word." The enthusiasm of the unknown writer of this Psalm knows no ordinary bounds. He sets out to rear a monument to the Word of God, and it is like a solid shaft of marble. sculptured into twenty-two sides, and each side bearing eight inscriptions. After the fashion of ancient acrostics, each side is appropriated to one letter of the Hebrew alphabet, and each of its eight inscriptions begins with that letter, as though all the resources of language would vainly be exhausted in endeavoring to describe the wonders of the Scriptures. He concludes this twentieth section by declaring that, from the first word on, every word is true. Resuming the argument of the last chapter, let us look at

III. *Cosmogony.* How grand a fact it is, in favor of the Bible, that not one scientific error, blunder or absurdity has ever been found there! Can the sacred books of other religions endure that test? Apply this touchstone to the Koran, the Shasta, the Zendavesta, or the teachings of the wisest and best of uninspired men. Compare Moses with Zoroaster and Confucius, Seneca and Socrates, Plato and Pythagoras, Anaxagoras and Aristotle—when the ancient religions or philosophies touch the Bible-theme of creation, they abound in sheer absurdities! Put the first chapter of Genesis beside the Hindu idea of the universe, which we might write out thus:

"Millions upon millions of cycles ago, this world came to be. It was made a flat triangular plain with high hills and mountains and great waters. It exists in several stories, and the whole mass is held up on the heads of elephants with their tails turned out, and their feet rest on the shell of an immense tortoise, and the tortoise on the coil of a great snake; and when these elephants shake themselves, that makes the earth quake."

Suppose the Bible had made such mistakes as Plato, who held that the earth is an intelligent being, or Kepler, who affirmed it a living animal! or the old sages, who taught that the Milky Way is a path over which the sun used to journey and showing the marks of his footsteps; or a band of solid substance joining the two parts of the globe, etc. What if the old notions, that brutes are human beings in changed shapes, that there are fish in the sea with horses' heads, that the fabled phœnix was a real bird, and that thunderbolts come from three stars, specially Jupiter,—were found in God's own Book! Who guarded this most ancient volume from the superstitions that corrupted astronomy into astrology and chemistry into alchemy? Who taught the writer of the 104th Psalm to compose that grand poem on the wonders of the created world, and yet introduce not one of the scientific errors current in those days; so that even Von Humboldt was compelled to confess that "in a lyrical poem of such limited compass, we find the whole universe, the heavens and the earth, sketched with a few bold touches!"

IV. *Natural Philosophy*. Modern discoveries as to the nature of light make the description of Moses divinely grand. He does not represent this mystery that vibrates so strangely through space, as being *made*, but "called forth" —commanded to shine.

In Job xxxviii: 13, 14, we read of the dayspring, that it "takes hold of the ends of the earth; it is turned as clay to the seal, and they stand as a garment." In Babylon cylindrical seals were used. As they rolled over the clay, they left an impress of artistic beauty. What was without form, before, now stands out in bold relief like sculpture—and so, as the earth revolves, and brings each portion of its surface successively under the sun's light and heat, what was before dull, dark, dead, discloses and developes beauty; and the clay stands like a garment, curiously wrought in bold relief and brilliant colors. Take that, either as science or poetry, and where, in any other book of equal antiquity, can you find the like?

And how exquisite is that phrase "takes hold of the ends of the earth!" The Hebrew word conveys the idea of the rays of light bending like the fingers of the hand, to lay hold, and this is spoken only of the ends of the earth. The direct ray of the sun falling upon its surface, comes, straight as an arrow; but, when the sunlight would touch the extremities of the earth, it is bent by the atmosphere so as to come into contact, and, but for this, vast portions, out of the direct line of the sun's rays would be dark, cold and dead.

Who taught Job, 1500 years or more before Christ, to use terms that Longfellow or Tennyson might covet, to describe refraction!

Job xxxviii: 7. "When the morning stars sang together" has been always taken to be a high flight of poetry. And when in Psalm lxv: 8, we read, "Thou makest the outgoings of the morning and evening to rejoice," the Hebrew word means to give forth a tremulous sound, or as the voice in vibrations—to *sing*. Modern science flings a ray of discovery across these poetic expressions, and scientific truth seems hidden or wrapped up in them. Light comes to the eye in undulations or vibrations, as sound comes to the ear. There is a point at which vibrations are too rapid or delicate to be detected by our sense of hearing; then a more delicate organ, the eye, takes note of them; they appeal to the optic, instead of the auditory, nerve—and as light and not sound. Must not light then also sing? The lowest tone we can hear is made by 16.5 vibrations of air per second; the highest so shrill and "fine that nothing lives 'twixt it and silence," is made by 38,000 vibrations per second. Between these extremes lie eleven octaves; C of the G clef having 258 $\frac{7}{8}$ vibrations to the second, and its octave above 517$\frac{1}{2}$. Not that sound-vibrations cease at 38,000, but our organs are not fitted to hear beyond those limitations. Were our ears delicate enough, we could hear even up to the almost infinite vibrations of light. And so it is literally true that "the morning stars sang together." We misconstrued this other passage in the Psalms, which we could not understand and dared not translate as it stood in the grand old inspired Hebrew, till

"Science crept up to a perception of the truth that had been standing there for ages uninterpreted, waiting for a mind that could take it in." And now we dare to read it as it stands—"Thou makest the outgoings, or radiations of light—of the morning and evening, to *sing*, *i. e.*, to give forth sound by vibration." Were our senses fine enough, we could hear the separate key note of every individual star. Shakespeare wrote unconscious truth, when he sang,

> "There's not the smallest orb which thou beholdest,
> But in his motion, like an angel sings,
> Still quiring to the young-eyed cherubim.
> Such harmony is in immortal souls;
> But whilst this muddy vesture of decay
> Doth grossly close it in, we cannot hear it."

Stars differ in glory and power; and so in the volume and pitch of their song.* In the future life our senses will doubtless be so delicate and refined that we shall be able to hear not only the separate key notes, but the infinite swelling harmony of these myriad stars of the sky as they pour their mighty tide of harmonious anthems into the ear of God. Then shall we be able to understand the truth of the hymn:

> "In reason's ear they all rejoice,
> And utter forth a glorious voice;
> Forever singing, as they shine,
> The hand that made us is divine!"

The music of the spheres is not monotonous. Stars draw near each other and make a light that is unapproachable by mortals; then the music swells beyond our ability to endure. They recede far away, making a light so dim that the music

---
* Dr. Warren: Recreations in Astronomy, p. 27.

dies away so near to silence that only spirits can hear it. No wonder God rejoices in His works. He sits in the midst of a universal orchestra—that pours into His ear one ceaseless tide of rapturous song. He dwells in the midst of light; to us it is only ineffable glory; to Him it is music!

Job xxviii: 25. "To assign to the wind (atmosphere or breath) its weight, and to the waters their just measure." If there be anything which seems without weight, it is the air—the breath that rises as it issues from the mouth. Aristotle and even Bacon knew not that there was weight to the atmosphere! The discovery of the gravity of the air was reserved for the great Florentine astronomer, Galileo. And yet Job, at least thirty centuries before Galileo, declared that God assigned weight even to the atmosphere!

There is danger of pressing the words of the Bible into a positive announcement of scientific facts, so marvellous are some of these correspondences. But it is certainly a curious fact that Solomon should use language entirely consistent with discoveries as to evaporation and storm-circuits.* Some have boldly said that Redfield's theory of storms is here explicitly stated. Without taking such ground, we ask, who taught Solomon to use terms that readily accommodate the facts, that the movements of the winds, which seem to be so lawless and uncertain, are ruled by laws as positive as those which rule the growth of the plant; and that, by evaporation, the waters that fall on the earth are continually rising again, so that the sea never overflows!

---

*Eccles. I: 6, 7.

V. *Entomology*. If any department of science s ience may be considered complete in its researches it is that which classifies the insects so completely that it has found 70,000 varieties of beetle alone. Solomon can hardly be considered up to modern level, and some have considered his mistake as quite too bad to be admitted into inspired writings, when he represented the ant as "providing her meat in summer and gathering her food in the harvest." The scientific sceptic affirms that the ant being a carnivorous insect, could not gather her food in the harvest, and that the very nature of that food would prevent it from being laid up in store; and that Solomon committed the blunder of many amateurs, in mistaking the white cocoon of the ant-pupæ, properly known as ant-eggs, for grains housed for future use. But what becomes of Solomon's inspiration? If he blunders in science he may have blundered in theology. Nor can we defend him, on the ground that the word translated, ant, should be otherwise rendered; for the word not only means, ant, but Buxtorf says it means a *seed-eating ant*.

When, however, we study the ants of Palestine, we find among them some species which not only feed on seeds, but harvest them; and if their stores are wet by the heavy rains, to prevent their sprouting, they bring them to the surface and dry them in the sun. More than this, late discovery shows that the agricultural ant not only stores grain but prepares the soil for the crop, plants the seed, keeps the ground free of weeds, and reaps the harvest; so that all Solomon says of the ants of Palestine, as exemplifying forethought and economy, is more than justified by facts! and so here is another of the "mistakes" which Solomon did *not* make. What becomes of the inspiration of the *scientists*, who charged him with blunders!

For what has Modern Science more earnestly contended than for the Reign of Law throughout the creation of God! Yet mark the stress laid by the Bible on this fact, that even those things, which seem most capricious and uncertain, are under the control of fixed order. The rain obeys a decree and the thunder and lightning move obedient to law—the sea can go but so far, and the wind returns according to his circuits. Sir John Herschel was so much impressed with the harmony between the facts of physical science and the Word of God that he remarked: "all human discoveries seem to be made only for the purpose of confirming more strongly the truths that have come from on high and are contained in the sacred writings."

VI. The Bible proves consistent with modern discoveries in *Physiology*, *Comparative Anatomy* and *Chemistry*. Physiology is a marvelous commentary on the exclamation of David, "I am fearfully and wonderfully made." The science of anatomy can find no error in the narrative of our Lord's crucifixion; and a living physician was probably saved from infidelity by observing the unconscious truthfulness of the evangelists, in their account of the crucifixion, as to anatomical facts, then entirely unknown to science.*

Eccles. xii: 6, is a poetic description of death.

---
*Phelps on Preaching, 153.

How that silver cord describes the spinal marrow, the golden bowl, the basin which holds the brain, the pitcher the lungs, and the wheel, the heart! Without claiming that Solomon was inspired to foretell the circulation of the blood, twenty-six hundred years before Harvey announced it—is it not very remarkable that the language he uses exactly suits the fact—a wheel, pumping up through one pipe, to discharge through another?

VII. *Ethnology.* The Bible unquestionably teaches the unity of the human race. Is this reconcilable with the discoveries of ethnology?

It has been urged that there must have been more than one original stock from which the race has sprung; that the varieties of color and form, brain-development, and physical type, cannot be accounted for by climate, food, and habits of life; that the negro, at least, belongs to another species. Some, disposed not to contend for the unity of the race, and yet to defend the Bible, take a middle ground, that the Bible gives the history of only one of the races—that, through whom came the redemption—forgetting that if the whole race has not sprung from Adam, the unity of the race both in sin and redemption is gone!

It is unfair to say that the Bible and anthropology or ethnology are at war. First, because the scientific facts are not yet settled. The men who have most diligently studied these subjects do not agree among themselves. Blumenbach insists on five varieties—Caucasian, Mongolian, Ethiopian, Malay, American; Cuvier makes three grand divisions; Prichard affirms seven races, Luke Burke sixty-three, Retzius two, and Dr. Pickering eleven, which he thinks may be reduced to one! Camper insists on the facial angle as the basis of division. Cuvier adopts as the basis, the comparative areas of the cranium and face sawed vertically on the median line. While scientific men are not agreed as to the facts, why need we seek to make their theories fit its doctrine? When one well-ascertained fact is found to be irreconcilable with the Bible, then, and not till then, may there be ground for alarm.

Almost all this outcry of hostility between science and God's Word is based upon speculation. Some infidel thinks he has found out some new fact, and makes haste to announce it. He crams it into his gun and then fires, and expects to see the defenses of the Christian faith totter and tumble under the tremendous shock of his artillery. But, lo, the fortress stands, and there is not even a hole or breach in the wall. And when we come to examine, what was it that the great scientist hurled against the walls? Some huge, solid shot of fact? No; a mere paper-wad of his own fanciful theory, that took fire from his own powder!

Again we say, show us one undoubted fact, revealed by scientific studies for two thousand years, that cannot be harmonized with the word of God! Not only can there be shown no conflict between the facts and the Bible doctrine of the unity of the race, but the whole drift of discovery, so far as it becomes clear and positive, is toward the confirmation of that unity. In man, the world over, we find the same grand physical characteristics: the same number of teeth and bones and muscles; the same system of respiration and circulation, digestion, secretion; nerves, veins and arteries are arranged on the same type. Man is everywhere capable of living on all kinds of food, in any climate; liable to the same diseases; grows to maturity slowly, and lives to the same average age. Dr. Prichard contends for the unity of the original stock from the fertility of the race in offspring. "Nature abhors hybrids," and varieties produced in the vegetable or animal world, by the crossing of species, speedily run out; and hence the fact that, after six thousand years, intermarriage between individuals of different varieties is still fertile in offspring, proves one original species. Dr. Prichard traces all existing varieties of the human family to secondary causes, and finds among different tribes or nations no permanent lines of division.

Man, and even animals, when subjected to a change of climate or manner of life, change color, hair and form. Dr. Carpenter instances the Magyar race in Hungary, known to have belonged to the Asiatic stock. About a thousand years since, they came from the cold north of Asia to the sunny south of Europe, and not only have their habits of life all changed, but even the type of cranial formation from the pyramidal or Mongolian to the elliptical or Caucasian; and, with their improved physical stature and feature, there is just enough of the Tartar cast to give a hint of their origin. And so as to the Lapps and Finns; Dr. Carpenter says that, though from one common stock with the Magyars, the most marked differences have developed even in cranial characters, and general conformation, stature and proportion.

In India, Persians, Greeks, Tartars, Turks and

Arabs, all white men, and without intermarriage with the Hindus, in a few generations become marked with the deep olive color natural to the climate, almost as dark as the negro; and the Portuguese, in three hundred years' residence there, have been dyed black as Kaffirs. Rev. John Campbell, years ago, observed that, as he moved from the southern cape toward equatorial Africa, the people uniformly grew darker; and the colony of Jews on the coast of Malabar are now as black as the natives of the coast. If climate may produce such marked changes in one direction, who is competent to say what changes all combined causes may produce during thousands of years? Von Humboldt, after stating the arguments for diversity of origin, gives his opinion that more weighty reasons favor unity; and certainly he will not be accused of superficial science or of undue bias toward the Bible.

Even the diversity of language, once thought to favor diversity of stock, is no longer an argument against the Word of God. The new science of comparative philology is grouping these tongues into families, and tracing them back by affinities and resemblances to one great root; and Klaproth illustrates the universal kinship of languages by the bricks with which Bagdad is built, and which bear the cuneiform legend of Nebuchadnezzar stamped upon them—showing that they are fragments of old Assyrian cities. Even so, modern tongues exhibit the fragments of an earlier primitive language. And so physiology and philology, and psychology and ethnology, all witness to that grand old conception of the Bible, that all men sprang from one original pair.

As to the antiquity of man, science has not presented one clearly established fact to show that the human race existed on earth earlier than the accepted chronology of the Bible places man's creation. Most so-called proof is simply wild conjecture, jumping at conclusions; and sometimes the jump is such a big one that such science has been called "grasshopper science," or "kangaroo science." It claims to present the results of original investigation, though, as Park Godwin says, "the originality is apt to surpass the investigation."

The facts which seem to argue a greater antiquity for the human race are simply mysteries that await interpretation. For example, bones have been found, cut and polished, in deposits which seem to have been immersed in water since man dwelt on earth, yet so finely cut and polished as, in the opinion of many, to prove human skill, aided, too, by instruments of rare perfection. Sir Charles Lyell, however, ventured to put among the beavers in the zoological gardens in London some bones similar to those discovered, and, after leaving them for some time, recovered them, cut and polished by the beavers, so nearly like the others as to leave no doubt that in both cases the same agency had been employed. So, in this case, the pre-Adamite man proved to be a beaver, and the perfect tools, which argued such high civilization, the beaver's teeth!

VIII. As yet we have not touched that broad field of *Archæology* where some of the richest, ripest harvests have been reaped for the confirmation of the Word of God. We present two or three, out of the immense mass of constantly accumulating facts, which show that God is taking the wise in their own craftiness. Sceptics have been confident that, from the discoveries brought to light by the archæologist and paleontologist, the Word of God would be proved at best a harmless fable; but lo, while we hold our peace, the very stones cry out in confirmation of the Word.

We read in ancient history that the King of Babylon at the time of its destruction was not Belshazzar, but Nabonadius, or Labynetus, and that he was neither captured nor killed, but escaped, and that after the taking of the city he fought a battle outside the capital, was beaten, made prisoner, and subsequently a satrap under the conqueror, living in luxury and dying in peace. And so the scientific sceptics laughed at the credulity of the simple souls who take the Bible as their guide, though it asserts that Belshazzar was king when Babylon fell, and on the night of its capture was slain. But over twenty years ago, from the mounds that mark the almost forgotten site of the great city, there was dug up a great cylinder, inscribed with curious records, and from these we learn that Belshazzar was the son of Nabonadius and a regent under him; and now the inconsistency is explained. Belshazzar, sharing the throne of his father, was slain at Babylon. His father, Nabonadius, escaped and survived the fall of his capital. Out of the ruins of buried cities rises a new witness to the Word.

Again, as to the Deluge. Assyrian tablets now in the British Egyptian museum, dating 660 B. C., copying and preserving an older record 1700 B. C., contain a pagan description of the flood, declare it to have been decreed by God on account of man's wickedness, and record the fact of a great ship being built, birds being sent out, an altar being built, etc.

St. Luke calls Sergius Paulus the proconsul of Cyprus. Historians insisted that his proper title must have been procurator; yet even an inaccuracy could not be tolerated in the evangelist's record. But lately ancient coins have come to light bearing the image of Claudius, and applying to the representative of Rome who governed Cyprus the very name, proconsul, which Luke applies to Sergius Paulus! The further modern investigation goes, the more is Holy Scripture established; every new discovery among the monumental records of antiquity adds a new witness to God's blessed book. Wonderful, indeed, that the Bible should be so framed and worded that, though never clearly announcing scientific facts, "in advance of the science of the age," it proves, when correctly interpreted, to be always "abreast of the science" of any age.

With a lofty air of papal infallibility, a sceptical writer declares that "every step that science takes leads mankind farther away from the idle hopes and fears of Christianity toward the calm of eternal truth." Whereupon Dr. Stebbins, himself a Unitarian, and an advocate of "liberal" views, dares a flat denial: "I affirm most deliberately, after nearly fifty years' study of science as well as theology, with the ardor of a lover, that there is not a single discovery or accepted fact of science which, in the slightest degree, militates against the teachings of Christianity as revealed in the gospels."

The Word of God cannot be demolished by

the ridicule of its foes. Voltaire may have many disciples who follow his method, and seek to cover God's Word with caricature as a modern "smart" boy disfigures with charcoal the face and form of some antique Apollo. But as the statue remains in its ideal perfection when the mischievous markings are washed away, so the pure celestial beauty of the Word survives all attempts to invest it with blasphemous absurdity. Nor can scientific assumption and presumption upset the certainties of a divine revelation. A falsehood is no more true because loudly spoken, and with gesticulation that attempts to *pound* conviction into the hearer. As Mr. Lincoln assured Mr. Bates that "calling a sheep's tail a leg does not make it so," we insist that even the sanction of a great name does not necessarily establish the verity and accuracy of a statement. Many a man who is very safe in the department of investigation, and perfectly trustworthy so long as he confines himself to the simple results of observation and experiment, is as unsafe whenever he ventures into the department of philosophy or logic, and attempts to draw inferences from his investigations; his conclusions may be as inaccurate and unsound as his experiments are careful and exact. The fact is, investigation and induction belong to different departments; and we are not always to adopt the inferences even of the most accurate investigator.

Scientific men are not always intellectually honest and candid. Biased in favor of a certain scientific creed, or religious system, they become intellectual *squinters;* they see only what they want to see, and array facts and figures adroitly on the side of preconceived opinion or notion.

SCIENTIFIC TRUTH OF THE WORD. 143

What, then, shall we do with the Bible? It comes before the tribunal of reason, and asks for an impartial judgment. It may be the best of books, yet by no means be the book of God. Yet how can it be simply the book of man? Even its apparent contradictions, when closely examined, reveal a deeper law of harmony, like the lines of the Doric column—once thought to be vertical and parallel, but now found to incline and converge, so as to meet if carried upward to a point above the column.

The witness which the Word contains within itself is what Chalmers called the "portable evidence" of Christianity. And it has this grand advantage: if within the Word, it may be found there by the diligent seeker. They say the shell sings of the sea; you may easily test it—put it to your ear and listen. Does the Bible speak of its own divine origin? then you have only to put it to your ear and hear; shut out other voices—the clamors of prejudice and pride, wilful unbelief and waywardness of heart—and you shall hear the music of the celestials.

And so we ought to "search the Scriptures," as did the noble people of Berea, with readiness of mind to find their hidden testimony; and therefore many of them believed! But it must be *search*, and not the careless, cursory glance which unveils and reveals nothing. Remember the famous jewel in the green vaults at Dresden; the egg with its silver white, its golden yolk, within the yolk a precious gem. The best is farthest within, always, and he whose hand touches only the shell finds not the treasures that lay hidden from the common, careless eye, as in "drusic" cavities.

Let us learn of the bee. See him alight on the flower and linger there, thrusting his trunk down into the heart of the bloom, where the sweet juices lie in a flask fairer than alabaster. Honest, earnest, studious searching of the Scriptures, lingering on the heavenly blossoms, the patient and prayerful penetration which touches the heart of the Word of God, is our great need. He who sucks the honey needs no other proof that the flower-cup holds the nectar! He who has stored the symmetrical cells of memory and heart with the treasures of God's truth, and has found full satisfaction and delight in it, needs no other proof. He exclaims:

"How sweet is thy Word unto my taste! Yea, sweeter than honey to my mouth!"

CHAPTER VII.

THE MORAL BEAUTY OF THE BIBLE.

"I have seen an end of all perfection: but thy commandment is exceeding broad."—PSALM CXIX: 96.

Everything human has a limit to its apparent perfection. Trace it far enough, or examine it thoroughly enough, and you will find defects if not deformities. Everything born of man or produced by him is faulty, mixed up with error. Our watches we correct by the chronometer and the chronometer must be regulated by the sun; for "beneath the stars nothing goes right." But God's law reveals no defects. It has no limit to its perfection.

There was in the Roman Forum, a gilt pillar erected by Augustus, and known as "Milliarium Aureum" or "the golden milestone." There, all the principal Roman roads centered and terminated; and thence radiated to the remotest verge of civilization, running in all directions, as far as the silver eagles had triumphantly borne the standards of the empire!

The Bible is the Golden Milestone of the ages. It has been for thousands of years the grand center of all the noblest thought, purest love, and holiest life of the world. All roads converge here. The great highways of human progress radiate from this shining center. From this great book proceeds the inspiration of the best literature, the most unselfish philanthropy, the most faultless morality, which the world has ever known. Whence came the Bible? Is this the accidental point of all this convergence; or is it the designed focus of all this light, love and life? Was this golden pillar erected by one infinitely more august than the foremost of the Cæsars, to be the center and source of all human progress? Did God put the Bible in the very Forum of the nations, that by all paths men might, in the honest search after truth, find in this their goal; and that, from this, as a starting point, every true lover of God and man might proceed in his noble career of service? This is the decisive test. No literary excellence, no scientific accuracy, no perfection, as a book, could atone for one vital error in ethical teaching or moral precept, in a volume which claims the high dignity of being a guide to the human soul, in matters of faith and life, doctrine and duty!

Suppose that no revelation of God's will had ever been made to man, through any such channel; but that, in some way, we were led to look for a written communication from God. What sort of a book would we expect? We would surely be warranted in anticipating in such a volume, the following characteristics: 1. It would be intelligible, a clear revelation, and capable of being understood by the average man. 2. It would be consistent, that is, its testimony would be essentially one, united, harmonious witness. 3. It would be transcendent, far surpassing all human teachings in the tone of its precepts, and bearing the impress of a divine mind and heart in its whole structure. 4. It would be practical, touching the actual needs of man, at the most vital points of contact. We cannot imagine even the human channel of the divine communication as seriously affecting the result. After making liberal allowance for human imperfection, and the imperfection of human language, we insist, on God's behalf, that whatever claims to represent his will shall in all these particulars correspond with the high claim. If the Holy Ghost shall pour the light of heaven into the dark chambers of this world, no necessary imperfection in the window panes through which it streams, can essentially diminish its glory. It may suffer some absorption or refraction or take some hue or tint in its passage, but it will still be recognized as light from above.

I. The Unity or consistency of the Bible is a grand argument in its favor. It is a collection of books, written at different times, and by different persons, at intervals through some sixteen centuries. In the style and character of these books, there is surprising variety and diversity; some are historical, others poetical; some contain laws, others lyrics; some are prophetic, some symbolic: in the New Testament we have four gospels, one historic narrative, and twenty-one epistles followed by a symbolic poem in the most oriental imagery. And yet this is no artificial arrangement of fragments. We find "the Old Testament patent in the new; the new latent in the old!"

The various books of the Bible are entirely at agreement. There is diversity in unity and unity in diversity; "e pluribus unum." There is sometimes apparent divergence, at first; but further search shews real harmony. As in a stereoscope, the two pictures sometimes will not come together, but as we continue to look, and the eye rests on some particular point, one view is seen; so in the Word of God. The more we study it, the more its unity and harmony appear. Even the law and the gospel are not in conflict. They stand like the cherubim, facing different ways, but toward each other; and the four gospels, like the cherubic creature in Ezekiel's vision, facing in four different directions, move in one. All the criticism of more than three thousand years has failed to point out one important or irreconcilable contradiction in the testimony and teachings of those who are farthest separated—there is no collision, yet there could be no collusion.

In such a book there would not be likely to be unity; for all the human conditions were unfavorable. No other book was ever composed or compiled in circumstances so disadvantageous to a harmonious moral testimony and teaching. Here are some sixty or more separate documents, written by some forty different persons, scattered over wide intervals of space and time, strangers to each other; these documents are written in three different languages, in different lands, with marked diversities of literary style, and by men of all grades of culture and mental capacity from Moses to Malachi; and there is in them great unlikeness both in matter and manner of statement; and yet in not one respect are their doctrinal and ethical teachings in conflict; from beginning to end, we find in them a positive oneness of doctrine, which amazes us. Even where, at first glance, there appears to be conflict, as between Paul and James, we find, on closer examination that, instead of standing face to face, beating each other, they stand back to back, beating off common foes. And, most wonderful of all, this moral unity could not be fully understood till the book was completed. The process of preparation, like a scaffolding about a building, obscured its beauty—even the workmen upon it could not appreciate its harmony—but, when John added the cap-stone and declared that nothing further should be added, the scaffolding fell, and a grand cathedral was revealed.

To appreciate this strong argument for the divine origin of the Bible, try this test in a supposed case. Imagine another book, compiled by as many authors, scattered over as many centuries! Herodotus contributes a historic fragment on the origin of all things, in the fifth century before Christ; a century later Aristotle adds a book on moral philosophy; two centuries pass and Cicero adds a work on law and government; still another hundred years and Virgil furnishes a grand poem on ethics; in the next century Plutarch supplies some biographical sketches; two hundred years after, Origen adds essays on religious creeds and conduct; a century and a half later, Augustine writes a treatise on theology, and Chrysostom a book of sermons; then seven centuries pass away and Abelard completes the compilation by a magnificent series of essays on rhetoric and scholastic philosophy. And between these extremes, which, like the Bible, span fifteen centuries, let us imagine all along from Herodotus to Abelard thirty or forty other contributors whose works enter into the final result, men of different nations, periods, habits, languages, and education; under the best conditions, how much moral unity could be expected, even if each successive contributor had read all that preceded his own fragment?

Have you heard Thomas' grand orchestra? See how, as that baton rises and falls in the hand of the Conductor, from violin and bass viol, cornet and flute, trombone and trumpet, flageolet and clarinet, bugle and French horn, cymbals and drum, there comes one grand harmony! You have no doubt, though the conductor were screened from view, that one master mind controls all the instrumental performers. But God makes His oratorio to play for more than a thousand years, and where one musician becomes silent another takes up the strain, and yet it is all one grand symphony—the key is never lost and never changes, except by those exquisite modulations that show the composer; and when the last strain dies away you see that all these glorious movements and melodies have been variations of one grand theme! Did each musician compose as he played, or was there one composer back of the many players? "one supreme and regulating mind" in this Oratorio of the Ages? If God was the master musician, planning the whole and arranging the parts, appointing player to succeed player, and one strain to modulate or melt into another, then we can understand how Moses' grand anthem of Creation glides into Isaiah's oratorio of the Messiah, by and by sinks into Jeremiah's plaintive wail, swells into Ezekiel's awful chorus, changes into Daniel's rapturous lyric, and after the quartette of the Evangelists. closes with John's full choir of Saints and Angels!

How can it be accounted for? There is no answer which can be given unless you admit the supernatural element. If God actually superintended the production of this book, so that all who contributed to it were guided by Him, then its unity is the unity of a divine plan and its harmony the harmony of a supreme intelligence and will!

We are told of the temple, first built upon Mt. Moriah, that it was built of stone, made ready before it was brought thither, so that there was neither hammer nor axe nor any tool of iron heard in the house, while it was in building. The stone was cut, squared, polished and fitted to its place in the quarry, before it was brought to the temple platform—the beams and boards, were all wrought into the desired form and shape in the shops; and when the material for the temple was on the ground nothing was necessary but to put it together. What was it which insured symmetry in the temple when constructed, and harmony between the workmen in the quarries and the shops, and the builders on the hill? There must have been one presiding mind that planned the whole. There was one brain or intelligence that built that whole structure in ideal before it was in fact. The builders built wiser than they knew; they were putting together the ideas of the architect wrought in stone, and not their own ideas!

In some such way alone can we account for the singular unity of the Word of God. The Bible is a structure planned and wrought out in the mind of a divine Architect, who, through the ages, superintended His own workmen and work. Moses laid its foundations, not knowing who should build up after him, or what form the structure should assume. Workman after workman followed; he might see that there was agreement with what went before, but he could not foresee that what should come after would be only the sublime carrying out of the grand plan. And yet what is the case? No one disputes the singular unity of the structure; and yet, during all those sixteen centuries, through which the building rose toward completion, there was no sound of axe or hammer, no chipping or hacking to make one part fit its fellow. Everything is in agreement with everything else, because the whole Bible was built in the thought of God before one book was laid in the order of its construction!

You cannot look on that cathedral at Milan, whose first stone was laid March 15, 1386, and which, after these five centuries, is yet incomplete, without instinctively knowing that it must have been the product of one mind, however many workmen may have helped to rear its marble walls and pinnacles. Its unity of design cannot be the result of accident. No, the workmen were not the architect. Every stone was shaped and polished to fit its place in the plan. And so of the Bible: that cathedral of the ages! Whoever the workmen were, the Architect was God!

This unity appears the more marvellous when we observe the progressive development of revelation. One of the finest scholars of Britain, in one of the grandest books of the century, has devoted the powers of his master-mind to tracing the "Progress of Doctrine in the New Testament." He shows that, although there could have been no such intent or intelligence in the writers' minds, and although the books of the New Testament are not even arranged in the order of their production, that order could not, in one instance, be changed without impairing or destroying the symmetry of the book, and that there is a regular progress in the unfolding of doctrine, from the Gospel according to Matthew to the Revelation.

A wider examination will show the very same progress of doctrine from corner-stone to capstone; from foundations first, then story after story, pillars on pedestals and capitals on pillars, and arches on capitals, till, like a dome, flashing back the splendors of the noonday, the Apocalypse spans and crowns and completes the whole, glorious with celestial visions.

The unity of the Bible is organic. Now the unity of a building is not organic. It is a unity of plan, of construction, of material, but you may take down the spire of a church and put up another; replace the windows by memorial windows making each a crystal monument of some departed friend; and change all the wood work in its interior; and yet the unity and completeness of the building are not affected. But if a human body loses an eye, a finger, or a joint, it is maimed; its completeness is gone; its unity violated; and nothing can ever supply the lack of that lost portion, however insignificant.

The Bible is a unity in this, that not one of all its books could be lost without maiming the body of truth here contained. Every book has a place which it fills. You may not at a single glance discover its use, or see why it is necessary to the plan of the book, but it is the fault of your ignorance; each book fills a place in the great plan; God's stamp is on this organic unity.

Take one example. The book of Esther has

been thought by some unnecessary to the completeness of the canon. Why, it is said, "It does not even contain the name of God." But that book critically studied proves a singularly complete exhibition of the Providence of God. It teaches an unseen hand behind human affairs; certain ultimate awards to the evil and the good; it exhibits this providential rule in the uncertainty and unsatisfactoriness of the prosperity of the wicked, and in the prosperity that ultimately comes to the good even out of their adversities; it shows how retribution is sometimes poetically exact in the very forms of punishment. And that we may not confound God's Providence with a bald fatalism that takes away human freedom and responsibility, it shows us how the prayerful resolution and action of God's servants and the unbiased freedom of His enemies, are consistent with His overruling sovereignty; and how all things work together to produce all grand results. We see the ministry of most minute matters in furthering Providential plans. The book that thus exhibits God's Providence—His universal sovereignty, the universal harmony, divine retribution and human responsibility, does not once contain the *name* of God; for it is meant to teach us of the *Hidden Hand* that, behind the scenes, unseen, moves and controls all things.

Cuvier has brought out into grand scientific statement the unity of organized being. He finds that, in every case, it forms a whole—a complete system, all the parts of which mutually correspond. None of these parts can change without the others also changing; and consequently each taken separately indicates and gives all the others.

For instance, the sharp-pointed tooth of the lion requires a strong jaw; these demand a skull, fitted for the attachment of powerful muscles, both for moving the jaw and raising the head; a broad, well-developed shoulder-blade must accompany such a head; and there must be an arrangement of bones of the leg which admits of the leg-paw being rotated and turned upward, in order to be used as an instrument to seize and tear the prey; and, of course, there must be strong claws arming the paw. Hence, from one tooth the entire animal could be modelled, though the species had perished.

So the unity of the Bible is the unity of one organism, where each part demands all the others. The Decalogue demands the Sermon on the Mount. Isaiah's prophecy makes necessary the narrative of the Evangelists. Daniel fits into the Revelation as bone fits socket, or as those strange bones in the vertebral column naturally form the axis of the neck. You cannot understand Leviticus without the Epistle to the Hebrews. The Psalms express the highest morality and spirituality of the Old Testament and anticipate the clearer beauty of the New; they link the Mosaic code with the divine ethics of the gospels and the epistles. The Passover foreshadowed the Lord's Supper, and the Lord's Supper interprets and fulfils the Passover. Even the little book of Jonah makes more complete the sublime Gospel according to John; and Ruth and Esther prophetically hint the Acts of the Apostles. Nay, look more closely, and after following the course of history, gospels and epistles, when you come to the last chapter of Revelation, you find yourself mysteriously touching the first chapters of Genesis; and lo, as you survey the whole track of your thought, you find you have been following the perimeter of a golden ring; the extremities actually bend around, touch and so blend that no point of contact is detected. You read in the first of Genesis of the first creation; in the last of Revelation, of the new creation—the new heavens and the new earth; there, of the rivers that watered the garden: here, of the pure river of the water of life, clear as crystal; there, of the Tree of Life in the first Eden: here, of the Tree of Life which is in the midst of the Paradise of God; there, of the God who came down to talk and walk with man: here, that the Tabernacle of God is with men. There we read of the curse that came by sin—of the serpent whose trail is over all human joys; here we read, "and there shall be no more curse"—"nothing shall enter that defileth or maketh a lie."

II. If the Bible be the Word of God, it will be clear and intelligible; else were it no Revelation. It must be clear to the average man—nay, to the lowest level of a complete manhood must a revelation from God descend. The Bible claims to be God's message to man as man. It unfolds a plan of redemption which reaches just as far and wide as the condemnation. The rescue must be as complete as the ruin; the salvation must touch at every point the sin. That is no restoration which cannot repair the whole ruin. And, inasmuch as all men are in sin and need salvation, the gospel must be so simple, plain, that any one who is capable of sinning may be capable of understanding and appropriating salvation. Now, we find that wherever there is a human being who has passed the first stages of infancy and childhood, and is not imbecile or idiotic; wherever there is a complete set of faculties, however undeveloped, there may be voluntary sin, and so responsibility. But if there be one human being who can sin and yet cannot receive the saving gospel, by sheer incapacity to understand it, there is ground for doubt that the gospel is of God.

The world has had many wise and good teachers of morals, and some of them have been centers of grand influence. But every one of them has spoken to a class of men. The great masses have been shut out from their select circle by the very character of their teachings. The word *mystery* is of Greek origin, and means "a revealed secret" which only the initiated could understand; and these were mysteries to the common people, and remained such because they demanded a measure of intelligence and capacity not possessed by the average man. By necessity, the philospher addressed the few. Aristotle originated the word *metaphysics*. He wrote first on "physics," then "meta-ta-phy-sica," "after the physics;" and what better expresses those subtleties which lie beyond the common mind? Suppose Aristotle's "Organon" contained the secret of salvation, how many sinners could from that find out the secret? Pythagoras was a great teacher; but he did not attempt to get a hold upon the masses. He welcomed those who desired to be taught his mysteries, and held them on probation till he should discover who were able and worthy to be pupils; and they were the only ones to whom he attempted to reveal the hidden things of his philosophy. Hence came the distinction between the exoteric and esoteric schools. These facts hint the drift of all merely human teaching upon moral an' spiritual truths. Had it been complete in all other respects, here was a fundamental fatal lack: it did not reach and touch, it could not move and mould, all men; it was not fit for man as man.

We open the blessed Book, and one of the first things which arrests our attention is the divine simplicity that is mingled with its awful sublimity. The way of holiness is a plain and straight highway, not a narrow, obscure, crooked byway; "the wayfaring men, though fools, shall not err therein." The vision is written plain upon the tablets, so that he may run that reads it. A child in years and understanding can understand all that is necessary to salvation. One of the first things which childhood shows is "trust," and trust is the soul of faith. Any child who can understand what it is, upon a dark and stormy night, when he had lost his way, to give up to a stronger arm a burden which he cannot longer carry, and give his hand to another hand, to be led to a home which he can no longer find, can understand what it is to let Christ bear his sins and guide him to heaven. Well might the Saviour of sinners set a child in the midst of men and bid them become as little children, for the learned and wise in this world of sin scorn and scout the gospel for its simplicity. And yet is it no sign that the true salvation is here, that we need not go up to heaven in order to bring a Saviour down, nor into hades to bring a Saviour up from the dead? God asks of us no such practical impossibilities, but only to believe in the heart and confess with the mouth. But, you ask, are there no mysteries in the Bible—no things "hard to be understood," high as heaven, deep as the abyss? Certainly there are; and were there not, would that not argue against the Bible? Does not the power wholly to comprehend the work of another hand or brain imply a certain equality? The very fact that there is about the product of another's genius what you and I cannot understand is a proof of genius—*i. e.*, of a superior order of faculties. I need do no more than hear Edison's phonograph repeat my sentences, to be convinced that the man who invented that machine is no ordinary man. And a glance at the statues of Michael Angelo is enough to show me that that man was a prince even among artists!

So the very mystery of God's works shows that they proceeded from no human hand. Let any man explain how a blade of grass grows, taking from earth, air, light and dew, just what it needs for its own structure, and building these elements into itself! The Word of God must show the God who inspired it. There must be thoughts above our thoughts, and ways above our ways, or it may be after all only a man's work!

How can God's Word be at once intelligible and unintelligible, within our capacity and above it, clear and yet obscure?

We need not stop to draw such subtle lines of distinction as that of Coleridge, between "apprehension" and "comprehension." A thing may at the same time be sublime and simple. The pillar of cloud and of fire was a mystery. Who can tell, even now, how a cloud can move with a supreme intelligence—now going before to lead the way, now resting to indicate a halt, and again going behind to hide God's host from the pursuing foe? How can a cloud herald the night-shade by burning with a glory that midnight cannot quench? And yet the cloud led Israel, and nothing could be more simple than to go where it went, and stay where it stayed. Whatever was mysterious about the cloud did not interfere with its office as a guide. The "secret things" belong to the Lord our God, but the "revealed things" belong to us and our children, even all the words of this law! There are mysteries, but they are speculative; there are revealed things, and they are regulative; *i. e.*, while God does not answer our questions, "how?" and "why?" he does answer "what?" We never ask; Lord, what wilt thou have me to do? without a plain, prompt answer, not clouded by mystery or shadowed by obscurity.

Mystery? Yes; and it would be a greater mystery if in a revelation from God there were not. Edward Irving compares the man who, with his finite knowledge, expects to understand all the deep things of God, to the little blind mole, running his tiny galleries underground, undertaking to interpret the marchings and countermarchings of mighty armies overhead! There are deep things about God, but none of them touch duty! You know not the mystery of motion—how the will is linked to the nerve, nerve to muscle, muscle to bone; and yet you can lift your arm and move your leg at will. And so, whatever mystery is in the Word, it does not becloud duty, or prevent us from walking in the path of obedience. This blessed Book acknowledges clouds and darkness to be round about Him; yet it never admits that clouds and darkness are round about the way that leads to Him.

You gaze up at Mont Blanc; it is dim with the distance, and clouds wrap its summit as in a white shroud. But the clouds *belong* about lofty peaks; that is their natural home, and they make the mountain look grand and sublime. They are fitted to catch a thousand hues from the sunbeam, and wrap the awful peak in rainbow colors; they leave the snow and ice far up toward heaven, which, as they melt, distil pure, cool water for the springs far below. But, though clouds invest these summits thousands of feet above, there are no clouds about your pathway at the mountain's foot; here your path is plain and clear. And all this shows that you were not meant to live on that higher level. Those grand peaks are, like the stars they seem to touch, meant to look at and admire—to strike awe into your soul; but you could not abide up there; you would get lost. Those are slippery heights, whence many an ambitious climber falls to his own hurt. The air is too rare up there; you breathe with difficulty, and the cold is too intense. But here you walk safely, and your feet do not stumble. At this level everything is fitted to feed and nourish your life.

Is it not so with the Bible? It is like some tall peak whose awful form, resting on the earth, reaches the stars. Its heights are infinite, distant, dim, enveloped in clouds, but glorious in their obscurity and mystery. Those heights were not meant for mortal feet to tread. Only angels can breathe that etherial atmosphere, or venture to explore the high and deep things of God. For you and me, those sublime heights are meant only that we may gaze, admire, adore. That is where the Bible touches God and heaven; we must only look and be lost in the glory. But where the Bible touches the earth it touches our level; here are no clouds or darkness; all is light and plain and clear, because here lies the path of duty. True, we may, as we become more and more familiar with God's truth, climb higher, get more extended prospects, truer views of the relation between the here and the hereafter; but even then we shall only be overwhelmed with the depths of the riches both of the wisdom and knowledge of God, and exclaim, "How unsearchable are His judgments, and His ways past finding out!" When we get as high as mortal can tread, we shall only say with Paul that there is a height and depth, a breadth and length, which pass knowledge.

Blessed is he who is content to understand the way of duty, and who, in these divine mysteries which have to do with the higher things and deeper things of God, sees only an additional evidence that the Bible is of God. Because it is of God, therefore does it rise so high above the earthly level as that its shining summit is shrouded in the clouds, and too glorious for our eyes to behold!

CHAPTER VIII.

THE MORAL SUBLIMITY OF GOD'S WORD.

"Thy Word *is* a lamp unto my feet, and a light unto my path."—PSALM CXIX:105.

Do the moral teachings of the Bible accord with its claims? This is the most searching question of all. Even prophecy and miracle would fail to satisfy us that the Bible is of God without correspondence between the moral truths there revealed and those faculties of our being to which such truths are addressed.

The scientist boldly infers that light was meant for the eye, and the eye for the light, because light is pleasant to the healthy eye, and painful only to the diseased. On scientific principles, we as boldly say that the Bible was meant as a light to the moral nature of men; and here is the broad basis of our induction. The men most free from moral corruption—men, like Plato, of pure mind and clear moral judgment—when brought in contact with the moral teachings of this book, most delight in them; and only so far as men grow corrupt morally, and the eye of the soul becomes diseased by vice and crime, do they turn from the pure Word of God.

It is commonly a mark of moral profligacy that men antagonize the Bible; and generally the degree of moral degradation is shown by the violence of such opposition. There is a man who has for years been conspicuous as the enemy and traducer of the Christian faith; yet his life was said to be exceptionally faultless in its morality, and his character singularly without blemish. This seemed strange, for his opposition to the religion of the Bible is peculiarly reckless and malicious. But further investigation disclosed the fact that his conversation, when unrestrained by the conventionalities of society, is impure and contaminating. I heard a gentleman of the highest probity say that, when by a severe snow-storm he was shut up with that man in a hotel, hemmed in by snow-drifts, so shocking was his foulness of speech that he preferred the cold and snow without, rather than expose his helpless ears to such defilement. It is the old story of hating the light, coming not to the light, lest one's deeds be reproved.

Let us give to this moral test its fullest weight. Some would have us receive the truth simply on the ground of its authority, whether it fits our inborn ideas of right and equity and humanity or not. There are a few who tell us that we are not to presume to judge as to right and wrong; that God's will makes right and wrong, and that what would be vice if done by our choice alone, becomes virtue if done at His word.

Are there, then, no eternal laws of right and wrong which lie, back of God's will, in the very nature of things? Was Kant, the philosopher, wrong when he said that "the two things that filled him with awe are the star-sown deeps of space and the deeper gulf between right and wrong?" Why did God give us faculties capable of judging wrong and right if He meant that we should dare no judgment? It is one of the awful things, that as God made man capable of sitting at the telescope, and, in the invisible scales of science, weighing the stars, so He has made man's moral nature capable of weighing even Him in its balances. As the child recognizes his father by a certain likeness— a look, expression, attitude, gait, tone of voice, grasp of hand, nay, even in darkness by something not to be described—so are we to recognize God because He corresponds to our inner sense of what God must be; because He fits with divine exactness into the strange void of our spiritual being as nothing else can.

We cannot conceive of any array of miracles that would force upon mankind a belief contrary to the teachings of reason or the promptings of conscience. Bishop Clark affirmed that if "it were written with letters of fire on the midnight sky: 'God is unjust, God is cruel,' there is that within us which would say, this is an illusion of the senses or the work of some malignant power hostile to God. He cannot be unjust."

If the Bible be the Word of God, we may be assured that it will contain nothing essentially opposed to our moral sense; for that moral sense is given us to perceive truth and recognize light. This is the argument from correlation, or mutual adaptation—an argument worthy to fill volumes.

Nature is full of wants with corresponding supplies; of appetites or cravings with their gratifications and satisfactions. The wing of the bird tells of the air on which it may float; the fin of the fish, of the water through which it may glide; the ball of the joint, of the socket; the eye is a prophecy of the light, and the ear of sound. So universal is this correspondence that wherever we find a craving, an adaptation, or a lack, we look with unerring certainty for something else filling the craving, meeting the adaptation, supplying the lack. Emerson closed a protracted argument with a literary sceptic in these forcible words: "Sir, I hold that God, who keeps his word with the birds and fishes in all their migratory instinct, will keep His word with man." And Bryant, in his "Lines to a Waterfowl," with great beauty, points out the lesson taught by this wonderful correspondence and correlation, in these lines:

> "He who, from zone to zone,
> Guides, through the boundless sky, thy certain flight,
> In the long way that I must tread alone,
> Will lead my steps aright!"

If man craves and needs an infinite Being, in whose strength, wisdom, power and love, human weakness, ignorance, feebleness and affection may find perfect refuge and rest, it will be the only exception to universal facts if no object exists to meet this conscious need. The Bible declares and exhibits just such an object, exactly adapted to fill and fulfil all this need.

It is our solemn duty to apply to the Word of God these moral and spiritual tests, in order, first, to ascertain whether indeed it be the Word of God, by its essential correspondence with our own moral instincts and needs; and, secondly, to appreciate more fully its real worth and beauty. Chamfort, the Parisian wit, says: "I heard, one day, a devotee speaking against people who discuss articles of faith, say *naivement*, 'Gentlemen, a true Christian never examines what he is ordered to believe. It is with that as with a bitter pill: if you chew it you will never be able to swallow it.'" Behind the witticism is a covert sneer; the light word is a sharp sword, meant to thrust at all genuine religious faith. But it is not so; the Bible asks no such absurd, blind faith, no such unreasoning, unthinking, mechanical acceptance!

In the uncovered mounds of Nineveh, you see only fragments of that departed glory—broken slabs, shattered pillars, grandeur and magnificence and splendor lying in ruin. How do you recognize Nineveh? You have from history and art formed an idea of Nineveh as it was when the crown of empire was upon its brow, and you compare the conception with these remains. They correspond; and you have no more doubt that the ancient city is uncovered than though you saw it now in all the pride of its supremacy. Somewhat thus, does God mean that we shall test his Word. Among its first declarations is this: "God made man in his own image." It is very plain that the image is shattered and man is a ruin. Yet if we compare the Bible idea of true manhood with the ruined fragments of the original man, we shall see a correspondence. And the more closely we compare the Word of God with human nature and needs, the more plainly will appear a similarity between the utterances of that Word and the highest utterances of the soul of man. This has been observed and confessed even by professed infidels, and it is a fact which no human philosophy has yet explained, and which, on the basis of sceptical philosophy, defies satisfactory explanation.

Happily, the foes of Christianity furnish us a

starting-point in their own concessions and confessions. So few are the exceptions that it is fair to call it a universal verdict that no book ever known among men compares with this. The praises of the Bible, drawn from the lips of infidels, and left on record by their pens, might be mistaken for the adoring words of saints, or even angels. Yet the Word of God does not court the favorable opinion of men. With divine indifference, it hews its way into the very heart of man. It begins by telling him that his wisdom is folly, his righteousness filthy rags; it assaults him from every side with the most humiliating exposures; and yet it challenges his admiration. Reville, the advocate of French Rationalism, says: "One day a question was raised in an assembly what book a man condemned to life imprisonment would best take with him, and from Roman Catholic, Protestant, philosophers and materialists, came alike the one reply, to which all agreed—the Bible!"

As H. L. Hastings quaintly intimates, this Bible is a "book which has been refuted, demolished, overthrown and exploded more times than any other book you ever heard of. Every little while somebody starts up and upsets this book; and it is like upsetting a solid cube of granite. It is just as big one way as the other; and when you have upset it, it is right side up, and when you overturn it again, it is right side up still."

I. One element which enters into the ethical perfection of the Bible is its *impartiality*. All human biography is more or less one-sided. Boswell's Life of Johnson has been pronounced the model biography, yet it is, more than anything else, a long-drawn-out and highly-flavored encomium—a worshipper, bowing before his idol, and obscuring his idol's features by the clouds of incense with which he invests him. Boswell breaks on Johnson's feet the alabaster box of ointment; and the book is filled with the odor of his spikenard. Human biography belongs largely to the heroic, and sometimes approaches the fabulous; and it is not unnatural. When men are prompted to prepare such books, it is commonly from profound admiration for the character they are to portray. They approach their work as an artist begins a portrait or a bust, with an ideal image before him—and in the artistic the natural is often lost; there is a likeness, but it is a transfigured likeness—a portrait untrue to life! Cromwell said to the younger Lely, who was about to paint his portrait, "Paint me as I am; if you leave out a scar, a wrinkle, a freckle or a pimple, I'll not pay you one shilling!" But if all human biographies were paid for upon this basis, their authors would not get rich; all of them more or less discredit the truth by a suppression of vices and faults.

In Bible biography mark the rigid ethical impartiality—rigid indeed, but never frigid! You do not feel that there is any effort or willingness to represent the subject of the biographical sketch either with a bias of prepossession or of prejudice, but to be exactly true to nature and fact. But no man is held up as perfect, except the one perfect man. Caleb and Joshua, Nehemiah and Daniel, are not presented on the faulty side of their characters; yet they are not put before us as faultless, crowned with a diadem almost divine. And, on the other hand, Noah, who was "perfect in his generations and walked with God," is still exhibited in his drunken sleep, and, though his sons went backward and cast a cloak over him to hide his nakedness, the impartial historian does not even cloak his sin by silence, far less, apology. We find Moses indulging in unrighteous anger and unholy pride, and there is no concealment lest we should think less of the glory of his face who talked with God as a man with his friend. David was "after God's own heart"—the great king, the saintly psalmist. How the pen of the uninspired biographer even now falters when tracing that part of his history which records two of the highest crimes! And yet how unhesitatingly the pencil of the Holy Ghost adds to the beautiful portrait the ugly and repulsive feature that belongs there, for the truth's sake!

The Gallery of Battles at Versailles immortalizes no defeats. You walk through those vast corridors, and you understand the inscription over the portal: "*A toutes les glories de la France.*" The galleries of paintings are so extensive that if these pictures were placed in a row they would cover seven miles. The subjects of the historical paintings range from the Crusades to the last Italian war, including incidents in the career of Napoleon I, by David; more recent Algerian battle scenes, by Horace Vernet, and Yvon's Crimean and Italian scenes. But it is noticeable that not one defeat is pictured forth.

Turn now to the Word of God; let us enter God's historical gallery. Here the ages are included from Adam to Abraham, Moses to Malachi, and from John Baptist to John the Apostle. Peter was to the New Testament church what Abraham or Moses was to the Old, and yet he, whose noble confession was the rock on which our Lord built His church, was also pronounced a Satan, an offense unto Christ, because he savored not of the things that were of God, but those that be of men. If the Bible would have spared any one, surely it would be the disciple whom Jesus loved, and whose head lay in his own bosom; and yet there is not even a golden gauze to veil his impatience and intolerance, his jealousy, ambition, vindictiveness! These men are not ideal men, but real men—men of like passions as ourselves, even the foremost of apostles, like Paul, or of prophets, like Elijah! There is no Greek idealism here.

II. This Book has never been found in a single particular to *teach immorality;* and the most exalted positive morality and spirituality are taught here. Where can be found such exhibitions of the deformity and enormity of sin? Where such lofty laws of thought, feeling, purpose, endeavor?

Some try to rob God's word of its moral value by subtle hints that it is not original. We are told that the law of Forgiveness is no new thing, that the Hindoo proverb long since enjoined it even toward enemies, and beautifully compared the forgiving spirit to the sandal wood that imparts it fragrance even to the axe which cuts it to the heart. We are told that the Golden Rule is as old as the Chinese sages, and that Confucius 530 B. C. wrote it in a negative form; "Do not unto others what you would *not* have them do unto you." But suppose all this to be true—and overlook the fact that the negative form of this precept is at best but a silver, not a golden rule— does it prove anything against Christianity that some of its grand precepts have been anticipated by Plato or Pythagoras, by Hindoo or Chinese sages? The moral system of the Bible is to be tested *as a system*. You may find tropical plants in a hot house—but to find them in their native soil you must go to the tropics!—there they are parts of the vegetable system, not exotic, but indigenous—they belong to the flora of the country. And the question is not whether certain of the ten commandments can be found in pagan codes, or some precepts of the sermon on the mount, in the sacred book of Buddha; but where do we find the higher laws of life and love, amid surroundings entirely consistent and correspondent? Here is the native soil, in which celestial plants naturally grow and thrive and bloom! It is this divine *system of morality* which makes the Bible stand apart and alone, alike without superior or rival. Daniel Webster said, "there is always room at the top." Thus far, the Bible stands confessedly at the top: still there is room for any better system of morality; and even if the Bible is like the topstone of the pyramid that leaves no place for any above it, the common verdict of mankind will heave it from its place if a better can be found. "The progress of human reason in the paths of ethical discovery is merely the progress of a man in a treadmill, doomed forever to retrace his own steps," and we feel no fear that any human system will ever be able to improve in one particular upon this sublime ethical teaching!

There is a tradition of the descendants of Seth living on the summit of so lofty a mountain as to be able to hear and join in the song of the heavenly host. The Bible is that mountain: its peak pierces beyond the clouds into the sublimest elevations and atmospheres. Where the Word of God ends, Heaven begins. The conceptions of things human and divine, found here, surpass in grandeur and magnificence all the dreams of the ages and of the sages.

III. Where did the mere mind of man learn such *moral conceptions of God?* In a previous chapter the Bible account of Creation was contrasted with the absurdities of the best pagan cosmogonies. Take the Greek conception of God, at the summit of ancient culture, and compare it with the idea of the divine nature here unfolded! Jupiter, father of gods and men, the Omnipotent, the Thunderer, was the Son of Saturn, who had dethroned his father, and devoured his own children at birth. His wife, however, succeeded in saving Jupiter, Neptune and Pluto—and they became gods respectively of earth, sea and hell. Jupiter held court at Olympus, and the court of the most licentious of French sovereigns was not more infamous. Lust, rage, jealousy, hate, intrigue, combined with power, wisdom, majesty and love in impossible mixtures. As Geiger well says, "Gods were a turbulent aristocracy—one mightier than the rest but not almighty." Juno, Jupiter's wife, put him to sleep during a battle of the Greeks before Troy. So angry was he with her for raising a storm to impede Hercules that he hung her from the vaults of heaven by a chain, tying anvils to her feet, and when her son Vulcan interposed he flung him down head first: he landed on Semnos but broke his leg in the fall and has limped ever since. Jupiter had a severe headache, and Vulcan was summoned to relieve his distress, and at a blow from his hammer, out sprang Minerva, full-armed. These are a few specimens of Greek mythology.

Think for one moment of the Bible conception of God—all powerful, but good; all-knowing, yet merciful; all-present, yet not the God of Pantheism, inseparable from his works; but a personal God. Think of His infinite holiness, of purer eyes than to behold evil, yet graciously planning for the salvation of sinners; exalted to the highest heaven and yet condescending to the weakest and the humblest. Where did the writers of the Bible get such conceptions of the one God, while the foremost nations were worshipping dumb idols! while Egypt bowed to the crocodile, and Athens gave 60,000 women to the licentious rites of Venus, and Rome was adoring the bloody God of War, and the riotous God of Wine! while even the Parsee got no higher than to turn his face eastward and adore the sun!

IV. The Bible is alone in the full, clear exhibition of the majesty and dignity of man; putting an infinite distance between the lowest of men and highest of animals. Look at the inversions of truth in history! See Egypt in her palmy days worshipping, as divine, the calf and the crocodile; man bowing before the animal; then read Genesis, and see how grand a difference and distance are there put between the loftiest level of animal life and the lowest level of human being.* The highest order of animal is only creeping thing, but man is made in the image, after the likeness of God, out of the dust of the earth, but with an inbreathed soul and spirit the direct inspiration of God's breath.

---

*Gen. i: 26, 27, 28.

Mark—when man is to be created—the crown of all creation—there is a council among the sublime persons of the Godhead: "Let us make man." He was to be in God's own image—intellectually independent, with powers of reason and reflection and intelligent communication. Hobbes finely says that man differs from all other animals, "*rationale et orationale,*" by the gift of reason and speech. Man alone was made in God's likeness —in intellectual capacity. Let modern science exalt the animal creation as it will, and try to evolve man from the monkey: but here is a great gap which no evolution can bridge. The capacity for development in the animal reaches a limit beyond which it cannot be carried. Man's capacity for growth no science has ever yet bounded or measured. The monkey is after six thousand years essentially the same. Improvement by the most painstaking process is only like the swinging of a pendulum within a very narrow limit—it never goes beyond the extremity of the arc. Is man what he was even a thousand years ago?

Look at the new-born infant—no animal is at birth so helpless as he; not even an instinct of self-preservation except that which enables the infant to attach itself to the mother's breast. No knowledge of the use of eyes or ears, hands or feet. The new-born pup is ahead of the newborn babe in intelligence, sagacity and power of self-preservation. But how soon the child will be training the dog, asserting his superiority!

There was a boy at Dr. Richards' private asylum in New York, who seemed utterly animal, irrational and without the self-helpful instincts of a normal animal. He would lie on the floor, his tongue lolling from his mouth, absolutely without apparent thought and almost without sensation. He was called the "oyster-boy!" For months they tried to awaken a single sign of conscious life, or impress upon him one idea. One day Mrs. Richards dropped her thimble on the floor, and it fell with a metallic ring that started or startled the boy's idiotic mind into feeble action—and he turned slowly, as Bottom would say, "to see a noise which he heard," and then back his intellect retreated into the idiotic darkness. as a snail withdraws into its shell! But like the faint streak of grey in the east, that simple sign meant the awakening of consciousness! It was the first tint that tells of the dawn of day. And, on the morrow, again the thimble was dropped, and again the oyster-boy moved, and looked, this time a little more quickly and intently—and so, little by little, the darkness gave place to the dawning light, till the tongue no longer hung from the mouth, but began to learn the mystery of speech.

By-and-by a shoemaker was brought and made a shoe before his eyes, fitting it to his foot, and then Dr. Richards, laying his hand on the shoe and then on the workman would say, "Shoemaker makes shoe." And so a tailor and a coat. Dr. Richards then desired to arouse at once the mental and moral faculties by introducing to this awakening intelligence some conception of God. But how should he select an object great and grand enough to convey such a conception! It was a summer morning—and the glorious sun was just pouring his flood of light into the bay window. Dr. Richards took the boy to the casement, reverently pointed to the sun and said with holy awe: "God made the sun!" and the boy, catching the tone and the thought together, repeated "God made the sun!". And Dr. Richards left him gazing. He returned two hours later, and that oyster-boy still stood reverently gazing and saying, as though his whole soul were overwhelmed, "God made the sun!" Bishop Potter afterwards heard that boy, Sylvanus Wheeler, repeat the Lord's Prayer, and with a voice choking with emotion he said, "For thirty years I have repeated that prayer, but never like that!"

Is man indeed only an educated monkey? When the noblest specimen of all the animal creation is found capable of even such development as that, it will be time enough to doubt that man is more than the animal. No, between that oyster-boy helpless on the floor and the highest style of animal life, there is the fathomless gap of the infinite! How does the gap widen when we remember to what illimitable extent the education and development of that mind and heart may yet be carried! Try and follow that intellect and heart, so slow to wake into a true life— as year after year, and, beyond this narrow sphere, age after age, and cycle upon cycle revolve—the oyster-boy has left all the scholarship and learning of the centuries behind, as the soaring lark leaves the twig of the shrub to greet the sun high up where clouds rest, or as the sun in noonday leaves the dim glory of the dawn. He has gone far beyond Aristotle and Plato, and Bacon; the learning of philosophers he despises as the full-grown man puts away the prattle of childish ignorance. He has attained unto the knowledge of the cherub and the affection of the seraph. If man has his descent from the oyster, how comes this ascent above the oyster!

The image of God in man is the moral likeness also—the power of judgment, discriminating between right and wrong. Man has a conscience, and if we measure fully the grandeur of its authority and the majesty of its decisions, we shall be constrained to say with Dörner, that "conscience has the man."

And so has the man the image of God's immortality. He is fashioned not like the beasts that perish, after the law of a carnal commandment, but after the power of an endless life. What wonder that God is said to have breathed into man's nostrils the breath of lives, so that man became a living soul—mark, *became*, not *had* a living soul. It is the soul that is the man, and therefore God made man to have dominion over fish and fowl and cattle—the whole creation.

It is because of the exalted moral and spiritual character of the Bible that it has successfully resisted the assaults of four thousand years! It is too strong in itself and in its hold on the hearts of men, to be overthrown; as well attempt with popguns and putty to demolish Gibraltar—or to root up by hand one of the cedars of Lebanon. The Bible is too high to be successfully assaulted; as well try to throw water against the firmament —or to dislodge the stars with arrows; or, as Dr. Breckinridge said, "as well attempt to plant your shoulder against the burning wheel of the midday sun, and roll it back into night!"

The second Psalm represents God as seated on his exalted throne, and derisively laughing at the impotence of human rage against Him and His rule. So may we say of the Word of God—it laughs at the malice of its foes, at the impotence of its most gigantic adversaries, for, like the throne of God, it rests on eternal foundations?

Some reader perhaps smiles at such enthusiasm, and thinks within himself that it is very strange if the Bible is such a wonderful Book, that the sceptical objector does not find it out. A man may look into the Bible with an eye open only to objectionable features. The unconverted man loves objections, as the condemned man at court is glad to detect a flaw in the argument which is directed against him, though the flaw may not at all affect his guilt or the real conclusiveness of the testimony. A mind disposed to scepticism opens the Word, if at all, not to find moral beauty, but to hunt for something on which to hang a new objection; and hence, most infidels never read the Bible, but take their objections at second hand. Let two examples be given.

"And he brought forth the people that were therein, and put them under saws, and under harrows of iron, and under axes of iron, and made them pass through the brick-kiln: and thus did he unto all the cities of the children of Ammon. So David and all the people returned unto Jerusalem"* This has been violently assailed as a proof of the cruelty of David—the man after God's own heart, who nevertheless took the people of Rabbah and sawed them in twain, or drew over them iron harrows, or clove them with axes, or roasted them in brick-kilns. But what if it refers only *to the work at which he set them?*†

*2 Samuel, xii: 31. †Angus' Bible Hand Book.

An infidel paper in Boston devoted a column of ridicule to the "quail story,"* estimating the bushels of quails piled up over the country, and showing that each of the 6,000,000 Israelites would have 2,888,643 bushels of the quails per month, or 69,629 bushels for a meal. But the Bible says no such thing as that they were piled two cubits high over a territory forty miles broad; it simply means that the wind that brought them from the sea, swept them within reach, or about three feet above the ground, not out of reach as they would have been over head. If you should say you saw a flock of birds as high as a church spire, even an infidel would ridicule any one for supposing they were *packed* so high.

V. There is one fact, worth more than all objections, and overbalancing them all. The Bible somehow works moral revolutions in character. Find any other book that has wrought such wonders. Men have studied natural philosophy, astronomy, botany, geology, read novels and histories and poems, works on law and medicine and philosophy; who has found these books restraining lust, curbing sensual appetites, inspiring noble aims, exposing sinful propensities, moving one to be a truer son, better husband, kinder father? But, somehow, from the day men begin systematically to read the Bible, they begin to be sensible of a new power at work in mind and heart, working most of all for righteousness. I would put higher value on one chapter of God's Book than on all other books put together, to restrain from evil, and constrain to good; and for more than twenty-five years I have been watch-

*Numb., xi: 31.

ing this book as it has touched other men and women in the quick of their being, with the thrill of a divine life. I have seen men of no secular culture grow grand under the educating influence of this book—their minds expanding under the influence of its elevating, ennobling, inspiring ideas of God and man, of duty and destiny; I have seen them grow to beauty of character and conduct, sweetness of temper and disposition, transformed, transfigured.

These results demand a cause efficient and sufficient to produce such effects; and that adequate cause can be found only in the fact that God is in the Bible by the breath of His inspiring, transforming Spirit.

"This little volume," said the venerable Schliermacher, holding up a Greek New Testament before two English students, "contains more valuable information for mankind than all the other writings of antiquity put together." This book is really the foundation of all the literature that is worth preserving. Not less than two hundred thousand volumes have been written to expound and illustrate the Book of books. It is thus the central sun of a constellation of glories; and more and more as the ages pass, do the noblest of human thoughts, both borrow their lustre from its glory, and wheel into reverent orbits about this as a centre?

Let the infidel assault it—let men blaspheme and ridicule. It is God's lever and it is moving the world. Science turns its microscopic eye upon it, but it cannot be convicted of essential error. The moral philosopher examines its ethical code; but the inspiration of all virtue is there.

The hungry soul that craves food for a starving heart, finds here the full feast of fat things satisfying every craving. Who will turn from this divine book, to gratify his evil heart by a fatal plunge into the darkness of unbelief!

PART II.

THE DIVINE PERSON.

CHAPTER IX.

CHRIST IN THE OLD TESTAMENT.

"In the Volume of the Book, it is written of me."—PSALM XL, 7.

The argument from prophecy we have put foremost, because God Himself does. This is the very seal and signature by which the Holy Scriptures are certified by Him, as of divine origin and authority. The author of this Book of Books attached to the volume clear *credentials*, open to examination, easy of investigation, conclusive in attestation. Other signs of supernatural origin and character there are, which can be appreciated only by prolonged and diligent study, disciplined intellect, varied acquirements; but here is a sign, a seal, a sanction, which lies upon the very face and surface of the document, appeals to the common mind, carries its own verification within the lines and limits of the Word itself. The most ordinary reader may examine the curious predictions of the Messiah's person and work found in the Old Testament; follow the gradual progress of these revelations from Genesis to Malachi, and trace the prophecies as they descend into details, more and more specific and minute, until at last the full figure of the coming One stands out, as the figure of the Corsican corporal stood out upon the Column Vendome; nay, if he will not only read but *search* the Old Testament

Scriptures, he may trace the Messiah from his birth in Bethlehem all along through his career of suffering and of conquest, as he might follow the career of Napoleon in those memorial reliefs along the spiral bronze that wraps that column. Then with this image clearly fixed in his mind's eye, he may turn from the Old Testament to the New; and beginning with Matthew, see how the *historic* personage, depicted by the Evangelists, corresponds and coincides in every particular with the *prophetic* personage, portrayed by the prophets; let him, after this new image has reached its full outline also, take the New Testament profile of the Christ and lay it over the Old Testament profile of the servant of God; let him note how feature coincides with feature, even to the most minute particular; how in every respect the history fills and fulfills the prophecy. There is not a difference or divergence, yet there could have been no collusion or contact between prophet and narrator, for they are separated by from four hundred to fourteen hundred years. Observe, the reader has not gone *outside of the volume* itself: he has simply compared two portraits; one in the Old Testament, of a mysterious coming one; another in the New, of one who has actually come; and his irresistible conclusion is that these two perfectly blend in absolute unity. No reasoning is required: instinctively, intuitively, he leaps to the conclusion, by the quick logic of common sense, that one hand drew the image in the prophecies and moulded the portrait in the histories, and that hand must have been divine!

Mark also that this conclusion is a double one: it compels the candid reader to accept the prophetic Scriptures as infallibly inspired, and to accept the historic Christ, toward whom these glorious fingers of prophecy point and in whom all these rays of light converge, as a divine person.

The apostles and Christ Himself laid great stress upon this argument from prophecy: it was not only the main, but almost the *sole* argument employed, in the discourses outlined in the New Testament. There was then no need to prove the *facts* of our Lord's life, death and resurrection: these things were "not done in a corner," as Paul boldly said to Agrippa. The history needed vindication and verification, no more than day dawn needs announcement. Even the foes of our faith dared not dispute the facts, set forth by the evangelists. An overwise and overnice 'higher criticism' may at the distance of eighteen centuries challenge us to prove to a mathematical certainty that Jesus rose from the dead, but it is noticeable that, during the first three centuries of hot contest, when every step of advance on the part of Christianity was marked with blood, it was not necessary for apologists to *defend* the *fact* of the resurrection which even the enemies of the cross had not the boldness to *dispute*.

As in those days the *facts* were plain, it was only necessary to show their marvellous correspondence with the Old Testament prophecy, in order to carry prompt conviction to every fair mind; and so this was the common method of preaching the gospel, the solid but simple rockbase of argument upon which rested all appeal.

Our risen Lord Himself, walking toward Emmaus with two disciples, "beginning at Moses and all the prophets, expounded unto them in all the Scriptures the things concerning Himself." They had been despairing at his death, and incredulous at his resurrection; yet he showed them that both his dying, and his rising on the third day, were anticipated for centuries in the prophecies, and so he rebuked at once their despondency and their unbelief, by exclaiming, "O fools and slow of heart to believe all that the prophets have spoken! *Ought* not Christ to have suffered these things and to enter into His glory?" that is, was it not *necessary* that all this should be, in order that the Scripture should find its glorious fulfilment!

On the day of Pentecost, Peter preached a sermon which overwhelmed three thousand hearers with immediate conviction. The entire basis of his argument was simply this: that in the death and resurrection of Jesus—nay, in their very crucifixion of Him, the *prophecies*, read every Sabbath day in their synagogues, were *exactly fulfilled!* He showed them how David, foreseeing that Christ should rise, had uttered the mysterious words of the sixteenth Psalm; how that Joel, foreseeing the outpouring of the Spirit, had long ago written of the very Pentecostal blessing they were then witnessing. And it was by this appeal, in which prophecy and history met in one burning piercing point of convergence, that those thousands were pricked in their heart.

We trace Peter's discourse in Solomon's porch, and in the palace of Cornelius; Stephen's address before his stoners; Paul's speeches and sermons, in the synagogue at Antioch, in Persia, and in Thessalonica, where "three Sabbath days he reasoned out of the Scriptures, opening and alleging that Christ must needs have suffered and risen again from the dead," and that this Jesus whom he preached was the anointed one—we follow this same Paul till he comes before Agrippa; his appeal still is, "Believest thou the prophets?" And when we get our last glimpse of him at Rome, he is still "expounding and testifying concerning the kingdom of God, persuading concerning Jesus, both out of the law of Moses and out of the prophets, from morning till evening." And so it was with Apollos, the golden mouth of Alexandria. Accomplished as he was in all the oriental learning, he chose this one all-convincing theme, and "mightily convinced the Jews, publicly shewing by the Scriptures that Jesus is the Christ."

Why was this argument from prophecy then so common, so mighty,—now, alas! so seldom used with real force and power—why was this great argument chosen, out of all the armory of weapons, to defend an assaulted faith and compel the very assailants to surrender? Because this argument is *unanswerable;* because it is *perpetual* in its force, and because it is *applicable* always and everywhere. And that we may all feel its mighty suasion, let us patiently enter somewhat into particulars.

The prophecies and references to Christ in the Old Testament, which are expressly cited in the New, either as predictions fulfilled in Him or as previsions applied to Him, number *three hundred and thirty-three.* These are passages of scripture, some of which contain in themselves a little group of predictions, including several particulars, so that they stand out in the firmament of prophecy, not like single stars, however bright, but like constellations in which are clusters of radiant suns.

These prophecies may be divided into two great classes: first, those which portray Christ in His human nature, His lineage, career, sufferings and glory; in His successive manifestations until the end of the world; secondly, those which describe His character and offices, human and divine. Each class may be divided again into some twenty subdivisions, covering with astonishing fullness and exactness the most minute particulars; the audacious pen of prophecy, with the calmness and boldness of conscious inspiration and infallibility, adds feature after feature and touch after touch and tint after tint, until what was at first "a drawing without color," a mere outline or profile, comes at last to be a perfect portrait with the very hues of the living flesh. This mysterious coming One is to be the seed of the woman, born of a virgin; He is to be of the family of Noah, and branch of Shem; of the race of the Hebrews; of the seed of Abraham in the line of Isaac, through Jacob or Israel; of the tribe of Judah, the house of David. He is to be born at Bethlehem, after a period of seventy weeks* from the issue of the decree to restore and rebuild Jerusalem; His passion or sufferings, His death on the cross, His embalment and entombment, His resurrection on the third day, His ascension into the heavenly glory, His second appearance in glory at the "regeneration," and His last appearance at the end of the world, are all

---

*Properly *heptades*, or divisions of seven.

included in the delineation of His humanity and human career as the Son of Man.

The second grand division of these Messianic prophecies includes His double character as the Son of God while yet the Son of Man; as the Holy One or Saint; as the Saint of Saints, the righteous or just One, the Wisdom of God, the Oracle or Word of the Lord God, the Saviour or Redeemer, the Lamb of God, God's servant, the Mediator, Intercessor, Advocate or Daysman, Shiloh or Apostle; Prophet like Moses; Priest, High-Priest like Aaron; King like David; Prophet, Priest, King in one, like Melchizedek; Chief Captain or Leader like Joshua; Messiah, Christ or Anointed; King of Israel and God of Israel; Jehovah, Lord of Hosts, and, as though all titles were exhausted, as "King of Kings and Lord of Lords."

I. The first class of predictions which arrests our attention is *Direct Prophecy* concerning the august personage known as the coming Messiah. The gradual unfolding of this flower of Messianic prophecy is marked by *three stages* or periods of development. The first ends with Moses, and may be called the *Mosaic;* the second centers in the reigns of David and Solomon, and may be termed the *Davidic;* the third closes with Malachi, and may be called the properly *prophetic*, and, because here prediction rises to its loftiest altitude, the *climacteric*. These three periods correspond, in plant life, to seed, bud, and full-grown flower.

1. The *Mosaic* period gives us the great germ of all that unfolds, afterward, into the perfect and fragrant bloom in the rose of Sharon, the lily of the

valley. In Genesis iii: 15 we are told that the seed of the woman shall bruise the serpent's head. To feel the full force of this germinal prophecy, we must stand where our first parents stood. The awful fact was before them that the serpent had fatally stung humanity at the very heart, and brought death into the world, and all our woe. Eden was lost, God's favor forfeited, and innocence forever gone. That deliverance could come at all was wonderful; that it could come by the seed of her who led the way in the first sin was more wonderful still; that it should not only bring healing to lost man, but a crushing blow to the very head of the serpent-tempter, was most wonderful of all. Yet all this was mysteriously wrapped in that first enigma of Messianic prediction. There was to be a triumph of humanity over the evil principle represented in the serpent, and exhibited in the fall.

And now this seed-prophecy, puts forth its slender blade, and begins to branch out into particular predictions. The general, vague promise narrows down; the deliverer is to come of the posterity of Shem; later still the promise grows more specific, and limits this deliverer to the descendants of Abraham, then of Isaac, then of Jacob, then of Judah, and finally of David. The prophecy thus branches out into more and more minute particulars, until the ramifications of the prophetic tree reach the tiniest twig; and yet, with each new descent or ascent into particulars, the prophecy becomes the more impossible of fulfilment if no divine purpose and power are behind it.

The prophecies of the Mosaic period branch

out into other particulars beside those of *pedigree*. Not Abraham's seed alone, but all the families of the earth are to be blessed in this coming One. He is to be a Shiloh, the peaceful or pacific One, and unto Him, as a sceptred Ruler, the people are to gather. He is to be a prophet like unto Moses, yet clothed with higher authority and gifted with higher wisdom—Lawgiver, Leader, Ruler, Redeemer—*Rex, Lex, Lux, Dux*.

2. The second stage of Messianic prophecy has been called the *Davidic*. Here, he who was to be a leader and a lawgiver like Moses, is to be a king of war like David, yet a prince of peace like Solomon; only his kingdom is to be without succession and without end, which could be true only of some order of royalty, higher than human. In the Messianic Psalms, various aspects of the dignity, royalty and divinity of this coming King are set forth. He is God's anointed Son. His sceptre sways even the heathen: redeemed humanity constitutes his chosen bride and the day of the nuptials is the feast day of the universe. Psalms ii, xlv, lxxii, etc.

His empire is to be as wide as the world, as long as time, yet it is to be *spiritual*, conferring peace by righteousness. He will be the friend of the poorest and most obscure. Like rain on the mown grass, His rule shall distil blessings that make the barren soil fertile. Liddon sees in these prophecies in which his *name* is represented as enduring and propagating, a hint that He *himself* shall be out of sight, ruling *invisibly* in his church. His people are clad not in a panoply of steel but an armor of beautiful holiness, serving willingly. This King is also a priest, anointed with the oil of celestial gladness, fairer than the children of men, yet himself a son of David.

3. Messianic prophecy soars to its summit in the *third* and properly *prophetic* period, represented by Isaiah, whose writings furnish us the "richest mine of Messianic prophecy in the Old Testament."* From the fortieth to the sixty-sixth chapters, inclusive, we have one continuous Messianic poem, a most wonderful production even for an inspired pen. This sublime song is not a mere rambling rhapsody, without link or joints of connection, but a continuous symmetrical discourse in poetic parallels, setting forth for future ages the *complete character* and *career* of this 'servant of God.' The first five verses of the fortieth chapter contain the germ of truth unfolded in the whole poem, viz: the pardon of iniquity, the revelation of divine glory, and the ultimate blessing to all flesh, which are to come by this mystic Servant of Jehovah. The discriminating reader may within the compass of this poem find Christ in his *three offices*, prophet, priest, king; will behold, crystallizing about the atonement, all the great truths of Redemption, and may trace in outline all the future course of redemptive history.

A singular refrain, repeated in the same words, "there is no peace, saith my God, to the wicked," and at the very close of the whole poem, repeated in more terrible terms: "their worm shall not die," etc., divides the poem into *three cantos* or sections; and in the very center of the middle book, to mark the very jewel which occu-

---

*Liddon, "Divinity of Christ," p. 83.

pies the innermost shrine, what do we find? that *fifty-third chapter*, in the compass of twelve verses, *fourteen times* declares the truth of *vicarious atonement*, that this man of sorrows bore our griefs, carried our sorrows, was wounded for our transgressions, bruised for our iniquities; the chastisement laid upon Him brought our peace, and the wales on His back assure our healing. Observe, we advance just half way from that *fortieth* chapter to the sixty-sixth, and in the very heart of the Messianic mine, we find one glorious central chamber, blazing with rubies—it is flooded with light, but the light is blood-red! The Spirit is conducting us to the *doctrine* which is *central* both in prophecy and history, that Jesus *died to save sinners*.

Around this central chapter cluster many other subordinate but starry glories. This Servant of God, called from his mother's womb, upon whom God puts His spirit, is anointed to preach good tidings to the meek, to bind up the brokenhearted, to proclaim liberty to the captive. The Jews have always narrowed down salvation to the chosen seed, but He is to be a light to the *Gentiles*, and salvation to the ends of the earth.

Under his rule, "the wolf also shall dwell with the lamb, and the leopard shall lie down with the kid, and the calf, and the young lion and the fatling together, and a little child shall lead them." There is to be a transformation even of *disposition*, that very stronghold of sin within us. Coarse, rough, savage, cruel natures are to be changed, to the gentle, tender, mild and generous. Wolfish rapacity and ferocity, leopardlike cunning and treachery, lionlike violence and cruelty, are to be subdued; and the childlike spirit is to reign in human hearts.

A prolonged study alone can reveal the minuter beauties and glories of this last and greatest period of Messianic prophecy. Yet with what boldness does the inspired pen tell us how He who poured out his soul unto death, bared his back to the scourge, was led as a lamb to the slaughter; and even depict him, standing before his judges, dumb as a sheep before the shearers.

This is only *Isaiah*. But after him, in the sacred canon, stretch three hundred years of prophecy, adding new and startling particulars to these direct predictions, until Micah elects *Bethlehem* as the one among the thousand cities and villages of Judea, where the coming one shall be born; and Daniel tells us that it shall be after *seventy weeks* from the going forth of the commandment to restore and rebuild Jerusalem, an enigma now of easy solution. The decree of Cyrus dates 457 B. C.; add the *thirty-three* years of Christ's ministry and you have 490 years, just seventy heptads of seven years each.

We are not surprised when Liddon triumphantly affirms that the human life of Messiah, His supernatural birth, His character, His death, His triumph, are predicted in the Old Testament with a minuteness which utterly defies the rationalistic insinuation that the argument from prophecy in favor of Christ's claims may after all be resolved into an adroit manipulation of more or less irrelevant quotations. No amount of captious ingenuity will destroy the substantial fact that the leading features of our Lord's human

CHRIST IN THE OLD TESTAMENT. 197

manifestation were announced to the world some centures before He actually came among us.*

We have barely touched upon the outskirts of the theme: the vast field lies yet before us.

II. The testimony of *indirect* prophecy is even more wonderful. We must be content with only a glimpse, leaving our readers to explore for themselves, while we indicate only which way lie the openings to these galleries of wonders.

What we have termed *indirect* prophecy may include:

1. Poetry not primarily or apparently Messianic.
2. Ceremony, in which are typical foreshadowings of Christ.
3. History, in which we can now see a hidden allegory; or historical personages, types of some aspect of Messiah's character.
4. Paradoxes, which only the facts of Messiah's history can unlock.
5. Undesigned coincidences which are accidental, so far as man is concerned, yet providential.

1. Prophetic *Poetry*. Take, for instance, the Psalms. Where such a man as William Alexander, Bishop of Derry and Raphoe, has left his footsteps like prints of gold, we may well hesitate to attempt, within such narrow limits, even an outline of argument. In his "Witness of the Psalms to Christ and Christianity," the Bampton lectures for 1876, he has given a magnificent specimen of both expository and apologetic literature. With the peculiar insight of a Christian

---
*Liddon, p. 95.

scholar, he first applies six grand criteria as tests of single prophecies: 1, Known prior promulgation; 2, Sufficiency of correspondence; 3, Remoteness, chronological and moral; 4, Non-isolation; 5, Characteristic, but not over-definite particularity; 6, Worthiness of spiritual purpose.

Then he divides the Psalms into the *subjectively, objectively* and *ideally* Messianic, and then shows how our Lord's character and life are there delineated, and how the character of Christian disciples and of the Christian church is clearly portrayed in poems that antedate Christ's coming by a thousand years.

As a specimen of the Witness of the Psalms to Christ, let us take Psalm XXII. There is nothing here, as in direct prophecy, to hint its designed application to the Messiah. It is, on its face, simply the wail of some sufferer abandoned to the malice of his foes. Yet set Jesus within it, and, like a blazing light in a cavern, he makes it all literally radiant with meaning. The opening cry: "My God, my God, why hast thou forsaken me!" was the last of seven sentences uttered on the cross—"that voice of utter loneliness in the death-struggle, which the noble-hearted rationalist, Schenkel, confesses to be 'that entirely credible utterance, because it never could have been invented.'"*

Who is this forsaken one? Observe the peculiarities of his position, circumstances, character, sufferings, and see what key fits this complicated lock. Five particulars arrest attention, which closer study might increase again fivefold:

* Alexander, 19.

CHRIST IN THE OLD TESTAMENT. 199

1. He is abandoned, scorned, abject, and crying out from anguish—a reproach of men.

2. He is surrounded by enemies, fitly typified by bisons, strong ones of Bashan, lions, and dogs.

3. His suffering somehow involves fierce thirst.

4. Death is its consequence and finale.

5. There is a piercing of hands and feet which suggests, if it does not compel, the *cross*, which was not a Jewish mode of punishment, and had no parallel in the times of David.

A closer view multiplies the particulars of correspondence. This sufferer is laughed to scorn; passers-by shoot out the lip and shake the head, saying, "He trusted in Jehovah, that He would deliver him; let Him deliver him, seeing He delighted in him;" and we recognize the exact anticipation of what took place at Golgotha.

His sufferings are described in language that would not fit any Jewish mode of punishment. "I am poured out like water, and all my bones are out of joint! my heart is like wax; it is melted in the midst of my bowels. I may tell all my bones; they look and stare upon me. They part my garments among them, and cast lots upon my vesture."

We must leap the gulf of a thousand years to find, at Calvary, the solution of this poetic enigma. The psalmist, probably unconsciously, was drawing a picture of a crucified Christ for future believers to interpret. It is the hanging by those pierced hands and feet that disjoints the very bones; the Roman spear-thrust that lets the heart melt in the midst of the bowels like wax, and the blood and water pour out from the riven side; it is the stripping off of the raiment that leaves the dying nude sufferer to count his very bones, made more prominent by the extension of the crucified body and the wasting pangs of crucifixion; and when they parted His garments, casting lots for the seamless robe, the last correspondence was unwittingly added to complete the fufilment of prophecy.

The scholarly bishop calls attention to another feature of that twenty-second psalm, which others have overlooked. It is a *psalm of sobs*. The anguish of the sufferer shows itself by broken cries, and the gifted writer asks, "Who can *construe a sob?*" The very grammatical structure of the psalm hints that He who hung in mortal agony was too exhausted to speak, save in fragmentary sentences. The Hebrew is full of pathos. "My God, my God! why hast thou forsaken me? Far from my salvation! . . . . Words of my complaint!" . . . .

And yet the agony of this sufferer is not all. He who is thus brought into the dust of death is yet to declare Jehovah's name unto his brethren, in the midst of great congregations to praise Him; and, stranger still, that sorrow is somehow linked to the ends of the world, and a people yet to be born are to be blessed by that vicarious agony. Will any candid reader say that the crucified Saviour is not mysteriously set forth in that psalm?

Christ is everywhere found in the Old Testament, as the scarlet thread is everywhere found in the cordage of the English navy, cut it where you will.

The Bible may be divided into four departments, as to the matter contained therein, viz: *Prophetic*, *Poetic*, *Didactic*, *Historic*. We have already found Him to be the great theme of prophecy. Beginning at Moses, to Him give all the prophets witness. Even the minute details of His life are anticipated in prophecy; but that He should be found elsewhere in the Word is a double marvel. Yet in Luke xxiv: 44, He Himself told His disciples, "All things must be fulfilled which are written in the *law* of Moses, and in the *prophets*, and in the *Psalms*, concerning me."

As these three popular divisions comprehend the whole Old Testament, the Master's words assure us that not only in prophecy and poetry, but in the *law*, we shall find prophecies of Him. The whole Old Testament is the book of Christ and His salvation.

Take the five books of Moses: Genesis tells of the ark saving from the flood of wrath; Exodus, of the passover, in which the sprinkled blood brought deliverance; Leviticus, of sacrifice, the day of atonement, the year of jubilee; Numbers, of the serpent lifted up for a look of faith to bring healing; Deuteronomy, of refuge from the avenger of blood. Not only are all these *symbols* of salvation and types of Christ, but there is a constant *development of doctrine*. These types betray an *order*—a progressive unfolding of the truth. First, there is salvation from wrath—it is by blood, by sacrifice of substitute; then it both puts away the penalty and the guilt of sin; then it ends in the jubilee of cancelled debt and release from bondage. A step further and we learn that it is all conditioned on a believing look of faith, and provides escape from pursuing justice. Sacrifice ends in atonement, and atonement in jubilee.

The indirect prophecies foreshadowing the person and work of Christ cover far more ground than direct prophecy or devout poetry. In fact, open where you will, you may begin at that same scripture and preach Jesus.

2. The rites and ceremonies of the Levitical economy are comparatively meaningless until you set Him in the midst of them, to interpret them. The cross was a center of radiance, and casts its beams backward to the first sacrifice, and forward to the last supper.

A single example of the foreshadowing of Christ's sacrifice in the Levitical rites may be given from the Day of Atonement, in Lev. xvi. Here the main central figures are two kids of goats, so nearly alike as to be practically identical, and distinguished, as some say, by a scarlet cord or ribbon tied about the neck of the scapegoat. One is offered for a sin-offering; the other is presented alive; over his head, while the high-priest's hands are laid heavily upon it, the sins of the people are confessed, and then he is led away far into the wilderness, that he may never find his way back to the camp. He is called "*Azazel*"—*i. e.*, removal. Even a child may see here a pictorial presentation of the *twofold* result of Christ's atoning work: first, the *expiation* of guilt; secondly, the *removal* of our offenses as a barrier to fellowship with God, as though even the memory of them were annihilated; and the two goats are, as near as may be, alike, because both represent different aspects of one reconciling work.

A studious examination of Old Testament rites, in their relation to the atoning work of our Lord, prepares us to understand the mysterious words of the Apocalypse, and why it was that the Lamb which had been slain was the only being in the universe found worthy to *open the book*, and to *loose the seven seals thereof.* * It is a tribute to the *interpreting power of the blood of Christ*. The Lamb slain is the only key to unlock the mysteries of inspired poetry and prophecy, sacrifice and symbol. The whole book is seven times sealed up, till we apply to it the blood; then the seals are loosed, and the mystic signs may be clearly read.

3. Even the *historic* books are indirect prophecies. First, because they *prepare* for and *point* toward Him. They tell of a chosen man, family, tribe, nation, out of whom, as the consummate flower of this historic elect race, comes a divine Leader and Lawgiver, the Founder of the Church of the world. The centuries are marshalled by an invisible Power, and take up their march toward the cross of Christ; there they all find both their rallying and radiating center. Reading history in the light of the cradle at Bethlehem and the cross of Calvary, all its pages are illumined with new significance.

In hundreds of instances Old Testament history seems designedly *typical*. Events have a double meaning—one apparent and present, another hidden and future. Paul himself says of the record of Sarah and Hagar, "which things are an *allegory*"—hinting that, behind the actual nar-

* Rev. v: 5.

rative of facts, there is a prophetic finger pointing to the future. Scripture biographies, like those of Joseph, Moses, Joshua, Elijah and Elisha, David and Daniel, reveal so many points of correspondence between these men and the Redeemer, that we cannot but regard them as *typical characters*, who foreshadowed Christ in the various aspects of his many-sided character. The three reigns of Saul, David and Solomon, each of forty years—that sacred number—unmistakably forecast the three periods of church-history—the *Jewish*, ending in apostasy; the Christian church *militant;* and the Christian church *triumphant* in the millennial reign.

Can any careful reader avoid seeing Christ in the paschal lamb? When the lamb was roasted, a spit was thrust lengthwise through the body, and another transversely from shoulder to shoulder; every passover lamb was transfixed on a *cross*. When Moses lifted up the serpent, it was not on a pole, but on a *banner-staff*—*i. e.*, a *cross*.

Our Lord himself teaches us to see in Jonah— sacrificed for the salvation of the ship's crew, and for three days borne down into the depths in the belly of the great fish, and then thrown out upon the land—a typical prophecy of His own death, burial and resurrection. And so full does Old Testament history seem to be of Christ, that there is a risk of carrying this perception of resemblance and analogy to a fanciful extreme, like those who in the Greek word for fish, $\iota\chi\theta\upsilon\varsigma$, find the initials of a redemptive sentence, $I\eta\sigma o\upsilon\varsigma\ \chi\rho\iota\sigma\tau o\varsigma\ \theta\epsilon o\upsilon\ \upsilon\iota o\varsigma\ \sigma\omega\tau\eta\rho$.

If Christ be *patent* in the New Testament, He

is as surely *latent* everywhere in the Old. There are, as far back as Genesis, hints of at least a duality of persons in the Godhead; and as the doctrine of *one God* was the great ark that God's people bore through the ages, this cannot be a relic of polytheism. What means this joining of a singular verb to a plural noun—*Elohim;* the consultation over man's creation, "Let us make man;" the threefold blessing by the priests in Numbers; the threefold rhythm of prayer and praise in the Psalter; the adoring chant of worship to the Most Holy Three in One by the cherubim in Isaiah? May there not be *occult* as well as *explicit* references to the Trinity? *

When we read of one supreme Angel of Jehovah, in whom was the Holy name of God; the Angel of His Presence, who saved His people; a personified *Wisdom* of God, who so mysteriously corresponds to the *Logos* in John—we claim the privilege of seeing at least a dim and cloudy image, sometimes taking on more distinct and definite features of the Christ whom we adore, and whom, having not seen, we love, and seem to see forevermore from Genesis to Malachi; so that every page becomes like an album-leaf—glorious with some new portrait of the Son of God.

4. Special attention ought at least to be called to the *Paradoxes of Prophecy*, in some respects most remarkable of all the witnesses to Christ to be found in the Old Testament.

A paradox is a *seeming* contradiction; no real absurdity is involved, but it presents an enigma which, without the clue, may be impossible of

---
* Liddon, 48.

solution. The Old Testament abounds in paradoxes about the Messiah, which were, and still are, absolute mysteries, except as the New Testament helps to solve them.

This coming One was to be son of God and yet son of man; born of a virgin yet his birth holy and immaculate; his form one of transcendent beauty and loveliness, yet he was without form or comeliness, his visage marred; he was to be a man of sorrows, acquainted with griefs, yet anointed with the oil of gladness above his fellows; he was to be the son of David yet David's Lord; the king of war, yet the prince of peace, etc.

If his garments were parted among the soldiers what occasion was there to cast lots on his vesture, to determine to whom it should fall? The crucifixion scene solves the problem—they did part his raiment, but when they came to the seamless robe, they assigned by lot, what they were ashamed to destroy by rending it.

These paradoxes abound in all parts of the Old Testament prophecies. Sometimes they are grouped so closely and in such plain terms as to remind us of oriental puzzles, like the oracular responses or the mystery of the sphynx. For instance in Isaiah ix, 6, this Messianic personage is first called a *son*, born to Israel; and yet what a fourfold name is applied to him? the wonderful —or miracle,—counsellor, the Mighty God, the Father of Eternity, the Prince of Peace! A child, born as a son to a family of Israel, yet having infinite Power, and Wisdom; and this son of time is the Father of Eternity, this weak babe is the God of All Might.

The fifty-third chapter of Isaiah presents the most startling of these paradoxes. In fact they seem *designed* to present a prophetic enigma which only the person of Christ can solve.

He was cut off from the land of the living, a young man and without offspring, and yet he shall prolong his days, and shall see his seed, and they shall be so numerous that even his great soul shall be satisfied. He is to be put to death as a despised malefactor, to make his grave with the wicked, and yet the sepulchre of the rich is to be his tomb. He is to be scorned and rejected of men and yet to justify many, and though himself treated as a transgressor is to make intercession for the transgressors.

If one can imagine a series of paradoxes more completely perplexing than these, what would they be! The solution, furnished in the double nature of the God-man, seems to us now, simple enough. But let us put ourselves by an effort of imagination back two thousand years in history and with the eyes of a devout Jew read these prophetic problems. How utterly hopeless all effort to explain or reconcile such contradictory statements. In fact the later Jewish doctors had recourse to the *invention* of a *double Messiah* as the only clue to these mazes.*

He was to be emphatically overwhelmed in adversity, and in mortal sufferings pour out his soul; and yet to see the pleasure of the Lord prosper in his hand; and while himself a victim, a worm crushed under the feet of his persecutors, he is to triumph over his victors, and divide the spoils like a universal conqueror.

*Liddon, 86.

This divine riddle waits seven hundred years for an interpretation. Then, at the time and place indicated, a babe is born of a virgin, being conceived of the Holy Ghost; in the flesh he was a man; in the spirit, he was God; in outward surroundings lowly, poor, obscure; in essence having the glory, dignity, riches of God; a man of sorrows yet filled with the unfathomable peace of God; David's son according to the flesh, yet the Lord of David according to the spirit. Dying on the cross, yet a young man, he travailed in soul and brought forth a seed so numerous that they shall outnumber the sands of the seashore; died as a criminal, and as a criminal his body would have been flung over the walls to be burned like offal in the fires of Topheth: but when his vicarious sufferings were finished, no further indignity could be permitted even to the lifeless body, and so it was tenderly taken down, wrapped in clean linen by gentle hands, and laid in a rich man's sepulchre, wherein never yet man was laid. Only a virgin womb could conceive, only a virgin tomb receive, the body of God's immaculate son.

The lines of an Ionic column were once supposed to be parallel: but it was found that if produced to a sufficient distance above the capital, they at last touch. These prophetic paradoxes are like stately Ionic columns in the structure of Revelation. Their lines seem parallel, and we seek in vain any point of convergence. But projected into the centuries, they meet at last in Jesus of Nazareth, the only solution of their seeming contradictions.

How is it that, with such overwhelming proof

that Jesus is in the Old Testament, any candid mind can escape the conclusion that a divine *pen* traced the prophecy and a divine *person* fulfilled the prophetic portrait. It would seem that in spite of a criticism that is destructive of everything yet constructive of nothing; in spite of a scepticism that would take away our Lord so that we know not where they have laid him, every honest man must say, *the Scriptures could not have foretold the Christ if they were not inspired of God*; and the *Christ would not* have been so foretold, the center of such converging rays of glory, if he had not been all he claimed.

The sad fact is that we have yet to meet the first honest sceptic, or even destructive critic, who has carefully studied the prophecies which center in Christ. There is an amazing ignorance, if not indifference, as to the whole matter. Whatever attention is given to the Scriptures by such minds, is directed to the discovery of errors or blemishes, as though an astronomer should be so absorbed in the spots on the sun as never to consider the sunlight that floods creation and makes the spots visible. The discovery of an error in transcription, a mistake in names, figures or grammatical construction, is heralded from pole to pole; while it never occurs to these critics and sceptics, that *this book must be a miracle* in itself, since its *slightest blemishes* can attract the microscopic inspection of the scholars of all the ages!

"But," says some wise owl, "perhaps, after all, these multiplied correspondences are only accidental." *Accidental?* Do such objectors understand the laws of simple and compound probability? If one prediction be made and that only a general one, it may or may not be fulfilled, *i. e.*, the chance of its fulfilment is represented by *one-half*. The moment another particular is added, *each* of the two predictions having one-half a chance of fulfilment the fraction representing the probability of both proving true is ½ × ½ = ¼. We have passed from *simple* to *compound* probability. Now the possibility of a thousand particular predictions, centering in one person at one time, is as ½ *raised to its thousandth power*: a fractional probability too small for figures to represent.

Some ways of meeting the argument from prophecy are so unfair and uncandid that they deserve a reference, only to show how desperate is the hatred of evil hearts toward the Word of God. Porphyry found such remarkable prophecies in Daniel, that while he admitted that history had accurately verified them, even in the slightest particular, he resorted to the trick of suggesting that so exact a record could be written only after the events; and Voltaire used the same trick to evade the proof from New Testament prophecy.

In this case, God has not left even this needle's eye for such camels to squeeze through. For there is a *gap of four hundred years* between Malachi and Matthew. God permitted the spirit of prophecy so early to die out, and the Old Testament canon to close centuries before our Lord was born. There was a *design* in it. He meant that there should be no chance of *collusion* between the Old Testament prophets and the New Testament evangelists. There must be a long period of absolute silence between the utterance of prophecy and its fulfilment, that there might be no doubt as to the inspiration of the prophecy and the divine character of the Son of Mary.

Bolingbroke resorted to a more cunning, but not less dishonest evasion. He admitted that the death of Christ was distinctly foretold in Isaiah liii; so distinctly and with so minute detail that it forced him to believe that Jesus, by a series of preconcerted measures actually *brought on his own crucifixion* merely to give disciples who came after Him the triumph of appeal to the old prophecies.

Modern criticism tries another way of breaking the force of this evidence, viz. by taking each individual prediction and saying of it, this is simply a chance coincidence, and worthless in itself as an evidence. As though one were buying a huge hawser, to hold a ship at her moorings, and should untwist it, take up strand by strand and break it with his fingers and then say to him who would sell the cable, "it is *worthless:* there is not a *strand* in it that would hold a ship a moment." Just so, but the strength of a cable is the strength of its strands braided together; and the strength of prophetic evidence is the united testimony of all these predictions. Any one might be insufficient: all in one, irresistible!*

Before we leave this astounding argument from prophecy, let us take one more rapid glance of review over the whole field of the evidence. At first, one germinal prediction, that branches out into minutest ramifications till the tiniest twig

---

*See Gibson's "Foundations."

is reached, each minute particular increasing, in geometric ratio, the impossibility of a chance fulfilment. Jesus of Bethlehem is born and as every particular of his history corresponds with every particular of the prophecy, every branch and twig of the prophetic 'plant of renown' grows radiant till the plant becomes a Burning Bush, and like Moses we loose our shoes and veil our eyes, for the place is holy ground.

"In the volume of the Book it is written of me." Yes, there is only one Book, and only one person—the Book manifestly written for the person; the person manifestly *before* the Book, to inspire it; *after* it, to crown and complete it. There are, as Luke said to Theophilus, "*many infallible proofs.*" Among all external, historical proofs, *prophecy* is the unanswerable argument. Among all internal and experimental proofs, the one all-sufficient is the *person of Christ*. Abraham saw His day afar off, and was glad; Moses wrote of Him, David sang of Him, and all this is so plain that, as our Lord said, "if they believe not Moses and the prophets, neither will they be persuaded though one rose from the dead."

Even history was prophetic. "Each victory, each deliverance, prefigured Messiah's work; each saint, each hero, foreshadowed some separate ray of His personal glory; each disaster gave strength to the mighty cry for His intervention. He was the true soul of the history, as well as of the poetry and prophecy, of Israel." *

Sir Joshua Reynolds closed his splendid lectures on art by saying: "And now, gentlemen, I

---

* Liddon, 93.

CHRIST IN THE OLD TESTAMENT. 213

have but one name to present to you: it is the incomparable Michael Angelo." And so all the prophets and poets, priests and historians, of the old covenant, seem to stand in reverent homage, pointing to the manger, the cross, the rent tomb, and the opening heaven, and uttering one incomparable name.

God has set His "golden milestone" in the forum of the world, and all roads of prophecy and history terminate there.

There are those who call themselves Christians who, instead of feeding on the pure milk or strong meat of the Word, are devouring the chaff or imbibing the poison of an unsatisfying, godless science or sceptical philosophy, or who pay a modern antichrist to retail the blasphemies and sneers of Voltaire and his age, in their ears; and yet they wonder at their own doubts. Nothing seems certain. They question whether the Bible be not, after all, the work of man, and whether Jesus be not at best only a myth or a mystery; whether death be not a leap in the dark, and heaven a dream of excited fancy. Poor, deluded souls! As though a disciple could grow strong and walk erect in the conscious confidence of an unshakable faith, who breathes only the stifling atmosphere of a prayerless life, and feeds on husks fit only for swine, while God's manna, every morning fresh, may be gathered in the fields of the Word. The sovereign cure for all doubting disciples is to *immerse themselves* in the Word of God, as a vessel is dipped in the sea till it is filled and overflows. Nothing but *God's own truth* can displace the uncertainty of scepticism.

How sublime is the attitude of our Lord himself! Standing forevermore with his hand on the Jewish canon, He calmly looks both opponents and disciples in the face and says: "Search the Scriptures, for in them ye think ye have eternal life; and they are they which testify of me." *

---
* Liddon, 96.

CHAPTER X.

THE PERSON OF CHRIST.

"Truly, this was the SON OF GOD."—MATTHEW XXVII:54.

"Go a little deeper," said the wounded soldier of Napoleon's body-guard, as the surgeon was probing to find the ball lodged in his breast; "go a little deeper, and you'll find the emperor."

In the study of Christian evidences, having considered the witness of prophecy and of miracle, the harmony of the Word of God with science, and with our moral nature, we now go a little deeper and touch the heart of the whole body of Christianity—the PERSON OF CHRIST. Here is the focal center of all Christian evidence; when we reach and touch that heart, feel its divine throb, and know its divine love, our intellectual doubts vanish, and we are constrained to confess: "Truly, this is the Son of God."

Nearly nineteen centuries ago, in an obscure town in Palestine, an event took place which has had more influence on the history of the world than any other since time began. A child was born—surely not so rare an occurrence as to awaken in itself any great interest: This was no son of distinguished parents, no heir to riches or royalty, no scion of a noble house, no prospective ruler of a world's empire. He was born in a stable and cradled in a manger, because in the inn there was no room for the mother even in the crisis of the sorrow of her sex. Yet, about that natal hour, that lowly cradle and that humble child, the thought, love and life of millions have, from that day to this, been centred.

The universal verdict concedes to Christ at least a grandly complete manhood. Pilate stands as the typical judge, saying, as he points to Jesus, "Behold the man!" Christ seems to represent humanity, in its broadest range and in a very special sense, as a man, and, in its ideal perfection, as *the* man.

We have space to touch this grand theme only at a few prominent points:

1. We notice about Jesus no narrow limits of individuality. James Watt suggests the inventor; Benjamin West, the painter; Napoleon, the warrior; Columbus, the discoverer; Pitt, the statesman. Men of mark stand out from the mass with sharp, individual traits, as, in the apostolic company, we think of Peter's impetuosity, Paul's energy, John's love; and these traits both distinguish and separate certain men from others.

But Christ's peculiarities did not isolate him from other men. Nothing stands out so prominently as to draw some to him from a sense of sympathy and similarity, and drive others from him by a feeling of natural antagonism. He is not so allied to any peculiar temperament as to impress others with a lack of power to understand their individual cast of character. Yet there is no lack of positiveness in this perfect man, like a coat fitting everybody, yet fitting nobody; no such elasticity of character as stretches or contracts to suit every new demand; but such a common fitness as tells of something in common with every man; a beautiful fulfilment of the scriptural figure that "as in water face answereth to face, so the heart of man to man." Any man, whatever his tastes or temperament, his type of mind or heart or disposition, finds in Jesus something answering to his need—a sympathizing brother!

2. Nor was our Lord—this perfect man—limited to a narrow nationality. How marked is the profile of national character! Demosthenes is always the Greek, Cicero the Roman, Hannibal the Carthaginian; the Jew is always and everywhere the Jew; he scarcely associates, never assimilates or amalgamates, with any other people. Try to weave him into history; he is the iron forever unmixed with the clay; the scarlet thread is seen all through the fabric—never lost sight of amid the other colors of the woof. And yet Jesus was a Jew, and yet less a Jew than a man. Paul could say, "I am a Jew;" but Jesus said with profoundest truth, "I am the Son of Man"—not so much Hebrew as human, filling out the grand motto of Terence, "*Homo sum—et humani a me, nil alienum puto!*"

3. Christ represents the generic man, and you will remember that the term "man" probably includes the woman as well as the man. "God made man in His own image. In the image of God created He him; male and female created He them." The ideal man combines and includes the womanly graces with the manly virtues; that which is gentle and tender with that which is strong and firm. The king of birds has not only the stern eye, the firm beak, the strong talons, but the soft, downy breast as well; and the king of men will be a woman also,

in the qualities of heart which make her the radiant center of the home. Christ had the kingly majesty and the queenly grace; none could be manlier than He; yet, without being effeminate, He was feminine; without being womanish, He was womanly, also; and it is no marvel if woman showed toward Him all the reposeful trust she loves to exercise toward one on whose strength she may lean, and yet have all the intimate, sympathetic devotion which she exhibits toward her own sex; and no marvel that

"She, when the apostles fled, could danger brave,
Last at His cross, and earliest at His grave."

We are at a loss to say which predominated in Jesus, the manly or the womanly virtues. He who flamed with righteous indignation at the desecration of His "Father's house," till every cord in His scourge burned like lightning and snapped like thunder, could graciously and gratefully accept the kisses and caresses of a sorrowing sinner, bestowed on His feet; and He whose grand words of warning and wisdom have for two thousand years moved the world as great winds heave ocean waves, could melt the heart of a woman by one word, "Mary," so that her tone of impatience gave place instantly to a rapturous, adoring exclamation, "*Rabboni!*"—"My dear Master!" Romanism makes a mistake in the Coronation of the Virgin, Queen of Heaven, as though the human heart needed another object of worship in whom the womanly graces should crystallize. Jesus has in Himself all that beautifies womanly character.

4. Jesus Christ was certainly most remarkable in the perfect balance of opposite, or, rather,

apposite qualities. We observe that few human characters combine the sterner virtues with the softer graces. You find gentleness, generosity, mildness and meekness in one class of men, and firmness, frugality, positiveness and energy in another; but how seldom do they meet and mingle in one character. Disraeli speaks, and you marvel at the polish and politeness of his dissection of his adversary's argument; but you detect, beneath all that suavity, the ferocity of a tiger; or you think of the anaconda, that licks his prey all over with his slimy tongue, preparatory to swallowing it! Can you, even in the most scorching rebukes and denunciations of hypocrisy, and of robbery of the poor, even find one trace of a savage, hateful, vindictive spirit in the perfect man?

Have you never remarked that the highest human purity is generally like a soaring alpine peak, cold and chilling? It suggests whiteness as of virgin snows, and transparency as of ice-crystals, undefiled by earthly elements; but it suggests distance. Purity may be attracted by purity, but impurity, even when coupled with penitence, is repelled; it cannot, dare not approach. There must have been something peculiar about the purity of the Christ. He moved among men freely; sat down to eat with publicans and sinners; yet His garments took as little stain as the light in passing through an impure atmosphere. And, though His very presence forbade the touch or whisper or breath of that which is defiled, the veriest outcasts of society were drawn to Him by resistless attraction, lavished tears of sorrow and kisses of love upon His feet, and broke flasks of precious ointment on His person! What a mystery! A purity beside which even the snow is no longer clean, mingled with a compassion and sympathy to which the vilest sinners run for refuge as to the downy breast of some majestic bird! There was a divine quality in that purity that reminds one of the light, so pure, so incorruptible, yet falling on the sterile sand and slimy pool to call forth fair and fragrant blooms; or of the dew falling from above to rest alike on the most wholesome and the most noxious growths, and leave everywhere its impartial benediction.

5. It is a grand fact that even the long test of nineteen centuries, and the close, severe, searching and microscopic criticism of these days, cannot find any flaw, not to say vice, in the Christ.

How difficult it is for the generation in which a man lives to form a fair judgment of the man! Sometimes prejudice heaps faggots about him, and his true features are hidden by the smoke of martyr fires; or, again, popular admiration or adoration burns incense before him, and his real self is obscured by clouds of excessive praise; and so we have to wait until the martyr-fires or the altar-fires go out, to see the real man; and what is the result? We often see the hero fade into a Nero, or the wretch rise into the saint.

Wendell Phillips says, "If you penetrate the halo of military glory which surrounds the Duke of Marlborough, you will find the most purchasable and infamous scoundrel of the age." Nearly two milleniums have passed since Jesus was moving among men. Whatever praise or blame, friends or foes attached to Him in those days, we are able at this remote time to form a fair judgment of His character and career. And the question rings out, "What think ye of Christ?" Has any man ever dealt a successful blow at the blessed one, whom the reviling tongue calls the "Christian's idol?" Point out one vice, one real blemish, in that character or life! Examine as with microscopic eye, but the more minute the examination the greater the disclosure of beauty.

6. What magnanimity there was in this perfect man! Even King James could send a petty gift of five shillings to rare Ben. Johnson—humiliating the foremost poet of the day because his poverty forced him to live in an alley, and provoking the retort, "Go tell the king his soul lives in an alley!" But in Jesus you see no trace of narrowness—even of Jewish exclusiveness and prejudice; no small or mean sentiment; no selfish feeling; a broad catholicity without laxity; a generous impartiality without indifference to truth and right. A great, grand soul as ever tabernacled in a human body! And yet nothing in His surroundings to educate Him into magnanimity; for the whole tendency of His age was toward narrowness and bigotry!

This greatness of Christ's soul, this singular unselfishness and purity of His love, arrests the attention even of the most casual observer. The best and noblest men often betray, in the crises of life, a lingering self-love, and sometimes an idolatry of self-interest. Burke, a keen observer of human nature, has said that if you do a man a favor, and put him under lasting obligation to you, you sow in him the seeds of dislike. It humbles him to think that he owes promotion to anything but his own merits, and his pride is rebuked whenever he meets you; and so he becomes, unconsciously perhaps, alienated from you. Rochefoucauld has remarked that there is something in human nature which permits us to get a certain sort of satisfaction even from the misfortunes of our friends—a remark which is unhappily illustrated when those who have been eminently successful experience the disaster of failure.

Such frank confessions show the opinion which sagacious students of humanity form of the common selfishness of the heart, to all of which Christ presents an exception, so unique, so conspicuous, so original, that our philosophy is at a loss to explain it. Satan said of Job, "All that a man hath will he give for his life"—boldly judging that to preserve his life, even a good man will make every other sacrifice; but how cheerfully did Jesus accept even a cruel and shameful death for the sake of His enemies! Well might the world stand amazed before His cross when the dying sufferer prays, "Father, forgive them, for they know not what they do!" and be dumb at sight of self-sacrifice, which was for the sake of service. And right here is, perhaps, the enigma of Christ's character. Whence came the inspiration of such self-sacrifice? All miracles of power are eclipsed by the miracle of His passion. In the agony and bloody sweat at Gethsemane, and the anguish and awfulness of the shameful death at Golgotha, there is something more overwhelming than in any of His mightiest works; and it was when He was "lifted up" that He "drew all men unto Him." Not what He did, but what He *was* in Himself, presents the most astounding miracle!

An oriental fable represents a crowd of idlers, thronging the market-place of a Syrian city, and looking contemptuously upon a dead dog, with a halter around his neck, by which he had been dragged through the dirt. A viler, more abject, more unclean, more repulsive thing does not meet the eye of man, and those who stood by looked on with abhorrence. "Faugh," said one, holding his nose, "it pollutes the air!" "How long," said another, "shall this foul beast offend the sight?" "Look at his torn hide," said another; "one could not even cut sandal-straps out of it." And a fourth spoke of his ears, draggled and bloody: and a fifth declared "he had no doubt been hanged for thieving." But there stood, among the throng, one, a stranger, who had, as they flung their jeers at the dead dog, drawn near; there was a strange light about his face, and in his whole mien a strange dignity and grace. Looking down compassionately upon the dead animal, he said: "Pearls are not equal to the whiteness of his teeth." Then the people turned to him with amazement, and said among themselves: "Who is this? This must be Jesus of Nazareth; for only He could find something to pity and approve even in a dead dog!" And in shame they bowed their heads before him, and went each on his way.

How easy, how human, to say satirical things; to see only the repulsive side of character; to taunt the heedless and trample on the fallen! How strangely humane was He; how benign and merciful; how marvelously penetrating, seeking the beautiful amid the ugly, and finding what is attractive amid what is repulsive; detecting the germ of the saint in the chief of sinners, the outcast woman and the hated publican! Like the benignity of Nature, that uses her elemental forces to bring beauty out of deformity until the clay crystallizes into the blue sapphire, the barren sands into the burning opal, the defiling soot into the radiant diamond, the foul water into snow-flakes and ice-crystals that rival the most exquisite gems for beauty of form and richness of luster; so He, with a divine condescension that makes even the lowliest great, beams upon poor, defiled, corrupt human nature, until a beauty develops that furnishes gems for the very crown of heaven's King—gems lustrous as stars!

7. The Christ of the Bible stands alone in His sublime law of self-renunciation. At the very gate of the new life we are met by this motto: "*Deny Thyself!*" There is a beautiful fable of Poussa, the Chinese potter—that he was required to produce a work for the emperor. He summoned to his aid all his genius and taste and skill; executed one after another task in porcelain, each a masterpiece, yet none worthy to be presented to his sovereign. His last work was in the oven, for the finishing process; but, in despair of ever being able to produce anything of sufficient merit to adorn the imperial table, he threw himself into the furnace, and lo! there came out the most beautiful and perfect porcelain ever known—before it, after it, nothing to be compared with it.

The Chinese sages wrote wiser than they knew. For the first and only time, this blessed Book has framed into a law the heroic principle of self-sacrifice, teaching us that no work is so precious in His eyes as that which is made complete and beautiful by the offering of self—illustrating this law by a life, such as no uninspired mind ever drew even in outline. This precious Book tells us of one who resigned the throne and crown of heaven, exchanged the radiant robe of the universal King for the garment of a servant, descended to earth, condescended to human want and woe and wickedness, lay in a lowly cradle in a cattle-stall at Bethlehem, and hung upon a cross of shame on Calvary, that even those who crucified Him might be forgiven. Can you span the chasm between the throne of a universe and that cross? a crown of stars and a crown of thorns? the worship of the host of heaven and the mockery of an insulting mob? When you can bridge that gulf, you may know something of the divine grandeur of such self-sacrifice. Whence such a conception of heroism? There is nothing like it in history, not even in fable; poets and philosophers have not approached it; the highest unselfishness is selfish beside it. Could it be the invention of impostors, or the wild dream of deluded fanatics? Is there any supposition that meets the case save this—that it was first a divine fact, expressing and exemplifying the divine idea?

8. When we endeavor to picture Him to ourselves, no beauty of face, form, figure, can do justice to His perfection. Put the "brow of Jupiter on the form of Apollo," and you have not approached the beauty with which imagination invests His person. Give Him "Luther's electrical smile, opening the window in a great soul," and you have nothing yet to express the divine charm of His winning grace, which, notwithstanding His majesty, drew little children to His arms. Give Him the wisdom of Solomon and the profoundness of Aristotle, and the originality of Bacon; and all this cannot explain the words of Him who,

by the confession of enemies, spake as never man spake, and who, in dealing with truths the most sublime, never forgot to be simple, even in the forms of His illustrations!

Here is the ideal of manhood, in mind as well as body. What thoughts, inspiring what words and works! What sublime conceptions, convincing argument, wise counsel, powerful persuasion, perfect illustration, grand discrimination!

What a heart—so pure, so noble! Was ever love so charming in its fervor, its sincerity, constancy, generosity, unselfishness?—nothing but a look of gentle reproach for the disciple who denied Him, and no word of bitterness even for the apostle who, with a kiss, betrayed Him. He left all ideals behind, in His reality. We think no more of the Roman notion of heroic virtue, the Greek notion of culture, the Italian idea of beauty; in presence of Jesus, all these fade, as stars grow pale at morning.

"How, then," says Dr. Porter, "can it be explained that forth from that generation came the loftiest and the loveliest, the simplest, yet the most complete ideal of a master, friend, example, Saviour of human kind, that the world has ever conceived; an ideal that, since it was furnished to man in the record, has never been altered except for the worse; a picture that no genius can retouch except to mar; a gem that no polisher can try to cut, except to break it; able to guide the oldest and to soothe the youngest of mankind; to add luster to our brightest joys, and to dispel our darkest fears? Whether realized in fact or regarded only as an ideal, the conception of Jesus is the greatest miracle of the ages!"

This humble Nazarene taught the race a new law of progress, viz: Self-oblivion. And since that cross was set upon Calvary, every grand step of advance for the race has been "from scaffold to scaffold, and from stake to stake." He led the way in helping men to live, by himself dying, and the ideas he embodied have been ever since "fighting their way against the original selfishness of human nature."

9. It is evident He was more than man. There is that in the PERSON OF CHRIST which has won almost involuntary homage from even sceptical minds. Daniel Webster, who was the Doric pillar of New England, as Edward Everett was its Corinthian column, drew up, just before his death, the following Declaration of Faith. As his was confessedly one of the few massive masterminds of history, it has double significance: "Lord, I believe; help thou mine unbelief." "The philosophical argument, especially that drawn from the vastness of the universe in comparison with the insignificance of this globe, has sometimes shaken my reason for the faith that is in me; but my heart has always assured me and reassured me that the gospel of Jesus Christ must be a divine reality. The Sermon on the Mount cannot be a mere human production. This belief enters into the very depths of my conscience; the whole history of man proves it."

We set, side by side with this, the testimony of one other man, by common verdict one of the most remarkable of the race—the first Napoleon. While in banishment at St. Helena, conversing with General Bertrand, who contended that Jesus was simply a man of great genius and power to command and control, the exiled emperor said: "I know men, and I tell you that Jesus Christ is not a man! Superficial minds see a resemblance between Christ and the founders of empires and the gods of other religions. That resemblance does not exist. There is between Christianity and whatever other religions the distance of infinity! We can say to the authors of every other religion, 'You are neither gods nor the agents of the Deity. You are but the missionaries of falsehood, moulded from the same clay with the rest of mortals. You are made with all the passions and vices inseparable from them. Your temples and your priests proclaim your origin!' Paganism was never accepted as truth by the wise men of Greece, neither by Socrates, Pythagoras, Plato, Anaxagoras or Pericles. Paganism is the work of man. One can here read but our imbecility. What do these gods, so boastful, know more than other mortals—these legislators, these priests? Absolutely nothing!"

When we study the marvelous history of those thirty-three years, we stand in presence of the most significant period of all history, folding in its bosom the most precious facts ever cherished in the heart of man. The existence of Jesus Christ is the pivot upon which turn the history and destiny of the world. This one man, born in poverty and bred in obscurity; without rank, wealth, culture, or fame; who could call no spot home, and no great man his friend; who was hated by the influential men of church and state, and died as a criminal, by their united verdict; even whose tomb was the loan of charity, to save his body from being flung over the walls to the accursed fires of Topheth—this one man somehow sways the world! We date our very letters and papers, not "Anno Mundi"—the year of the world—but "Anno Domini"—the year of our Lord; and even he who, from his dark chamber of doubt and disbelief, sends out his assaults upon Jesus of Nazareth, still dates his pen's production "Anno Domini"—unwillingly bowing to Christ's Lordship, even of the world's calendar! Even creation is forgotten, as the epoch from which all is to be reckoned, since that babe was born in Bethlehem of Judea—as though all history had a new birth then. Kings are anointed in His name; the grandest cathedrals unfold their white blossoms of stone to bear perpetual witness to His glory and beauty. Millions of believers offer Him the myrrh of their penitence for sin, the frankincense of their prayers and praise, the gold of their costliest offerings of gratitude and service; and even the profane swearer rounds his oath with the precious name of Jesus, while no other name is spoken with such reverence by the pure and good!

What shall I do then with Jesus? However, I may account for His existence or explain His character and career; whatever I may think of His being born of a virgin and begotten of the Holy Ghost—whatever I think of His words and works, as divine or human, He is Himself the miracle of history! Science and philosophy vainly try to account for Him or interpret Him.

He stands absolutely alone in history; in teaching, in example, in character, an exception, a marvel, and He is Himself the evidence of Christianity. As Bishop Clark says, "He authenticates himself." "The most natural solution of His life is the supernatural. The truths which He uttered were not truths which He had learned. He was the truth!"

It is therefore no marvel that the Word of God is full of this wonderful personage. In the British navy-yards, where all the cordage, from the huge hawser down to finest strands, has braided into it a peculiar scarlet thread, you cannot cut an inch off without finding it marked. So everywhere, woven into and through the word you may find the scarlet thread—and beginning anywhere, preach the blessed Christ.

One of the most sublime facts in connection with this wondrous PERSON OF CHRIST is the strange hold He has upon millions of believers at this remote age. After eighteen centuries have passed, a large proportion of the human race, the most intelligent and the most lovely, can say of Christ, with Paul, "Whom having not seen we love." Everything connected with His personal life on earth has perished. We can only guess at the spot where he was born, the place where he lived, the site of the cross and the tomb; and yet, millions are living for Him, and would die for Him. They believe that this unseen presence inspires their faith, hope, love, life; that with this unseen Saviour they hold daily communion; they go through the valley of tears, leaning on His arm; and they fear not the shadow of death, cheered by His smile. This fact is absolutely without a parallel, and it impressed the great Napoleon more deeply than anything else about this mysterious person. He looked back through the centuries and saw the blood of Christian martyrs flowing in torrents, while they kissed the hand that, in slaying them, opened the door to Him. "You speak," said he, "of Cæsar, Alexander, of their conquests; of the enthusiasm they enkindled in the hearts of their soldiers; but can you conceive of a dead man, making conquests with an army faithful and entirely devoted to His memory? My army has forgotten me while living. Alexander, Cæsar, Charlemagne and myself, have founded empires. But on what did we rest the creations of our genius? Upon force! Jesus Christ alone founded His empire upon love: and at this hour millions of men would die for Him. I have so inspired multitudes that they would die for me—but, after all, my presence was necessary —the lightning of my eye, my voice, a word from me—then the sacred fire was kindled in their hearts. Now, that I am at St. Helena, alone, chained upon this rock, who fights and wins empires for me? What an abyss between my deep misery and the eternal reign of Christ, who is proclaimed, loved, adored, and whose reign is extending over all the earth!"

And so it is. A public life of three and a half years, ending with a death of shame at thirty-three; yet to-day swaying a world's history and destiny!

Simple as was His speech, even yet His words move and mould the world! Theremin insists that "eloquence is virtue"—or, as Emerson puts it, "there is no true eloquence unless there is a man behind the speech," or as Carlyle adds, "he's God's anointed King, whose simple word can melt a million wills into his!" All the conditions of the most powerful and persuasive utterance meet in Him! Behind the speech, lay the perfect man—the divine soul; and with an indifference to the lapse of time which reminds us of the indifference of the telegraph to the stretch of space—at this remote day, his simple word melts millions of wills into His. He says 'follow me!' and on through flood and flame, over land or sea, move the true hosts of God's elect, in obedience to His word.

We have referred to Christ's birth as attracting the gaze of the world. But if such interest gathers about His cradle, what shall be said of the interest that gathers about His cross? It was a cursed tree indeed, yet the tree of knowledge of good and of evil, which is associated with the first sin and the original curse, has on Calvary been transformed into the tree of life, whose very leaves are for the healing of the nations—and whose fruit is abundant and perpetual! That cross of shame is the most precious object that the eye of faith rests upon. It is the focal point of history—toward that, all lines converge from the creation, and from it all lines diverge and radiate until the end of the world.

Again we ask what then shall we do with Jesus who is called Christ? We calmly and reverently say, there is no middle ground. Here is a gigantic fraud, in comparison with which, all the dishonesties, perjuries, and villainies of men sink into insignificance—as mole-hills are forgotten under the shadow of colossal mountains; or else here is the one gigantic fact of history, the one grand personage of all the ages and eternities, the God-man—creator, ruler, judge of all mankind, the Anointed Messiah, and only Redeemer. No middle ground! and yet you dare not call Him an incarnation of fraud—reason and conscience alike forbid; and only when men have ripened or rotted into the most daring and desperate blasphemy, apostates both from God and a right mind and a pure heart, have they dared to hint that Jesus Christ was a deceiver! And when a man does venture such self-evident blasphemy, his own companions in scepticism shrink back from him as himself as great a fraud as he makes the Nazarene to be.

And yet there is no middle ground — you must curse him as a wretch or you must crown him as the King. If you claim to hold neutral ground and cast no vote, remember He has said, "he that is not with me is against me." If He be a gigantic deceiver, you cannot be guiltless, unless you do all you can to meet gigantic imposture with gigantic resistance; you are bound therefore to be a pronounced foe. If He is the King—your only Saviour, your final judge—your guilt is awful and your exposure terrible, if you simply withhold yourself from His service, or above all lend aid or comfort to His foes! You are, by obligations of the highest sort, bound to be a pronounced friend, and to do your best and utmost to lead others to see and confess His beauty.

And so, the voice of truth and duty calls on you, in tones of thunder, to choose this day, what you will do with Jesus! You cannot, dare not be indifferent to the issue. He is or He is not the way, the truth, the life. If He be, then better you had not been born, than to wander from this way, deny this truth, forfeit this life.

CHAPTER XI.

THE MYSTERY OF THE GOD-MAN.

"He took not on Him the nature of angels; but He took on Him the seed of Abraham."—HEBREWS II: 16.

The mystery of the God-Man! Such a mystery implies both glory and obscurity; and a careless, irreverent handling of such a theme only lessens the glory and deepens the obscurity. No human philosophy can clear away the cloud which has ever hung about Christ. Concede the truth of the Bible portrait, the accuracy of the scriptural representation, that Jesus Christ was "God manifest in the flesh;" that He, for the first and only time in history, exhibited in Himself the union of the human and the divine natures in one person; that He was a proper Son of God and proper Son of Man, and you have necessary mystery. We are so constituted that we can understand nothing which is not in accord with our experience. Everything that is new to us is comprehended only by the aid of that which is old; we find in it a combination or arrangement which is novel, yet the principal elements, which are combined and arranged, are more or less familiar. What we call "invention" or "discovery" does not proceed by huge strides or leaps, but step by step. Some new feature is added to that which is already familiar. An old machine is put to new uses or takes a new form; a common agent is linked to new and perhaps strange appliances, as when steam or hot air is employed as a motive-power; two or more long-known appliances are united, to accomplish what neither could alone; but, in a peculiar sense, "there is nothing new under the sun." Even such a startling marvel as Edison's phonograph is simply the application of certain facts and principles, well understood in the scientific world, viz: that sound, like light and heat and color, is a mode of motion; that the differences in sound are due to the varying rapidity of vibrations of air; that these vibrations may be made to impress and record themselves upon a sensitive surface, like tin-foil; and that, under proper conditions, the impressions so recorded may again reflect or reproduce vibrations similar to the first, as the stereotype casts made from type may be used to mould new type. "New inventions" are simply improvements upon the forms, methods, modes of appliance, or combinations and conditions of elements and principles already known. We rise to the height of each new discovery upon the step furnished by that which preceded; and so we are prepared to understand what is new and strange. If to-day some entirely new principle should be revealed, which should contradict all previous notions and revolutionize our whole theory of mechanics—effecting combinations before believed to be impossible, and by means and modes hitherto unknown—it could be to all of us only a mystery. Men skilled in mechanics and in science and philosophy would simply confess, "We do not comprehend this;" and it would only be when familiarity with the fact of its reality had destroyed its novelty, that we should be able to think of it without surprise and wonder.

Admitting that Jesus was indeed the God-man, the hope is vain of either escaping or explaining the mystery which invests Him; for he presents the phenomenon of history, original, unique, solitary; no being like Him, before or after. Here is a combination heretofore supposed to be contradictory and impossible! God is infinite; space cannot contain Him, nor time limit Him. Man is finite, fenced in by definite bounds. How can the unlimited and limited combine and unite? All our previous notions of things are contradicted in the God-man. God is omnipotent; yet here is God, submitting to the laws and limits of a human body, which can occupy but one place at any one time, and must, by the law of locomotion, take time for a transfer from place to place. God is omniscient; yet here is a being claiming equality with Jehovah, yet affirming that there are some things which as a man, and even as the Messiah, He knows not. God is omnipotent; yet the God-man says He "can do nothing of himself," and that it is God dwelling in Him that "doeth the works."

How can we understand or explain this sublime and stupendous mystery? We cannot. Allow the fact to be true; concede and confess the reality; the gospel itself attempts no solution of the enigma, because we can interpret that which is new only with the aid of that which is old; and here no aid can be gotten from that which is old. Christ is wholly new—a man with human infirmties, without human sin or sinfulness; poor, yet having at His disposal universal riches; weak and weary, yet having the exhaustless energy of God; unable to resist the violence and insults of His foes, yet able to summon legions of angels at a word or wish; suffering, yet incapable of anything but perfect bliss; dying, yet Himself having neither beginning of days nor end of years. Can you or I understand a being who in Himself presents such a combination?

What is there in our experience or observation to help us in the interpretation of a mystery so profound as that of the God-man? Nothing—absolutely nothing? Should we start with the faintest hope of removing or penetrating the cloud surrounding Him, we should only be proclaiming our own folly, and not only so, but degrading this sublime personage to the low level of our common humanity; for the expectation of fully understanding and comprehending Him implies another expectation—that we shall find in Him nothing essentially above the plane of purely human character and career. To admit that He may be more than man is to admit that we may find in Him what we cannot explain. But mark, that the very mystery which invests Christ, and of which we cannot divest Him, is an argument for His reality as the God-man; for, as we could not understand such a being, neither could we, of ourselves, imagine or invent a God-man.

This important thought needs to be expanded and emphasized. We have seen that we can understand only what accords with our experience. So does our experience assist us in all creations even of imagination and fancy. What we call original conceptions are only original forms or combinations of older ideas. A painter may use a brush to represent a scene, the like of which never existed; but he is putting together things which he has seen. Even a crazy artist, who might paint trees with feathers for foliage, and mountains with ice-fields at their base and tropical gardens at their summits, or men with eyes in their feet, and hands growing out of their heads, would only be putting together, in grotesque shapes and strange union, things which he had seen. And so man never conceives anything absolutely new; without his experience to aid him, he could invent nothing new, or if he did, it could be only absurdity and contradiction.

Among the fabled creatures of mythology were the centaur, faun, mermaid. The centaur was a monster, half man and half horse, said to have inhabited a part of Thessaly. But such creation involves an absurdity; for the arms of the man correspond to the forelegs of the horse, and a compound like this involves a double set of bones and muscles and organs, such as pertain to the upper part of the trunk. The faun had the legs, feet and ears of the goat, with the rest of the body human. But here again is absurdity; for a goat is a grass-eating animal, and man is not; and there are constitutional differences that defy combination. The mermaid was half woman, uniting to the human head and body the tail of the fish. But the fish is anatomically a different creature, with totally different habits; the fish breathes in the water, where man drowns. And so all these inventions of fable are absurdities. When man tries to form a new creation, even of fancy, by combining things which do not exist together, he blunders into grotesque absurdities.

Now, whence came the idea of the God-man? There was nothing in man's experience to suggest it, and yet, with all its mystery, there is no absurdity. The person and character and career of Jesus are exactly what might be expected if God actually became man; and yet there was no experience to help even in the forming of such a new and harmonious conception. Men had often imagined the "gods as coming down, in the likeness of men;" the pagan religions are full of such incarnations; but they are not at all like the mystery of the God-man, for they represent God as taking on Him a human form only; they are manifestations of God. Here is the only true incarnation of God—God in a human body, with a human soul; and yet there are no absurdities. It is not two beings somehow united, nor two persons with two minds, two wills, two conflicting existences, wedded in impossible bonds; but one being, harmonious, symmetrical, consistent—not God in man, or God and man, but the God-man.

We ask again, whence came such an idea and ideal? Deny the reality, and your denial compels you to account for the conception! The attempt to escape one mystery involves you in one even greater. Here is a labyrinth; you are lost in a maze of perplexing paths; you may flee from the perplexity of the God-man to the denial of His reality, but neither path leads you out of the labyrinth. And there is but one path that does. Here is the clue: admit that Christ was an absolutely new being, the union of the divine and the human in one person, and that the evangelists simply give an honest portrait of this marvelous personage, without attempting to explain the profound mystery which hangs about Him, and you have a plain, straight road out of the labyrinth! Here, as the innocent Irish maid said, is "the entrance to get out at." And the only possible or rational solution of the enigma is faith in the witness of the Word to Christ, and in the witness of Christ to himself; for if the reality did not exist, the conception is more marvelous, mysterious, miraculous, than the person of the God-man himself!

While confessing the mystery of the God-man, and having no design or desire to attempt the absurd task of clearing up the mystery, into the depths of which "angels desire to look," there are many things about the person of Christ and the whole subject which may be seen in much clearer light than they commonly are.

There is a wide difference between mystery and mist; and, while standing in awe before an impenetrable mystery, we may penetrate the mist. In other words, false or partial conceptions, or half-truths, make the mystery needlessly greater, and involve us in useless doubt, and tempt us to dangerous denial and disbelief of truth and fact.

Let us then seek to pierce, or rise above, the mist of vague, partial, mistaken notions, with which we often surround the God-man, and get clearer views at least of the mystery itself. And, if we still find, that He soars, like a mountain, far above our sight or thought, into altitudes so sublime, that even on wings of imagination we cannot follow him; perhaps we may still get near enough to see the mountain, without needless mist or haze, or even the dimness of distance between.

There is an old fable of 'the Knights and the Shield.' Some proud old baron had exalted a shield by the roadside, as the pious monks of Germany set the crucifix in shrines along the routes of travel, that the devout passer-by may tarry to pray before the sacred symbol of his faith. One day two brave knights of yore met at a castle, near by where the famous ancestral shield stood. And one said to the other, "Have you seen the baron's shield?" "I have." "And how do you read the inscription?" And he gave the words, as he had been able to read the half-worn motto. But the other insisted that he was wholly wrong: he had himself read it carefully and it was entirely different. And then they grew angry and would have fought, but a stranger passing by, and hearing their contention, counselled them to go together and examine the shield once more. And lo, they found that the shield had two sides and each side its own motto. They had approached it from different directions, and each read the side that faced him. Each was right, because he told the truth; each was wrong, because he told but the half-truth which was all he knew.

In all that follows, let us bear in mind that here is a being to whom there are two sides or aspects. Whether we see one side or the other will depend on the direction from which we approach, and the point of view we occupy. And if we do not wish to be misled by half-truths, we must look at both sides; and, in all our study of the God-man, keep in mind both the divine and the human elements so mysteriously mingled. Only so shall we prevent adding to mystery our own misapprehension.

The Bible is confessedly the most remarkable book of the ages: and Jesus Christ is confessedly the most remarkable person of the ages. And this book and this person are so remarkably connected, that the mysterious link which unites them is not less wonderful than the book and the man themselves.

On close examination and comparison of the Holy Scriptures and the Holy Child, we have found that he bears to them so close a relation that they actually contain a minute history of Jesus centuries before his birth. Here is a biographical sketch, a kind of portrait of a man, prepared, without doubt, hundreds of years previous to his advent. The very year and place of his birth, his life and death, his crucifixion and resurrection, with many of the most marked features of his character and career, even to the beast on which he made his triumphal entry into Jerusalem, and the treacherous bargain by which a disciple betrayed him, the exact sum which was the traitor's hire, the insults that were heaped upon him at his trial, the mockeries that derided his dying agonies, and the peculiar facts of his burial: these and many other minute matters, are recorded long before one of the events either happened, or could have been foreseen by the most sagacious conjecture.

Take a man of intelligence, a stranger to the Christian religion; place before him the Jewish Scriptures, calling special attention to the portrait which they furnish of one whom they call "God's

Servant" or "Anointed." Then ask him to note that the Old Testament writer lived more than three centuries before the Christian era; and that we have historic proof that these Jewish Scriptures, in their complete form, were in the hands of the Jews for three hundred years before that era began. Then place before him a copy of the Christian Scriptures, and ask him to read the gospels, and note that they were never in existence till at least four hundred years after the last Old Testament writer laid down his pen. And, without suggesting any divine or supernatural element, either in the writings, or in the person of Christ, leave him to compare the two. With what amazement would he find all the main facts, recorded in these gospel narratives, long before anticipated in these writings? The fact of this correspondence is so familiar to us, that its force is greatly lessened. But imagine an instance in our own day. It seems but yesterday that Mr. Lincoln died by the hand of an assassin: and his history, from his lowly beginnings as the child of poverty, up to his heroic end, as the martyr of liberty, is familiar even to our children. But what if, in the works of Francis Bacon, there were found an exact and minute sketch of this coming President, three hundred years before; not one particular of which failed to correspond with the facts! and how would our amazement increase, should we find a score or more of writers in different centuries and countries, long before Bacon, supplying other and equally important material for this prophetic biography! With what august wonder would we compare the facts, so well known to us, with the forecast of them in these writings of the by-gone centuries! and with what candor would we inquire for an explanation!

II. Of this mysterious correspondence between the Jewish Scriptures and the person of Christ, those Scriptures themselves give a solution. They declare that this wonderful person is the Son of God and the Messiah, anointed of God for the salvation of men; and that, so important was his advent, that the holy men of old were inspired of God to tell, in advance, the story of his life and death!

Let us again suppose this unprejudiced stranger, who has with amazement traced the history of Christ in the prophecy of the Old Testament, to meet, in those very Scriptures, this explanation. Would he not be disposed to regard this as a rational solution of the problem? It is an accepted canon of criticism, that if an hypothesis supplies a satisfactory basis for the harmonizing of facts or truths, it is not worth while to look further: we may accept it as the truth. Thus Kepler, after repeated trials, struck the real law that rules in the solar system; and, as that law which was at first only a supposition, has so far reconciled all known facts, and solved all apparent difficulties, we do not hesitate to call his guess, a discovery! Certainly, there is about the exact fulfilment of the prophetic portrait in the person of Christ, a problem demanding a solution; and, if the solution, afforded by the Scriptures themselves, proves a satisfactory one, why should we hesitate to accept it?

Does the Person of Christ then correspond to this Bible basis of solution, viz: that he was son of God as well as son of man, and anointed for a special office, namely, to fulfil the law in a perfect life, and then atone for sin by a vicarious death?

It is proper to examine this great question in a scientific spirit. We have already considered Jesus Christ simply as an historic personage, a man of singular symmetry of character, who towered above the level of ordinary men as the peaks of the Himmalayas tower toward the stars; and now we look at him as the Messiah of Scripture, and as claiming to unite in himself both the divine and human natures.

How shall we explain the mystery of this complex person and character, on a Bible basis?

The solution is given us by Paul, Romans i, 3, 4. "Concerning His Son Jesus Christ who was made of the seed of David according to the flesh, and declared to be the son of God with power, according to the spirit of holiness by the resurrection from the dead." Accept this solution, and the problem is solved. Not that this Incarnation of God in human nature, this mediation between the finite and the infinite, the union of God and man in one person, is without mystery; not that we can distinguish the divine from the human—define their boundaries and determine their limits; say just where one ends and the other begins; not that we claim to be able to answer the question how two natures can combine in one person, and not destroy individuality and identity. I am a mystery to myself. I see a body; a mind, or thinking power; a heart, or loving power, united in myself; each capable of individual activity, and yet all making one man. I do not dispute the fact while I cannot penetrate the mystery. Even so, "I bow before the mystery of His complex person, and do not ask to have it resolved!" For if I know that there combine in me two natures, the physical and the spiritual, and the complexity is still a perplexity, is it reasonable to reject the fact of Christ's complex person because I have no philosophy for the fact?

III. The Scriptures boldly present both sides of the God-man. The son of man appears everywhere—there is a human mother, and a human birth—a human nature and growth in wisdom and stature—he has needs like men; feels weakness and weariness, hunger and thirst, craves human companionship and friendship, sympathy and love —is a man of sorrows, acquainted with grief, touches humanity with the tenderness of conscious brotherhood; indeed as we, following his career, behold him growing, weeping, suffering, dying, there is so much of the man in all this—such experience is so intensely human, that it veils and obscures the divine element. And yet the Bible does not hide these human infirmities, but makes them a necessity to his completeness as the God-man.

Philip. ii: 7: "He took upon him the form of a servant," and the fashion of a man. "He emptied himself" of his divine glory, and laid his divine attributes, omnipotence, omniscience, omnipresence, under temporary voluntary limitations; it was a part of his humiliation, that he condescended to human infirmities, to accept as his lot human want and woe, so far as consistent for a sinless man; that he might be a brother to man, the representative man himself, and a "merciful and faithful high priest," able to sympathize with, and succor, the tempted, because himself having been tempted or tried. This is the Book's explanation of the person; and of the perplexing problem of his double nature as the God-man.

Yet he boldly affirmed concerning himself the essential quality with God which left him free to lay aside, even as he had assumed, the form of a servant. "I have power," said he, "to lay down my life"—that, any martyr might say, choosing to die for the truth's sake: but he added, what no created being could say, "I have power to take it again."

As we turn over page after page of the sacred book, we get a glimpse now of his humanity and now of his divinity. It is like a dissolving view, now his human nature is clearly seen, and again his divine appears with equal clearness; and one melts into the other, so that we cannot say where one ceases, and the other begins, to appear. We are constrained to say, He is divine. Yet this strange personage weeps at the grave of his friend Lazarus, proving himself "of like passions" as ourselves, of active, tender, personal sympathy, uniting a perfect humanity with his divinity; not God in a human body, but God with a human soul. The divine speaks sublimely, "I am the resurrection and the life;" "Thy brother shall rise again;" "Lazarus, come forth!" The human speaks, in groans within himself; in tears of conscious bereavement; in the question, "Where have ye laid him?"

And how consistent with the grandeur of the God-man is the sublime majestic reserve which he manifested. A human being, conscious that he was about, in the exercise of divine power, to restore the dead to life and to the weeping sisters of Bethany, would have approached the sepulchre with the excitement of conscious prerogative, with evident emotion and expectation—but the Lord Jesus moves as calmly and composedly as though calling the dead to life were as simple and as common as to speak the most ordinary words of a master to a servant. There is no pompous flourish—no show of needless energy. Angels might have been summoned to remove the stone—but man could do that, and so he simply said "take ye away the stone;" and then used the life-giving word to accomplish what man could not. How like a man is the human element in all this: yet how unlike a man is that other element, which links the Christ to the invisible, omnipotent, eternal!

IV. That there is not only a mystery but a paradox, in this complex person, we are quite ready candidly to confess. But the contradiction is, after all, only apparent. Project your parallel lines far enough, and they converge.

Our main difficulty lies in forgetting that this personage is wholly unlike any other. Of God, we have some conception to guide us in interpreting His words and works. Of man, we have a more complete knowledge, to aid us in understanding man. But here, for the first and only time in history, appears one who asserts of himself, "I am the Son of God," "I am the son of man," in whom "dwelt all the fullness of the God-head bodily;" yet who "took on him the seed of Abraham."

In all your progress through the apparent contradictions of the Bible portrait of Jesus, this idea of His complex person needs to be borne in mind; for it is the key that unlocks all perplexities. You expect to see now the human element made prominent, and, again, to see the divine equally conspicuous; and it is a very notable fact that in the Gospel according to John, which most completely gives us Christ's witness concerning himself, He twelve times calls himself "Son of Man," and just as many times "Son of God," as though himself pointing us to both sides of the shield, and by repetition impressing the necessity of avoiding the falsehood which really lies in a half-truth.

No part of the problem of Christ's witness concerning himself has caused more perplexity to Bible-readers than His contradictory declaration as to His equality with God. At one moment we hear Him say, "I and my Father are one,"—and that the Jews understood Him to mean the unity not of mere sympathy, but of equality, is plain; for "they took up stones to stone Him" for the blasphemy of making himself equal with God. And yet He said, "My Father is greater than I;" and to unravel this tangled skein of perplexity, men have suggested that He was only a created being, or an inferior order of divine being—Divinity, but not Deity.

Is it well to resort to a solution that itself presents a new problem, demanding a new solution? If Christ were a creature, then His testimony to himself is false; if an inferior order of divine being, the unity of the Godhead is lost, and we have not only polytheism, but different grades of gods! But we are perplexed to know how a being can be divine and yet not have divine attributes; yet, if omniscient, omnipotent, omnipresent, can there be degrees in omniscience, etc.? Can one God know all and do all and be everywhere, and another know and do more than He, or be anywhere where He is not? If we are going to hold such absurdities as these, let us admit that the bulls of the Irishman afford us a good type for doctrinal and theological statements.

On matters which perplex the wisest, it is with becoming modesty that one ventures even a suggestion. Absolute equality may co-exist with relative inequality, and absolute inequality with relative equality; and these terms imply no real contradiction. We venture an illustration, with the caution that an illustration is not an analogy. An analogy is supposed to fit at every point; an illustration only at the precise point at which it is applied. What we seek to illustrate, is the statement that absolute equality and relative inequality are consistent, and conversely, but we are not illustrating the mode of the divine existence, etc.

A firm is composed of three men, who are absolutely equal in amount of capital invested, in capacity for business, in share of profits; if you please, in culture, social standing and personal worth. Yet they agree that in all the purchase of goods no one shall act on his own responsibility, or except by instructions; or it may be agreed that one man shall keep the books or hire all clerks, in which case either of the others may properly say, "I have no authority in this matter." Or, again, a college faculty, composed of men every way on absolute equality, may consent that one shall act as president, and may put in his hands the entire control. Here is absolute equality, with relative inequality. On the other hand, a father sets up three sons in business as partners. They are of different ages, grades of culture and capacity; yet they are to share alike in privileges and profits. Here is absolute inequality, with relative equality—and no inconsistency.

These illustrations do not even touch the mystery of the Trinity and the double nature of the God-man; yet if we but understand our Lord as speaking at one time of that which is divine in himself, and again of that which is human—now in terms absolute, and now in terms relative—all difficulties are at least relieved, if not dissolved and dispelled! In the capacity of a man, He was inferior to God; in his character and office as Messiah, he was under subjection to Him that "sent him;" as a Son, he owed filial obedience to the Father. Now, if such terms as these express His essence, His whole nature, His complete self, then to apply to Him divine titles, offer Him divine honors, or pay Him divine worship, is certainly idolatry. But if these terms express not His substance and essence, but His office and relation, then we are justified in looking back of these inferior titles to find His essential self. And the careful search into the Scriptures will show us a glory, like that of the sun, behind the veil of His humanity. He was on one occasion instantly transfigured so that His face shone as the sun, and His raiment was white as the light, and no human eyes could look on His glory.

V. But why should He, if true God, decline the homage of men, saying to the young man who addressed Him as "good Master," "Why callest thou me good? there is none good but one; that is God?" This seems the more perplexing since

He allowed disciples to hold Him by the feet and worship Him, as well as to address to Him the most unmistakable words of homage.

We must consider that Christ's true Godhead was not understood by the common multitude, who saw in Him simply a remarkable man. To receive such homage as belongs only to God, from one who regarded Him as only a man, would be to encourage virtual idolatry.

The good caliph, Haroun Alraschid, was wont at night to go in citizen's dress, disguised, through the streets of Bagdad, in order to learn accurately what wants among his subjects needed to be relieved, and what woes redressed. And the Emperor Joseph II., of Germany, went *incognito* on extensive tours through Hungary, Bohemia, France, Spain, Holland—his true self not being suspected. It is very plain that for these rulers, while in disguise, their true character unrecognized, to accept from a citizen-subject any homage or obedience, due only to the caliph or king, would be to encourage treason! The fact that the person in disguise was the sovereign, could not change the disloyalty of the act while the subject did not know him as such.

If on such occasions, officers of state had to the disguised king breathed state secrets, they would have been arraigned for treason; although the king had the right to receive the communication, the officer had no right to communicate to one whom he did not know to be the king. If Joseph II, while hearing such a traitor speak, had said, "Why do you breathe this in my ear? none should hear this but your sovereign," we should see no inconsistency.

It was part of Christ's humiliation that while in disguise, he should not accept unintelligent homage. To those who saw his true self—whose eyes pierced the veil of his humanity, he never said, "Why callest thou me good?" etc., but, with the calmness of the divine majesty, he permitted Peter to say, "Thou art the Christ, the Son of the living God;" and then declared that, upon that confession of his divine Messiahship, he would, as on a rock, build his church, against which the gates of Hell shall not prevail!

We repeat that we are not concerned with the mode of the divine existence or the union of two natures in one person. The question is, were there marks of the true man and the true God, apparent in Christ? if so, is not his own solution the rational one? And, without abandoning scientific calmness and candor, we have only to lay aside all bias of prejudice to see that here is the only perfect solvent, leaving behind it no residuum of difficulty.

VI. There is a subtle argument deftly used by such as Strauss and Renan, against the supernatural element in Christ Jesus, which may be easily seen to be sophistical and fallacious. It is said that, if Jesus were indeed the son of God, there would be about his whole character and life, as well as his words and works, a plain supernatural aspect; that the very naturalness of the whole story shews the work of man's hand. It is all just as a good and great man would be likely to be and do, but not on a scale befitting the God-man. If God really came down to dwell among men why did not the very light of his eye, his form and feature, his very tread, proclaim the divine Creator, and Lord? But all this life is intensely human.

This very fact and feature of Christ's life and its record, afford a grand argument, for the truth of the gospels. Had impostors been at work, fabricating a story of God manifest in the flesh, to impose on human credulity, we should have had no such simple, natural portrait. The infant Saviour would have been represented as, from birth, a perfect prodigy of unnatural and supernatural wisdom and power. Whenever the human mind has tried to construct a superhuman childhood, there have been extravagance and exaggeration; as in the myth of Hercules, who, while yet an infant in the cradle strangled two huge serpents with his tiny hands. And in those apocryphal gospels, which pretend to supply the defects of the true narratives, the years of our Saviour's infancy and boyhood are crowded with marvels and miracles. Dumb beasts and even dumb idols bow in adoration before the child, as he is borne down to Egypt to escape the sword of Herod, and trees bend to do him homage; and, while yet a boy, less than seven years old, he amuses his play-fellows by transforming balls of clay into flying birds, bids the running stream become dry, changes his companions into goats, works all manner of miracles through the magical power of the bed on which he slept, the towels which he used, and even the water in which he was washed! now using his divine energy to excite the curiosity, and now to arouse the fears, of his playmates.

When the inspired evangelists draw the portrait of the infant Saviour, we have a truly human child, born indeed of a virgin, but increasing in wisdom and stature, like other children, according to the laws of human growth; at twelve years of age, in the temple, hearing the Jewish doctors and asking them questions, and surprising them by his understanding and answers. "There is nothing premature, forced or unbecoming his age, and yet a degree of wisdom and an intensity of interest in religion, which rises far above a purely human youth."* What was it that restrained the evangelists from adding to the portrait of the God-man, features obviously fanciful and ideal.

We have only to suppose that God's own son did take upon him not only the form, but the nature, of man, and did live purposely as far as possible on the level of humanity, that he might shew man how to live; and nothing can be more beautifully natural, than the recorded life of Christ. We can see how there came to be that rare blending of the high and humble, the sublime and simple, the divine and human, which marks this portrait in the gospels only. Had men invented this history they would have presented us with the human aspect or with the divine, alone; or, if the union of the two were attempted, we should have "a mass of clumsy exaggerations" or absurd contradictions.

Concede that the evangelists had the reality before them, and everything appears natural and consistent. Does it, therefore, follow that without the reality before them they could be thus natural and consistent? Reason may approve many things which it cannot prove; that which, when

---

* Schaff, "Person of Christ."

presented before us, may commend itself as perfectly reasonable and consistent, we might have been unable to devise or discover. A problem that perplexes us for years may have a solution so simple that, when known, it seems no problem at all; but that is a child's way of judging. What no man could invent may, when God unfolds it, seem eminently simple and natural. It is therefore a fallacy to argue that, because these gospel narratives are so natural, therefore they are fabrications of man! For thousands of years mankind has been working at, but never working out, this problem—trying to invent a satisfactory incarnation, to get God manifest in the flesh. The Greek, Roman and Hindoo mythologies are full of these attempts; but men even among those very pagans say these must be myths; "they are unnatural, contradictory, inconsistent." At last there is a true incarnation, and now the wise owls of modern scepticism squint and wink at the God-man and say, "All this is so simple and natural that it must be a myth." Truly, the men of this generation are hard to suit; pipe for them a joyful strain and "they will not dance;" play a mournful melody and they will not "lament." If an incarnation is unnatural, it is mythical; if natural, it is mythical. God solves the problem over which the race has been studying for four thousand years, and the solution seems so simple that the wise men deny that there was any problem, after all.

Yet in sceptical essays it is a favorite argument against the Bible doctrine of vicarious sacrifice for sin, that there is nothing in it that needed the divine mind to frame it. It is simply an innocent man suffering for the guilty, and so illustrating the inviolability of law and the grandeur of voluntary self-sacrifice.

Suppose this were all the deep meaning there is in the death of Christ. How happens it that all the pagan attempts to devise a way by which the guilty soul might escape, and yet divine justice be satisfied, have been confessed failures! Men have planned to save the sinner, while the plan has not saved God from complicity and compromise with sin; or they have planned a salvation from penalty without a salvation from guilt. God tells us how all desirable ends may be compassed. Justice and mercy may be harmonized, as the cherubim on the ark, though looking in opposite directions, faced each other; and the sinner is saved from the punishment of his sin, and, better still, from sin itself.

It is both absurd and dishonest to say that, because the gospel scheme of salvation is so simple and satisfactory, it bears traces only of a human hand. As well say that because the sun's ray brings us at once light, heat and life—just what earth needs, and all in one sunbeam—the sun is a human invention; that the problem is so simple in solution that it bears no marks of a divine mind.

God is always simple, even amid the most complex mystery. It is man "who darkens counsel by words without knowledge;" who cumbers his words with affectation of learning and logic, and his works with pompous pretension. Only the grandest of men learn the divine art of artlessness—of perfect naturalness and simplicity.

VII. At this point, the external and internal evidences of Christianity touch so closely that it becomes not only contact, but almost coincidence. In a previous chapter the proof of miracles was considered; but there is a moral argument which may be drawn from the miracles of Christ. The witness which miracles furnish must largely hinge upon their character. If they are mere displays of power, gratifying the popular greed for novelty, appealing to curiosity, serving mainly to supply stimulus for those who, like the "Athenians, spend their time in nothing else but either to tell or to hear some new thing," the whole character of the miracle-worker is degraded by his pandering to this insatiate appetite for what is new and strange.

If the Son of God should to-day, for the first time, appear on earth in human form, with signs and wonders as the proof of the divinity that veils itself in His humanity, we should look for signs such as become so august a person. Mere displays of power, such as descend to a level with the trivial tricks of a juggler, however they might puzzle us to explain, would not impress us as worthy of the Lord of all. It was said of Hercules, god of physical force, that "whatever he did—whether he stood or walked or sat or fought—he conquered." That fine conception has in it an artistic finish as exquisite as the touch of a master sculptor, like Praxiteles; it suggests that a true god will always carry the air and mien of a god. With or without his crown and scepter, robed in glory or clothed in sackcloth, awake or asleep, speaking or silent, in work or war or rest, he will still be divine. And if Christ were the God-man, everything He did must have been consistent with such a character.

Now, look at His miracles. When men crowded about Him, asking for a sign, pretending that they desired Him to work wonders to convince them of His divine mission, He calmly but firmly refused to degrade divine power to the low level of human curiosity. He would not harness the fiery steeds of Omnipotence, which roll the very suns through space, to the petty chariots of a race-course, to make dull eyes stare with idiotic amazement.

What signs did He furnish, to satisfy the honest heart that would find the God in the man Christ Jesus? "The blind receive their sight, the lame walk, the lepers are cleansed, and the deaf hear; the dead are raised up." (Matt. xi: 6.) Not mere works of power, but works of love, attesting indeed divine authority, but revealing also divine sympathy; such works as a Father would be likely to use to reveal to His estranged and erring children His Fatherhood. When Jesus Christ undertook to show to men the sealed credentials of His mission as the Messiah, in what sublime characters they were written! They had about them the handwriting of God; they shone with a light and luster like that of suns and stars. But as we look closer, they seem to be written also in blood and tears. There is in these displays of divine power a divine tenderness and gentleness more impressive than the miraculous element itself; they are moral miracles, and the purest and most loving nature most feels their force. Christ might have spent the three years of His public ministry tearing up sycamine and cedar trees by the roots and hurling them into the sea, by a word; commanding mountains like Hermon to be removed from their place; causing the sun to veil his shining face, and then uncover it at his bidding; making the sea to raise itself up, and stand like a column. These would have been grand displays of the power and authority of God, but they would not have unfolded the divine love and sympathy. What did He do? He wrought such wondrous works as showed men, in all conceivable circumstances of human want and woe, a divine readiness to give help and hope.

Behold the divine Christ come down from the mount, where he had spoken that imperial sermon of our holy religion; and what was His first work, proving and approving His right to teach with authority, and not as the scribes, who only referred men to a higher authority? Among the multitudes that followed Him, there came a leper and worshiped Him, saying, "Lord, if thou wilt, thou canst make me clean."

"And Jesus put forth his hand and touched him, saying, 'I will! be thou clean!' and immediately his leprosy was cleansed!"

Here was divine power indeed, so grandly exercised that we are reminded of Him who, in the profound gloom of primeval darkness, said, "Let light be! and light was!" who "spake and it was done; who commanded and it stood fast." But, least of all, was this a word of power: it was a touch of Love! A leper was a loathsome wretch —a living corpse, an exile from human society, whose presence was uncleanness, and whose touch was contamination. Leprosy was regarded by a Jew as the awful incarnation of sin, its power and its penalty—a living, breathing, walking parable of death and judgment. A leper wore his leprous robes that even his dress might distinguish him: and, lest he might come into actual contact with humanity, he went everywhere crying, "unclean! unclean!"

Observe the pathos of that phrase, "touched him." Christ's word was enough, even at a distance! but that poor leper had been wont to have human beings shrink from him and bid him stand afar off. It may have been many years since he had felt the sympathetic touch of a hand, uncursed by this scourge of God! and therefore the man of sorrows "put forth his hand and touched him." He wished to show that leper that, back of the divine power that healed, was a divine Love. That touch is the key to Christ's miracles: they told of a throbbing heart, that combined the unspeakable strength and tenderness of a father's and mother's devotion.

On one of the battle fields of the late war, a young soldier was wounded so badly that no human skill could assure recovery. He grew rapidly worse, and in his delirium called piteously for his mother. The gentle surgeon, at the hospital, telegraphed her at once, and she arrived at midnight. He met her at the entrance of the ward, and restrained her impatient feet: "Madam, your son hangs between life and death; a moment of excitement, and there may be no hope. You must not see him now."

For three long hours she waited outside the ward, near enough to see her darling boy, though dimly, and catch with the quickness of a mother's ear, each groan of pain. At last she laid hold of the surgeon's arm: "Doctor, I shall die if I stay here Let me go in and sit beside him. I will not speak: only let me do what the nurse is doing, soothe his brow and smooth his pillow." The nurse was called, and the mother took her place by the cot, once more enjoined by the surgeon to do nothing by which she might be recognized. She sat in silence—the face of the dying soldier turned to the wall. He groaned feebly. She, to quiet him, laid her hand on his hot forehead. Instantly he turned himself about, and said, "Nurse, how like my mother's hand!" Even to that delirous lad, there was that, in a mother's touch, which no stranger could counterfeit. And so in that touch of Christ, upon that loathsome leper, there is revealed all the Fatherhood of God! That was like the Father's hand, it was the Father's hand!

We lay no undue stress upon the moral force of Christ's miracles! To overlook this, is to fail to see the most important and powerful feature of the divine manifestation in Christ; and to fail to feel the weight of that grand logic which speaks to the hearts of men! In proportion as the human nature approaches the divine, it responds sympathetically to human sorrow and suffering. When God came down to men, the most touching proof he gave of his presence was found in the tenderness of his ministry to human want and woe. And even his works of power were most remarkable for their exhibitions of a divine heart throbbing through a divine hand!

Did the Star in the East guide the magi to the manger where He lay? The whole Bible—the book of the ages, is but the Star to shine for him and guide to him; the light in the deep darkness to move across the heavens, and over his cradle to rest, then to fade into a paler glory, before the day-dawn. The whole Scripture testifies to Christ, leads to Christ, rests in Christ, and fades before Christ as before a superb splendor—a greater glory obscuring the less. But that star guided only the magi—and them only for a season—this Word is the star that waits on Him, and will never cease to burn or shine as the guide to seeking souls, till the last of those who look anxiously for a redeemer shall find the place of his cross and empty tomb!

The question which Pilate asked, each of us is compelled to answer: "What shall I do with Jesus?" No formal disclaiming of responsibility can wash our hands clean of responsibility. If Jesus is the Christ, the anointed of God, the Saviour of men, he that despises or rejects him crucifies him afresh. The Jews took the responsibility from which Pilate shrank, and said "His blood be on us and on our children." What a prophecy lay in that awful prayer. For eighteen hundred years his blood has been upon them and their children. The fire, the sword, the pelting hail of human hate, the scourge of hostile law and popular scorn, have pursued them everywhere from pole to pole and from the rising to the setting sun.

The question "What think ye of Christ?" even scepticism finds it equally hard to evade or to answer. Even could we explain miracles by some ingenious natural theory, the greatest miracle of all is the person of Christ. If he were a mere man, we know not how to account for his words or works; his relation to the Hebrew Scriptures and his relation to the Christian church. If he were the God-man, all is easily explained, but such an admission must be fatal to the whole fabric of scepticism. On the one hand the sceptic cannot explain Christ, on the other he cannot defend himself. For if Christ be more than man, to reject his words, and rebel against his authority must imply guilt and peril.

The God-man! The 'daysman betwixt us both, who can lay his hand upon us both,' because he is of us both! The way of God to man—the way of man to God; the true Jacob's ladder between heaven and earth. God above it, to come down—man beneath it to go up! The God-man, in himself our pledge that as God in Christ became a partaker of the human nature, so man in Christ becomes a partaker of the divine nature. Born of a woman, made like unto us, that we might be born of God and be made like unto Him! The God-man is not only a mystery and a miracle, but a prophecy and a promise. He tells us what man shall be, when by faith in Jesus, he is for evermore made like unto the Son of God.

They used to say of Mozart, that he brought angels down; of Beethoven, that he lifted mortals up. Jesus Christ does both, and here lies the central mystery of the God-man, a mystery which is blessedly revealed to him who by faith has personal experience of his power to save!

CHAPTER XII.

CHRIST THE TEACHER FROM GOD.

"Rabbi, we know that thou art a teacher, come from God.— JNO. III: 2.

John calls Jesus, the "Word of God." What is a word? It is the invisible thought taking form: Wordsworth says, "Language is the incarnation of thought." Spoken words are sounds, articulate and significant: sounds in which there is soul. Written words are visible signs of intelligence and intellect; thought has determined their exact form, order, relation.

God is represented as pure Spirit, and cannot be known by sense. He would communicate with man, and so puts his thought and love in a visible form in Christ, who is therefore beautifully called the living 'Word of God.' As God does everything perfectly, we are justified in looking for such an expression of His mind and heart in his incarnate Son as shall excel all other revelations of himself. In Christ, as the Word of God, we may properly expect to find the clear and unmistakable stamp of the divine mind. In his teaching there must be a divine authority, majesty, originality, spirituality, vitality, essential worth and practical power, such as no merely human teaching could display. Let us candidly apply the test.

Even the wisest and best of human teachers have dealt largely in such words as "if" and "perhaps;" have spoken with doubt and hesitation on great moral questions, reasoning that "it might be so," or, sometimes with deeper conviction, "it must be." But Christ, with an authority that in a mere man would be audacity, says, with unfaltering tongue, on the most perplexing questions, "It is so!" Never once does He hesitate in unfolding the mystery of the divine being, the present life, the future state. To Nicodemus he calmly but firmly declares the necessity of the new birth; of a character and a life built from the foundation on godly principles, and He does not even stop to answer the question, "How can these things be?" To the woman at the well, He speaks of the spirituality of God, and that all-pervading Presence which makes every spot a place where the soul of man may come near to Him. To the unbelieving Jews He affirms His equality and identity with God the Father, and His power to raise the dead and pronounce that judgment on human character and destiny, from which there is no appeal. He dares to challenge men to "search the Scriptures," and find them, from Moses to Malachi, witnessing to Him; affirms that, in whatever disguise of law, prophecy or psalm, rite, ceremony or historic event, the careful reader may still see His features clearly revealed. And yet He was but thirty years old, and the Scriptures were fifteen hundred! He not only said "Moses wrote of me," but "your father Abraham saw my day, and was glad;" and when the astounded Jews replied, "Thou art not yet fifty years old, and hast thou seen Abraham?" He, with the calmness of divine certainty, said, "Verily, verily I say unto you, before Abraham was, I am!" Mark the exact words—not "I was, but "I am;" for the Eternal One knows no tenses; past and future are present to Him who is both without beginning and without end. At the sepulchre of Lazarus He said,"I am the resurrection and the life;" and when He says, "Lazarus, come forth," it is as when, out of the sepulchre of eternal night, God bade light come forth! Even before Pilate and Herod there is the same commanding bearing, yet it is not the vanity of conceit; it is the sublimity of conscious omnipotence voluntarily held in suspense. "My kingdom is not of this world;" "Thou couldst have no power at all against me if it were not given thee from above;" "Thinkest thou that I cannot now pray to my Father, and he shall presently give me more than twelve legions of angels?" "Hereafter shall ye see the Son of Man sitting on the right hand of power, and coming in the clouds of heaven!" Nay, even amid the anguish and agony of dying, He turns to the penitent thief, and with still unfaltering tongue—himself no longer having even a garment to cover His person—promises him the inheritance of eternal bliss: "Verily, I say unto thee, to-day shalt thou be with me in paradise."

I. *Authority* appears to have been the first impression made, if not the last impression left, by Christ's teaching. Matthew completes his report of that "Sermon on the Mount," which inaugurates Christ's public ministry, by adding these significant words: "When Jesus had ended these sayings, the people were astonished at His doctrine [*i. e.*, teaching]; for He taught them as one having authority, and not as the scribes." The scribes were the transcribers of the law; the pen in their hands was the printing-press of those days for the multiplication of copies of the blessed Word. Their necessary familiarity with the letter of the law—"Scriptures," literally so called—gave them a certain right to teach, but not with authority. They referred their hearers to the law; their language was, "Thus saith the law." But Christ's habitual language was, "I say unto you." He taught as a teacher having authority, original, ultimate, underived; as one who had himself made and could modify the law. He expounded the Scriptures not as a commentator, but as the author. Hear his sermon on the mount! With what calm, firm hand he lifts from the law of God the huge mass of human tradition and interpretation which had covered and hidden it, as God would, by an earthquake, upheave some buried monument, or with one breath, as by a tornado, brush away from it the sands of centuries!

Lord Northwick brought from Italy a fine picture of St. Gregory, by Annibale Carraci. To secure its safe delivery, he hired a mere dauber to paint over it, in body color, an imitation of some inferior artist. On exposing the canvas, his friends saw nothing but a rude and repulsive daub; but he took a sponge, and, as washed the colors from the surface, the masterpiece was gradually revealed to enraptured eyes. Somewhat so, carnalism and literalism had during centuries glossed over the holy Word, till what scribes and Pharisees taught men to revere as God's law was largely the traditions and commandments of men. And, with the calmness of divine authority, Jesus boldly wipes away these glosses of false comment and perversion, and makes the law to be seen once more in its true spirit and intent. "Ye have heard that it hath been said by them of old time"—that is the human daub; "but I say unto you"—that is the divine original!

This authority lifts Christ above all other teachers. Even the great Greek philosophers disclaimed all original right to teach. When Leon, charmed with the silver tongue of Pythagoras, asked him wherein lay his highest excellence, the great teacher could only reply, "I am in nothing a master, but only φιλοσοφος"—a lover of wisdom; and hence came the word "philosopher." An old legend tells how there came to be seven sages in Greece. The priestess of Apollo had awarded a golden tripod to the wisest of the Greeks. It was sent to Bias, who said, "Thales is wiser;" and so it was sent to Thales, and passed through the hands of the seven, each claiming that the other was wiser than he, till, simply because no master could be found to claim it, it was sent back to Apollo's temple. God's golden tripod waited four thousand years for one to claim and hold it; none of the wisest ever dared to assume the right to teach with underived authority, until He came "who was found worthy to open the Book" of God and "loose the seven seals."

If human teachers wield influence, their teaching must commend itself and command attention; if it has not the authority of truth, they can add to it no authority. Even prophets could only declare, "Thus saith the Lord." But Christ spake as never man spake—"I am the truth."

Such authority could not exist without independence. The sneer of enemies expressed the fact: "Master, thou teachest the way of God in truth; neither carest thou for any man: for thou regardest not the person of men." No bait of applause could turn Him aside, nor pelting hail of human hate drive Him into a politic silence. Burke said to the electors of Bristol: "I conformed to the instructions of nature and truth. I maintained your interests against your convictions!" But even such fidelity was but a feeble reflection of that absolute candor that made the name of Jesus the synonym of loyalty to right and truth. To the reluctant and the willing ear alike, whether met by fervent love or by fierce hate, He, with unfaltering tongue, told the truth.

With what audacious positiveness He grasps the grandest themes, which even the foremost of philosophers have touched but hesitatingly and tremblingly. Plato thought the soul must be immortal, but he spoke not as one who knew. Cicero said, "There is, I know not how, in the minds of men a certain presage, as it were, of a future existence; and this takes deepest root and is most discoverable in the greatest geniuses and most exalted souls." This was as far as mere human teaching ever got. But not so speaks the Bible. Job, 1500 B. C., could say, "I know that my Redeemer liveth;" Paul could say, "We know that if our earth house of this tabernacle were dissolved, we have a building of God, an house not made with hands, eternal in the heavens." Life and immortality were brought to light by Him who, on the most delicate, difficult and perplexing questions, spake with authority, and who gathered up in one bold affirmation the substance of all Bible-teaching on the immortality of the soul: "He that believeth in me, though he were dead, yet shall he live; and he that liveth and believeth in me shall never die." Such boldness and calmness of utterance, on the most difficult and doubtful questions, could mark but one of two orders of mind—either a mind seized with an insane fanaticism, or a mind inspired by the certainties of conscious knowledge. Christ was certainly neither a fool nor a fanatic. There are about Him the proportions of a giant, and yet the perfection of symmetry, and the firm and fearless tread of conscious power!

Truly, "never man spake like this man!" An impostor he could not be; for whence came such a life? It is, on the loftiest scale, pure, noble, heroic!—the one peak that soars to the stars and defies the approach even of an impure atmosphere! A fanatic or enthusiast he could not be; for his wisdom, self-poise, intellectual and moral perfection, are inconsistent with a lack of balance! The firmness of his tread, the weight of his words, the justness of his decisions, the clearness of his judgment, the profoundness of his ethics, the faultless beauty of his life, leave no room for doubt that he could neither deceive nor be deceived.

II. *Sublimity.* Christ can be accounted for as a teacher on no merely human theory. The Jews had scores of intelligent teachers, such as the scribes, rabbi, doctors of the law, Pharisees, learned members of the Sanhedrim; but none of them taught like Christ. To prevent errors in copying the Scriptures, or intentional additions and corruptions in the sacred text, the Masorites counted and recorded the words and letters, nay, even the points and accents, and noted literally every jot and tittle. So minute was the accuracy insured, that the verses of each book and of each section were numbered and recorded.

The interpretations of scripture, and the rules and maxims of these teachers, had become similarly minute and trivial. They worshiped the letter and forgot the spirit; they taught a hollow, shallow, heartless, lifeless creed, cumbered with cerements of technical trifles and empty forms. Nothing is more surprising than the puerile absurdities over which the various schools of rabbi quarrelled. Think of writing learned treatises on this question: "If a man should be born with two heads, on which forehead must he wear the phylactery?" The school of Shammai taught that an egg laid on a festival day could be eaten, while the school of Hillel remonstrated against such a breach of propriety; and the Pharisees had long and learned controversies over such unimportant questions as, whether a stream, made by pouring water from a clean into an unclean vessel, is itself technically clean or unclean, and whether touching the holy Scriptures could make the hands unclean, in the Levitical sense. We need not marvel, therefore, at the petty exclusiveness which forbade a Jew to shew an uncircumcised traveler his lost way, or point him to a spring where he might quench his thirst; nor at the hair-splitting nicety which discriminated between swearing by the temple, and by the gold of the temple—the altar, and the gift upon it.

The foremost religious teachers of that day

descended to what was puerile and trivial. Believing the prophetic spirit withdrawn, they tried to make up for its absence by a system of petty rules, tithing herbs and washing cups, and forgetting justice and love and purity of heart. In place of a morality, based on love of the right, they devised the most "frivolous casuistry ever known," loaded men's memories and consciences with countless rules so trifling that they rival the paltry regulations of the Koran; and then left the grandest duties to relax their hold on the human heart, by putting these trifles in their place.

In what school did Christ learn to teach on a scale of such grandeur, majesty, dignity and authority? Who revealed to this obscure Nazarene who died at thirty-three, who had no scholastic training, and at whose ignorance of letters his enemies laughed—who taught him to insist upon great vital truths and grand first principles, that lifted him infinitely above the superficial trifles, over which the whole Jewish church wrangled?

Christ, as a teacher, is a marvel. The whole Hebrew church was corrupted by the leaven of Pharisaic Ritualism and Sadducean Rationalism: the blind were leading the blind, and all alike falling into the ditch. Out of a village, so mean and low that to hail from it was a reproach, there comes this young man, trained neither in Greek schools as at Tarsus, nor in Hebrew schools as at the feet of Gamaliel; He comes forth from a carpenter's shop, where, like all other well-trained Hebrew youth, he had learned his father's trade, and his first public utterance is the most original and revolutionary address on practical morals which the world ever heard. It overturns the whole existing system of both Pagan and Hebrew ethics and religion. It plants a huge lever underneath formalism, ritualism, rationalism, hypocrisy, immorality, insincerity; the aristocracy of blood, birth, wealth; all mere outside propriety and false distinctions of society, and announces that all are to be demolished—and if you ask where he is to rest his lever, where to find his $\pi o \upsilon\ \sigma \tau \omega$—you see that he already has his fulcrum in the instincts of the human conscience, for wherever, then or now, might may lie, right is on his side, and must triumph.

We are spell-bound before the magnitude and magnificence of his moral teaching, as we stand in awe before Mt. Blanc, pillaring the skies upon its white brow; yet we are as much amazed by the simplicity as by the sublimity of his teaching, and know not which seems most divine.

Such wisdom the world waited four thousand years to hear; yet there is not a sign of pedantry. It requires no great learning to take his meaning, no trained mind or memory to classify and retain his precepts, no subtle logic to follow his argument. There is no studied method, no tedious analysis, no wearisome division and sub-division. There is no aim at rhetoric: the thought, not the word, absorbs him; yet the word just fits the thought. His illustrations suggest no great knowledge of history, philosophy, science—they are simply windows to let in light, and, that they may let in the more light, are not cumbered with elaborate framework, nor dimmed, as with stained glass. You do not see the window, but only find yourself in the light. His language is the language of the common folk, and there is not a taint of self-seeking in it all. Yet all the love and the wisdom of the ages have never been the golden setting to such a jewel as that simple discourse enshrines. As Augustine says: "His life is lightning; his words are thunder!"

To say that Christ's teaching was wise is to speak tamely: in Him are 'hid all the treasures of wisdom and knowledge.'* How wide the range and scope of his teaching! What revelations of divine love and goodness! how broad his basis of morals! how profound and penetrating his insight into human conduct and character. Samuel Johnson wrote as the epitaph of Oliver Goldsmith: "He left nothing that he did not touch, and touched nothing that he did not adorn!" But whatever Jesus touched he left gilded with glory, transfigured! And yet he adapted himself to the lowest and lowliest of his hearers; and, with the highest skill, gave his teaching the form best fitted to the place, time, object, occasion and audience. Yet though he condescended, he never descended; never forgot his lofty character, his heavenly themes—instead of taking a lower level, He lifted his hearers to a higher one.

Who could as lawfully hold God's golden tripod, as he who spanned the breadth, pierced the height, sounded the depth of infinite truth? While human teachers taught forms, he, the spirit; they, ceremonies, he, affections; they, conduct, he, character; they, details, he, duties; they, petty practices, he, grand principles! While they would frame a code so complete that the smallest matter should have its rule, as though man were a ma-

*Col. ii: 3.

chine and must have an iron track to run on—He would fire the soul with that enthusiasm for God and goodness which makes duty delight, and service to God and man, the prompting of Love.

And so the spirituality of Christ's teaching constitutes its sublimity. It lays stress first of all on what is within! not outward act, but inward motive. Down into not only the deep things of God but the deep things of man, his teaching went, into the secret soul where character is born and cradled; beyond the impure act, to the look, and the lust—beneath the blow to the hate—beneath the word profane to the irreverent heart, beyond the act of revenge to the vindictive feeling.

With the calm confidence of the eagle, whose wings tire not with the longest, loftiest flight, and whose eye dares, undazzled, the noon-day sun, Christ spake of the grandest themes, dissected the very character of God, denied errors that had the authority of antiquity, and revealed truths hitherto wholly unknown.

Christ so magnified and glorified the Scriptures, so interpreted aud unfolded their deep meaning, that his evolution of new principles compelled a revolution both in ideas and practices. Their righteousness must exceed even that of the acknowledged leaders of the people, if they would enter into his kingdom, for no correctness of outward life could compensate for the lack of inward love to God and man. Back of the white front of the Pharisee's life he shewed the dead men's bones of a lifeless creed, and the uncleanness of a heart full of corruption. Beneath the graceful mound of grass and flowers, the outward beauty

CHRIST THE TEACHER FROM GOD. 277

of alms and prayers, he shewed the grave where love lies buried, and righteousness is in decay.

As the Lord of temple courts overthrew the tables of money changers, so he overturned the common notions of morals and piety, and brought men back to right laws of holy living: while as a faithful executor of the law he declares that to the last, least jot and tittle it shall be fulfilled, like a law-maker he assumes the right to modify and repeal the law itself, wherever, as with the ceremonial code, its object was temporary.

"Where the word of a King is, there," said Solomon, "is power!"* Here was the power of a King's Word: and it called the spirit of God back into the dead forms of the law, and then called the reanimated law from its sepulchre as Lazarus from the dead! And we can only remember his own majestic words, as he was about to ascend to heaven: "All power ($\varepsilon\xi ov\sigma\iota\alpha$) is given unto me in heaven and on earth!"†

Judged even by a literary standard, where can such teaching elsewhere be found? such parable and poem, such doctrine and discourse, such philosophy and theology, such simplicity and sublimity? Here is the teaching both of the idea and the ideal, precept and practice. He tells men how to live, and then he, by living, shews them how to live. No such ideal was ever imagined, no such heroism ever before became historic; in words and works alike no blemish is seen, no beauty is lacking.

The sublimity of Christ's teachings has overawed even those who dispute his divinity. As well look on the soaring summit of Chimborazo,

─────────
*Eccles. viii: 4.   †Matt. xxviii: 18.

emotion of sublimity, as to study his
:hout an impression of the moral sub-
;t, in any aspect of his character, re-
calls Goldsmith's famous lines:

"As some tall cliff, that lifts its awful form,
Swells from the vale and midway leaves the storm,
Though round its breast the rolling clouds are spread,
Eternal sunshine settles on its head."

III. *Flexibility* is another marked peculiarity in the teaching of Christ—its ready adaptation to every new phase of character or need of society. Systems of rules for conduct have often been rigid. Christ saw that conduct, even when conformed to the right, is not always exactly the same. Human relations and conditions change, and so must human laws and ˙human life; but principles never change; and hence, if Christ planted the great germ of holy principles in men, amid all changes of conditions and relations these unchangeable principles would beget right practices.

In this, Christ's teaching was wholly unique and peculiar. The age in which he lived was marked and marred by fearful forms of social sins and crimes; the whole body politic scarred by old wounds or festering leprosy. Polygamy, infanticide, legalized prostitution, capricious divorce, bloody and brutal games, death and punishment by torture, unjust and cruel wars, caste, and slavery; these are some of the awful vices, that existed more or less distinctly as social usages during Christ's public life and ministry. Yet only one of them all does he name and directly rebuke and denounce.

Did the great Teacher approve these immoralities and criminalities? The whole drift of his teaching, with the momentum of a moving glacier was grinding and ploughing the very structure of society into new form; but Christ, instead of attacking even gigantic wrongs, sought to put beneath the whole fabric of society, one all conquering, controlling love of law—and law of love. He knew that right principle to be the true lever of Archimedes, that could and would move the world; and this inflexible devotion to right and righteousness is yet strangely flexible, accommodating itself to every new condition of society.

God uses a strange substance to confine and restrain the ocean's flood. It is sand, yet sand is peculiarly characterized by mobility: the mighty wave that dashes against and pulverizes the rock-cliff, moves the sand before it and as it recedes washes it back to its place; and so the sea-beach, always changing, never changes: that soft, mobile sand that yields to your footstep, and that a ripple moves, banks in and bounds the sea.* And so the holy principles with which Christ surrounds and restrains the individual and society, accommodate themselves to all fluctuations of social condition, yet eternally abide and imperatively say: "thus far, and no farther!"

IV. *Vitality.* Christ's teaching had life-giving power; it was vital and vitalizing. It humbled the heart, wrought deep desires after God and godliness, and transformed and transfigured human lives. And all other teaching is only preparatory to his—even the law is our schoolmaster to lead us to Christ: its precepts are but the signboard at the crossway of duty and inclination,

---
*Jerem. v: 22.

truth and error, with the index finger pointing to him in whom all the glories of prophecy and history center and meet.

We are told of men "whose words shook the world;" and we think of that humble monk who, in the opening of the sixteenth century, came from convent gates at Erfurth, and on the door of All-Saints' Church nailed up his theses—at the blow and echo of whose hammer the whole fabric of the Papacy shook and trembled. But what power in the words of Christ! Here is eloquence indeed. When men heard the silver-tongued Cicero they said, "How beautiful his speech!" When men heard Demosthenes they said, "Let us go and fight Philip!" When that great orator was asked what are the three requisites of power in the orator, he answered, not 'action,' but '$\varkappa \iota \nu \eta \sigma \iota \varsigma$'—that which moves people to act; that which gives motion and stirs emotion. Here we have the divine $\varkappa \iota \nu \eta \sigma \iota \varsigma$—the power to move and mould. Men heard Christ, and they not only said "never man spake like this man," but they said, like Joshua, "As for me and my house, we will serve the Lord," or, like Thomas, the doubter, "My Lord and my God!"

Well might Mary Magdalene cry, with the mingled rapture of joy and tears, "Rabboni!" *Rab* was a Hebrew title, meaning *a great one*, and applied in Jewish schools to acknowledged teachers and masters. *Rabbi* is more emphatic, "my master," and marks a higher dignity—the comparative degree. But "Rabboni" was the superlative, "My great Master,"—most honorable of all, and applied to but seven persons, all of whom were pre-eminent in the rabbinical schools. In that word, "Rabboni," Mary surrendered her very self to the authority and supremacy of her risen Lord. And blessed are they who, prostrate at his feet, join her in adoring, loving self-surrender.

To accept Christ as a divine teacher, as the incarnate Word of God, solves the mystery of his person and his teaching. Indeed, the person cannot be separated from the teaching. Character and utterance must correspond. Therein is right; "eloquence is a virtue;" the ultimate power to move and mould men by the wonderful gift of speech, is the power of a soul filled with knowledge, and fired with love of the truth. Those mighty floods of conviction which overwhelm others with similar conviction; those mighty floods of emotion that sweep all obstacles before them and compel persuasion, imply the correspondingly great channel of a great mind and heart. The highest, grandest influence of eloquent speech is the influence of character, felt through speech; the power to convince and persuade is the power of being convinced and persuaded. A tongue that talks divinely must be taught by a heart that throbs divinely. Great things are spoken by great men; great thoughts are born of great minds; great love grows in great hearts; great teaching is the fruit of great natures. And, as Ruskin says, "they cannot be mimicked but by obedience; the breath of them is inspiration, because it is not only vocal but vital, and you can learn to speak as these men spoke only by becoming what these men were."

Christ, the living Word of God, the Divine Teacher, invites all to accept and obey his teaching. He is a tender, fraternal, cherishing teacher, guarding the pupil of his charge as the pupil of his eye. The disciple is won not only by his wisdom, but, infinitely more, by his love.

When Plato came to Socrates to be taught wisdom, Socrates had a dream. He thought a pure dove, white as the snow, flew to his bosom and took refuge there, amid the soft, warm folds of his tunic. He thought he watched it from day to day, and saw its feathers grow and its wings develop, until it suddenly expanded its pinions and soared away till lost from sight among the clouds of heaven. And that dove, Socrates said, was Plato, taking refuge in his bosom only to give his own wings time to grow, and then, in the sublime flights of his pure and lofty philosophy, soar out of sight.

Jesus takes his docile pupil, like a timid, trembling dove, to his own bosom, and there, hidden under nurturing and cherishing care, he learns to fly. Blessed, indeed, are they who learn of Him, who in Him find, like a wandering dove, a rest, and who, under His loving discipline, learn to soar and sing, like the lark winging its way toward the sky!

"Jesus, lover of my soul,
 Let me to Thy bosom fly."

CHAPTER XIII.

THE ORIGINALITY OF CHRIST'S TEACHING.

"Never man spake like this man."—JNO. VII: 46.

ORIGINALITY conspicuously marked Christ's teaching: it was novel, even in its repetition or resurrection of old truths; as he himself said, they were "new and old," at the same time: old, because all truth is eternal; new, because the form, dress, illustrations and applications of truth were exactly suited to existing needs. A piece of spar, held in your hand, seems dull and opaque; but if you turn it till the light strikes it, at a certain angle, it shews lustre, beautiful and brilliant colors. This divine teacher took even the sterner and more forbidding attributes of God and turned them around, that the light might so strike them as to shew the glory and beauty.

Who has not been repelled by the prevailing notions of divine wrath, common to all human religions! Anger in God was only an ugly human passion, in a gigantic growth, and called by divine names. It meant revenge, backed by the power that none can resist, and armed with all the tortures that infinite wisdom can devise—it meant malice and malignity and hate—dwelling in the bosom of the deity. Men could understand divine wrath only by their experience of human wrath, which is vindictive and cruel.

Christ turned the dark attribute around, till it exhibited its glory, its lovely aspect. God's anger was seen to be, not a passion, but a principle —the eternal hatred of wrong, which corresponds with the eternal love of right, and which is only another aspect of love. The magnetic needle swings on its delicate axis: it attracts at one end; it repels at the other: attracts at one end because it repels at the other. In the light of Christ's teaching, we see in the one attribute, Benevolence, a divine magnet, with two poles—love of holiness, hate of evil—both equally essential to its perfection; and so we learn to love God because He hates sin. His wrath is not an impetuous and changeable passion but an eternal and unchangeable principle, not malevolent but benevolent, not so much destructive as constructive, not retaliative but retributive, not vindictive but vindicative. It is one of the two equal pillars, on which rests the very arch of the divine government—a necessity to the very law and rule of God. Here is wrath, perfectly consistent with love; that hates not the soul, but the sin, and hates the sin for the soul's sake. "*Amat errantes, odit errores.*" God's wrath is but the certainty of ruin to the evil doer, who prostrates himself across God's track. Shall He move aside from the straight path of truth and right to spare the wilfully wicked? this would make God become a transgressor for the sake of saving the transgressor.

Jesus taught us that wrath in God is the unchangeable perfection of holiness; and that holiness is love to the holy and wrath to the guilty. The same fire that warms and cheers, that refines and purifies, also burns and blasts, tortures and consumes; it all depends on our relation to the fire, whether it be our friend or our foe. We ourselves, by our sin, create the repulsion, with which we often find fault in God.

"In Retsch's illustrations of Goethe's Faust, there is one plate, where angels are seen dropping roses down upon the demons who are contending for the soul of Faust. But every rose falls like molten metal, burning and blistering wherever it touches. God rains roses down, but our sinful hearts, meeting divine love with hate, and grace with stubborn, wilful disobedience, turn love into wrath; and what dropped from His hand, a flower beautiful and fragrant, becomes, when it touches the ungrateful and unloving soul, a live coal.

All purely human notions of God are necessarily imperfect, and bear the stamp of their origin. What is beyond our experience we can conceive only in accordance with our experience, *i. e.*, our notions must be qualified and limited by what we have seen and known. If we think of eternity, it is only time indefinitely prolonged. If we try to imagine pure spirit, we give it involuntarily a bodily shape, form and features. We build our heaven out of earthly pleasures and elements. God himself reminds us of our infirmity, in framing conceptions of Him: "Thou thoughtest that I was altogether such an one as thyself." Our highest idea of God, independent of the help of the Bible, would be simply man on a grand scale.

If Christ was a teacher come from God, there will be in his portrait of God, features not at all human. If he be, himself, God, and speak as one who knows what Godhood is, though he may have to use imperfect human terms, he will impart superhuman ideas of God. And is it not so? When we think of eternity we do not drop the idea of succession, which belongs to time—we talk of a present, a past, a future. But Christ teaches that God's eternal existence has no past nor future. "Before Abraham was, I am." No man would talk in that way; man would say, 'before Abraham was, I was;' but while man is, was and shall be, God can only say, "*I am;*" for all the past and future are present to Him.

Christ has introduced both new words and new ideas among men. "Humanity is a word you look for in vain in Plato and Aristotle: the idea of mankind as one family, as the children of one God, is an idea of Christian growth; and the science of mankind and of the languages of mankind without Christianity would never have sprung into existence."

In the Greek, there is a word which means humility: ($ταπεινοφροσυνην$) but this humility meant, with rare exceptions, meanness of spirit, the cringing, fawning spirit of the conscious slave. Christian humility is a virtue, a noble condescension, which, in its very lowliness is lofty.[*]

What new conceptions Christ gave us of the dignity and worth of the human soul! Man has speculated upon the relation of mind to matter, and could arrive at no certainty. The body might be like a harp, and the thoughts and feelings, sensations and perceptions, like the harmony of the harp. But how came the harmony? is the harp like the æolian, that you set in your window, for the chance breeze to fan into music, or is there,

---
[*]Trench on Words, 45, 46.

aside from the instrument and the vibration of its chords, a master hand that sweeps the strings! Christ shewed men the human spirit, the true self, made in God's image; as Joseph Cook says, beside the harp and the harmony, the harper, presiding at the harp and making the harmony. And he taught us that the harmony may be no longer heard and the harp itself be shattered, and yet the harper survive, exchanging the earthly harp for the heavenly, and with fingers trained to divine skill, evoking such melodies and harmonies as earth never hears or knows!

Christ Jesus taught us a new philosophy of sorrow and suffering.

The old pagan idea, which largely permeated and penetrated the Hebrew people, was that all suffering is the penalty of sin, and a judgment of God. Hence when any calamity came upon a man, a family, a nation, something must be done to appease the anger of a revengeful deity. Offerings were brought to the temple to buy God's favor, victims poured out blood in rivers to make reconciliation for sin; the first born of the body was sacrificed to please and placate the awful chastiser and avenger.

Of course there is much suffering that is penal or punitive or retributive; the judgment of God upon evil doing, and the sign of His providential and moral government in the world. Terrible as these judgments are, they awaken profound gratitude: for by them wickedness is both rebuked and checked; and "the inhabitants of the world learn righteousness." What a fearful abode would this world be, if God had withdrawn from its active control; and left it to the unaided struggle between right and wrong, and to the might of a simply human arm! Thankful, indeed, ought we to be for God in history, although his presence on the throne be, at times, revealed in flames of fire such as consumed Sodom, or floods of water such as overwhelmed the old world, or signal wars such as destroyed Jerusalem, or such plagues and pestilences as the black death that swept millions from the earth.

There is much suffering that is not judicial retribution but organic penalty; it comes by a natural law of cause and consequence: as for example, the bodily pains that follow neglect or violation of laws of health, or the pangs of remorse that follow crime.

But while this divine Teacher did not deny both these offices of suffering, he taught men a higher use of sorrow, viz., to discipline and develop the soul. "Every branch in me that beareth not fruit, he taketh away: and every branch that beareth fruit he purgeth it that it may bring forth more fruit."* The husbandman comes with his knife to cut off dead branches and burn them—here is retributive judgment: he comes also to prune even the living and fruitful branches, that they may bear more fruit: surely that is not retributive suffering, it is rather corrective, educative, to purify, beautify, glorify.

Our views of the power and office of sorrow are very partial and imperfect. Jesus teaches that suffering is not always a penalty, either judicial or organic: it is designed to purge away our faults and follies, perfect our character and enlarge our capacity for service. This original and glo-

*John, xv. 2.

rious conception of the discipline of sorrow, is in various forms elaborated and illustrated in the New Testament. God has an "inheritance in the Saints," and He sets a high value upon it: and in order to complete and perfect that inheritance He subjects his saints to sorrow and suffering, as a proprietor plows up his land and pulls down his homestead that barrenness may give place to fertility, verdure and flowers, and the old house be reconstructed in a new and more beautiful form: he is simply improving his inheritance!

Captain Lott used to say that a head-wind, which seems to hinder, helps the progress of the ocean steamer; it "makes the furnaces draw." What a solace would God's sorrowing saints find in their very trials, could they but see in them the means of speeding their spiritual progress!

Some virtues and graces depend on sorrow for their very life and growth. Patience is a flower that blooms only at night, and fully only at midnight; it implies something to be patient about—something borne. The heavenly mind is acquired only by that process that refines away the worldly mind. We must be weaned from the temporal and perishable; the wine must be poured from vessel to vessel: otherwise it will settle on the lees, and take their taste. The assurance of hope comes only after hope's anchor, tested by the gale, has held us fast and firm to the rocks of promise. And how shall we get capacity to comfort others until we have ourselves been comforted of God?

What trials the filthy rags undergo before they emerge in the pure, white paper! Torn to pieces, ground to pulp, bleached with chlorine and lime and alum, washed again and again till the levigated stuff is white as flakes of snow, shaken to and fro till fibre crosses fibre and gives firmness to the fabric, ironed by hot cylinders till made smooth and even; how like the divine discipline by which our filth is cleansed; how like the tribulation out of which the host come up whose robes are washed white in the blood of the Lamb!

How much the beauty of the pottery depends on furnace-fires! Even to the dull, dead colors, the heat gives character and quality; the very paint must be fused at white heat, and melt into the substance of the vase or vessel. Even then the pottery must not cool too quickly, and the bloodstone must burnish and polish the decorated surface till it is brilliant and radiant!

Christ taught Paul to "glory in tribulation," because "it works patience, and patience experience." And what is experience but the mark of the divine assayer of the precious metal, who, when he sees that all alloy is released and his own face is reflected in the purified gold, stamps it "Approved?" Yet how many of God's suffering saints cry, not like Paul, "All things work together for good," but like Jacob, "All things are against me," or, like Rachael, weep for their loved ones and "refuse to be comforted because they are not." Under Christ's tuition, sorrowing saints learn to rejoice in affliction, like the blind girl who thanked God for blinding the outer eye, that He might put telescopes to the eye of the soul, and bring celestial glories near. The "diamond of the first water" is recognized by retaining its brilliancy under water where other precious stones lose their lustre. And our Lord teaches that a part of the office of affliction is to show how the radiance of the true disciple is undimmed beneath the deep waters of sorrow. Passing through the valley of tears, he makes it a valley of springs and streams.

The greatest of poets only echoed the teaching of Christ when he wrote:

"Sweet are the uses of adversity,
Which, like the toad, ugly and venomous,
Wears yet a precious jewel in his head."

In the shipwreck of worldly joy, the disciple casts out the four anchors of faith and hope and love and patience, and, swinging from them, waits and wishes for the day!

Is sorrow, then, the furnace-fire,
    The fuller's soap, the vale of tears?
It still fulfils my deep desire—
    God's image in my soul appears!

Christ both taught and lived a new law of self-sacrifice. And, to this day, the unselfish use of a love that accepts even death for the sake of the lost is, to all unrenewed souls, a mystery. Satan said of Job that he did not serve God for naught, and declared that a man will give all that he hath for his life. But Job's life proved that to be a lie; he was moved by a love of holiness that no man can understand if it does not move him also! The men and women who, from Christian lands, go to China to convert pagans—who toil and suffer, dare poverty and defy death, without any motive of self-interest—are to the most intelligent Chinese simply a marvel. "The Mandarins may comprehend Confucius, but not Christ."

There is a story of a poor sot, rejected by the maiden whom he loved, because he was a slave to drink. She one day saw him lying asleep in the gutter, and, averting her tearful eyes from the repulsive sight, dropped her white handkerchief over his bloated face, to hide his shame. He woke, drew the handkerchief away from his face, and saw her name wrought in its fabric. He rose from the heavy sleep, resolved yet to be worthy of a love that stooped so low in pity for his sin. And many a lost sinner has been first won to God by the thought of a divine love, so unlike the noblest human affection that it is bestowed most lavishly upon the least worthy. Christ taught this new law of love: "A new commandment I give unto you, that ye love one another as I have loved you." Love was not new, but such love was. It had been said by them of old time, "Thou shalt love thy neighbor and hate thine enemy." The love of men is prone to be selfish and exclusive. Thales, best and wisest of the Greeks, thanked God that he was "born a man, and not a brute"—"a Greek, and not a barbarian." Outside of Greece all were brutes and barbarians, to whom he owed no debt of love. Demosthenes' noble motto was, "Not father or mother, but dear native land." But this rose no higher than patriotism. Even the Jews, trained under a divine faith, had "no dealings with the Samaritans"—not so much as to show a lost traveler his way, or give a drink to the thirsty. Christ first taught mankind a true philanthropy—the love of man, as man, wherever found. Until Christ came, this grand truth of the universal brotherhood of man was even more obscured and perverted than the universal Fatherhood of God. Schiller, and even Wordsworth, have suggested a contrast between the Pagan and the Christian faith, and hinted that, however divinity might be on the side of the religion of Jesus, the humanity rather appeared on the side of the old gods of Greece. We confess surprise at such a disparaging and unjust comparison. Christ and Christianity brought not only a new theology, but a new philanthropy. And "after that the kindness and philanthropy of God our Saviour toward man appeared,* etc., for the first time, the world was taught to see in every human being a brother, and, as such, to love him. Christ adopted the old maxim, "Thou shalt love thy neighbor," but gave that word, neighbor, a new and grand meaning. "Who is my neighbor?" Let the parable of the Good Samaritan answer. Not he who lives next door, my fellow-citizen and fellow-countryman, but whosoever is made of one blood with me, who shares my humanity, and, most of all, who, by poverty, misery, want or woe, is most in need of my gentle, generous offices. If, by chance, I pass that way, and even my enemy lies naked and wounded across my path, I am to go to him and bind up his wounds, put at his service my precious healing-oil and strengthening wine, and walk that he may ride, caring for him, and providing for his wants. Did Greece or Rome, even in their golden ages, under Pericles and Augustus, ever teach such doctrine, or exemplify such practice? See the old worn-out slave, and even the aged, helpless parent, turned out to die of starvation and neglect! See the captives taken in war glutting the savage thirst of the lion and leopard in the arena! Go through these two grandest empires of the ancient world,

---

* Titus iii : 4.

and look in vain for an asylum or hospital for the deformed, the diseased or the dying! And yet we are told that the pagan religions outshine the religion of Jesus in their teaching or practice of humanity and philanthropy! Christ has made all men neighbors, by the delicate and etherial bond of an unselfish sympathy; his disinterested benevolence is like a telegraph-wire whose starting-point and battery were at Calvary, in the throbbing heart of Him who died with the unselfish prayer for his enemies, "Father, forgive them, for they know not what they do." That bond, reaching from the cross and round the world, establishes between all members of the human family a sympathetic communication, and makes all men neighbors. The heart of Christendom feels the pulse of the heart of Pagandom, and beats in responsive sympathy. Famine pinches the human brotherhood in India, China and Persia, and ten thousand miles away are felt the sympathetic gnawings of hunger; and out through the arteries of commerce the Christian heart pulses its life-blood. Ships hoist their sails, and trains blow their whistles, to bear food to perishing brethren! Knowing their spiritual famine, even while they do not fully realize it, we send to them the bread of life. Our missionaries are met with coldness and even persecution, die of fever, hunger, exposure, violence; and yet to the unthankful and the evil they continue to go, moved by a love like the perfect love, until in fifty years more than six hundred saintly men and women fall asleep in Jesus, and find a grave in India alone! Can such love as that be found, such humanity, such philanthropy, among the ancient pagans? Did Greece or Rome ever send a misrionary to the outside barbarians? And yet London alone encircles the globe with her missionary bands! They cross the Sahara, and pierce the Dark Continent; they dare the Arctic snows and bergs; they face the tigers in the jungles of India, and the cannibals of the southern seas. From the equator to the pole, and from sunrise to sunset, the missionaries London alone has sent out have borne and planted the cross, as a support for this telegraphic circuit of love which binds all men in one brotherhood. And while London is doing all this abroad, she builds within her own borders more than one hundred hospitals, asylums and houses of shelter for the victims of poverty, deformity, disease and misfortune!

O Schiller, O Wordsworth! poets you may be, but you are scarcely philosophers if you cannot see that Christ taught men a new commandment, and set them a new example, of love; a true philanthropy, unselfish, catholic, impartial; not limited by family circle, nor wider circle of state or church. Here is a benevolence of which the most ample almsgiving is but one expressson; a benevolence which means not an act or a feeling, but a spirit and law of life; that sends out angels of mercy on divinest errands to the ends of the earth; not to gather gold or gems to feed the greed of gain; not to learn facts for history or science, or frame theories for philosophy; not to find delicacies and dainties for the palate; but to lift mankind to a higher level for this world and the next; to break down the middle wall of partition between man and man, till, by the simple force of love, no barrier be left, though it had been high as mountains or broad as seas; till there should be neither "Jew nor Greek, barbarian, Scythian, bond or free, male or female, but all one in Christ Jesus."

This love teaches us to find our "neighbor" not only in him who is most remote, but even in our enemy. Even the publicans and pagans love their friends, but we are taught to love those who hate us; to love what is unattractive and even repulsive, for the sake of making lovable, because love ennobles and elevates, blesses and saves!

CHAPTER XIV.

THE POWER OF CHRIST'S TEACHING.

"Where the word of a King is, there is Power."—ECCL. VIII: 4.

DE QUINCEY has drawn a beautiful line of distinction between the "literature of knowledge and the literature of power." "What," he asks, "do you learn from Paradise Lost? Nothing at all. What do you learn from a cookery book? Something new, something you did not know before, in every paragraph! But would you therefore put the wretched cookery book on a higher level of estimation than the divine poem? What you owe to Milton is not any knowledge of which a million separate items are still but a million of advancing steps on the same earthly level; what you owe is power, that is, exercise and expansion to your own latent capacity of sympathy with the infinite, where every pulse and each separate influx is a step upward—a step ascending as upon Jacob's ladder, from earth to mysterious altitudes over the earth. All the steps of knowledge from the first to the last carry you farther on the same plane, but could never raise you one foot above your ancient level of earth; whereas the very first step in power is a flight, is an ascending into another element where earth is forgotten.!"

Now in the teachings of Jesus, we have both the literature of knowledge and of power, and both of the highest order. There is such a thing as lustre without weight, even as there may be weight without lustre. Here we have both: the most glorious moral radiance with the weightiest moral dignity, worth, sublimity!

Christ's teaching bears marks of Divine Inspiration. Here are "thoughts that breathe and words that burn." These are living words, there is about them a vital breath and a celestial brightness; compared with them all literature is dead.

How fragmentary are the works that survive the lapse of centuries! we have but a few relics, saved from the ruins of ancient letters. But Christ's words, recorded by a few unlettered men, according to his own prophecy do "not pass away;" they are thus far immortal. Kingdoms perish, thrones crumble, nations drop out of history, but firmer than the eternal hills, Christ's words live, and they live simply because they cannot die; there is in them the undying spirit of God.

The Word of Christ proves itself to be the Word of God by its living energy, and its penetrating power. "It is living and powerful, sharper than any two-edged sword, piercing even to the dividing asunder of soul and spirit and of the joints and marrow, and is a discerner of the thoughts and intents of the heart." This is the language in which the Bible itself expresses the power of God's Word; and if Christ were the living word, his teaching must correspond. Mark the beauty of the figure. Here is a Damascus blade, skillfully shaped and sharpened, bright as a mirror, keen on both edges and burning at the point. Behold the Titanic warrior wield it, with a strength and skill so terrible that it pierces through the very body of the foe, burying itself to the hilt, dividing the joints and cleaving to the marrow, and laying bare the very vitals. In such hands the sword becomes a living thing—the coat of mail can neither stay nor dull its edge; from the crest of the helmet to the skirt of the kilt, it is ripped asunder, and by the same blow the body of the victim is cleft in twain.

Had the word of Christ any such power? Let the history of nearly two milleniums tell us. For eighteen centuries it has proved itself a living sword, cutting through all obstacles, piercing to the inmost soul, with convicting and converting power; cleaving through the hardest mail of bigotry, prejudice, superstition, self-righteousness; and revealing the secret thoughts. And all this the word of Christ is doing to-day.

I. That peculiar power in Christ's words which we call "*Penetration*," is well expressed by the symbol of the sword, keen-edged, sharp-pointed. His teaching somehow pierces to the depths of consciousness and conscience, and reads and reveals the thoughts and the intents of the heart; so that there is no created being that is not searched by it. Christ's words shew that he knew by divine insight, "what was in man."

Have you never seen yourself revealed to yourself in the Word of God? the secret springs of your conduct exposed? What a revelation of human nature, of familiarity with the human heart! The sermon on the Mount dissects the very soul of man: it is both an exponent and an expositor of the secret life.

The enigmas of human character and conduct

find there a master solution. Note a few examples.

How moral philosophers have puzzled over the almsgiving of a selfish soul. Christ explains it by the love of applause. You marvel why the Pharisee parades his prayers, for you feel that secrecy and devoutness go together. Christ tells you it is prompted by the lust of notoriety; the prayers are to man not to God. You are perplexed because some, who are blind to their own faults see, with uncommon clearness, the faults of others. Christ tells you that the beam in the eye of one man makes him see a mote in his brother's. Hence the pharisee condemns ostentation, the bigot denounces intolerance, the hypocrite rebukes insincerity, and the backslider, inconsistency. Your simple soul is surprised because the faultfinder pecks at you in your very effort to please. Christ shews you that a heart, ill at ease with itself, vents its unrest in snapping and growling at others.

You ask, how can the same man be lax in some things and severely rigid in others? Christ answers, that it is the effort of self-righteousness to make up for laxity one way, by severity another; as when one feasts six days and fasts the seventh, or compounds with his conscience for sensual sins by bodily penance; or cheats his neighbor all the week but would not black his boots on Sunday; or gives money away to atone for getting it unfairly!

You are again perplexed to find enthusiasm and apathy in the same character—this divine teacher accounts for the strange mixture by instability of character, a life of impulse instead of principle.

Marvellous indeed was Christ's insight into human nature. With divine delicacy, yet with divine certainty, he lays his hand upon the heart of the moralist who, boastful of his prim propriety, triumphantly asks "what lack I yet?" and touches instantly the sensitive spot. "Go sell that thou hast and give to the poor." In that fair life there was a secret weakness—the greed of gain, and it corrupted all the rest. He, without hesitation, touched at once the hidden idol, and the fair life withered into deformity.

The penetration of Christ's words struck his most gifted foes dumb. Pharisees and Herodians forgot their hostility and conspired to catch him in his talk: "Is it lawful to give tribute unto Cæsar or not?" "Render unto Cæsar the things that are Cæsar's, and unto God the things that are God's." Then the Sadducees sought to entangle him in a question on the resurrection: but again his wisdom put them to silence. Then the Pharisees returned to the assault and cunningly tried to entrap him into giving some one command of God undue prominence. And when again he read their hearts and so majestically eluded their snare, from that day they "dared ask him no more questions!"

Fouquè has a fable of a magic mirror, so wonderful that he who looked in it might read his own character, history and destiny. Goth and Moor, Frank and Hun came from far to see their past and future unveiled.

Here is the true magic mirror—this keenest sword is also a polished blade: it not only cuts deep, but it reflects character. Nothing is more plain, in Christ's words, than an insight and a foresight, far beyond man. Here, as in the brook, is the inverted image, which shews how deep is our degradation—but it tells of our possible elevation and salvation—even as the stars are no deeper down in the reflection than they are high in the heaven.

Go look in this mirror, see your own thoughts revealed, your concealed chains of ambition, avarice, appetite. Self-deception is without excuse; he who tries himself by Christ's standard of duty may learn himself—what he is and what he may be.

Blessed indeed to the true man is a true insight into himself. He can devoutly pray with Burns,

> "O wad some power the giftie gie us,
> To see oursels as others see us!"

But what is it not worth to see ourselves as God sees us!

> Ah, blessed mirror of the Word,
> Thine image is not dim nor blurred.
> Looking in thee, myself I see
> As God's Omniscient Eye sees me!

II. The *adaptation* of Christ's words to every want of every soul is, even more than their penetration, the secret of their power and the proof of their inspiration; indeed they pierce, not to wound, but to cure; not to hurt, but to heal. They are for all alike, the child, the man, the ignorant, the cultured, in all ages and climes, at all times of life. To the infant in the cradle, and to the aged, at the doors of the tomb, you whisper the same precious words: they guide the doubting, solace the troubled, assure the timid, and encourage the penitent. The very blade that pierces so deep, bears on its point the balm of Gilead, and it is to carry the balm that it thrusts so deeply. It is half the cure to know the disease. And the divine teacher helps us to the knowledge of ourselves that we may feel our need and find our cure. He does not apply the soothing ointment until he has first cut out the fatal cancer; and he shews his skill just as much in the use of the blade as in the use of the balm.

The convicted sinner and the afflicted saint alike testify to the adaptation of Christ's words. One keen-edged utterance strikes home to the heart, penetrates to the conscience, and makes it smart as though under the hot iron. Remorse so keen and cutting that it drives him to the verge of despair, fills the sinner with agony. His guilt seems beyond pardon. The sword has gone deep, the soul and spirit almost seem divided asunder. But had the truth been less penetrating, it would not have suited the sinner's case; any milder thrust would not have pierced the joints of his harness of hard habit and indifference. And when the deep wound heals under the balm of gracious promise, and the anguish of penitence gives way to the peace of faith, the sinner sees the adaptation of Christ's words.

So too the sorrowing saint finds in them the very solace he needs. The sharp dart of affliction seems to part the very soul in twain, but the sorrow goes no deeper than the solace. It is because Christ's words penetrate so deep that they make the words of man seem so hollow and shallow. Here only is the celestial branch which sweetens the bitter water of Marah. Christ's teaching presents a perfect system of truth.

III. He set up no claim as a philosopher: yet where will any *philosophy* be found worthy to compare with his teachings?

Among all the systems which gave rules for the conduct of life, two stand in the front rank, viz: Epicureanism and Stoicism.

Epicurus sought to frame a scheme of morals with happiness as its end: and his conception of happiness was not a low one: it must be virtuous and enduring. Yet it was a mere passionless or impassive state after which he taught men to strive. The happiness of the gods, he said, is repose, they neither take nor give trouble, and have no care about our affairs. And so the chief end of the wise man is to get to this state of apathy.

Stoicism taught that the wise man must be self-contained, have all the elements of happiness within, and be indifferent to pleasure and pain, sickness or health, wealth or want; and as all actions are from within, he may commit deception, suicide, or even murder, at a proper time and in a virtuous character. The virtuous stoic was like cold marble, proudly superior to pain and pleasure, smothering his own sorrows and repressing pity for the sorrows of others.

Set beside these systems the pure teaching of Christ, which puts man's happiness in holiness, union with God by faith, hope, love: puts in the place of self-indulgence for pleasure's sake, self-denial for the sake of humanity. It makes men neither passionless nor impassive, but teaches us to rule all impulses by reason and right, and to open hand and heart to every sufferer. Man's chief end is to love and serve God, and bless his fellow-man. The presiding law of all life is love.

When philosophy has reference to God, it is theology. Can any system of human theology compare with the teaching of the Son of God? In most cases human systems are marred by grotesque absurdities and fanciful follies.

Mohammedanism boasts 150,000,000 of adherents. It says sublimely, "There is one God;" but if you take away what it has borrowed from Judaism and from Jesus, what have you left? An absurd fatalism, which denies all moral freedom; one-sided views of God, all power, no love; a sensual paradise whose black-eyed houris and voluptuous pleasures make heaven only one vast harem!

There is Hindooism, hoary with age, having 500,000,000 followers, offering the choice between all God and no God, pantheism or atheism; teaching transmigration of souls, and full of moral abominations. It is an insult to Christianity to talk of comparing the teaching of Jesus with Buddhism or Brahminism.

Pass all others by and stop a moment with that which leads all the rest by right of worth, viz: the system of Socrates and Plato. Here we find a Supreme God, Creator, Ruler, arranging and upholding the universe, fountain of all truth, beauty and goodness. First principles of morality are his laws, not to be broken with impunity; goodness and truth are the end of true living.

Socrates urged men, at risk of life, to be virtuous; lived himself in voluntary poverty, and died a martyr to his integrity. Yet even Socrates taught only doubtfully the immortality of souls, and with his last words ordered a cock to be sacrificed to Esculapius; yes, even he sanctioned "some kinds of the most horrible licentiousness; he was only a philosophical reformer."

Beyond Socrates and Plato we need not go; for men of purer doctrine and life the pagan world has not produced. Yet Plato owned that what he and the Greeks knew of the Gods they learned from the Israelites; so that Socratism is only a scion grafted on Judaism. Rousseau confessed that "if Socrates died like a philosopher, Jesus Christ died like a God!" And just this we may say of their life and teaching: If Socrates lived and taught like a philosopher, Jesus lived and taught like a God!

From all human systems we turn to the teaching of Jesus, and even the pure but partial revelations of the Old Testament appear, as John saw in Apocalyptic vision, a waning moon beneath that New Testament gospel which, crowned with twelve stars, is clothed magnificently with the sun—that orb of glory before which stars fade and even the moon grows dim. From all the long search of centuries we come to end, at the cross of Christ, our pilgrim path. We have found him who is the way, the truth and the life. We are willing to sit at his feet and learn of God—the one God, a Spirit, infinite, unchangeable, eternal, almighty, holy, good; his dwelling, immensity, his life-time, eternity. Here we learn of man, sinful, responsible, immortal; of the hereafter, with its sure reward and retribution. Here only do we learn of a way of salvation both from the penalty and power of sin. By faith in the God-man, we become one with God and fit for heaven. Here we are taught true humility, a charity that reaches its arms around even one's enemies, a self-sacrifice which is simply sublime; and to all this theory is added an example which, if possible, is grander than the theory. All this pure and perfect teaching is illustrated by one single and singular life; all these ideas of snow-white purity, magnanimous forgiveness and holy love, are made manifest in the flesh; the thought of the Divine Artist flashes forth in the colors of a living panorama, and we are challenged to make trial of the power of this teaching, whether it does not hide the life of man in God, and reveal the life of God in man.

The teaching of Christ marks an era, an epoch in human history, which is like the flash of light upon the eternal night. Truths but faintly foreshadowed, if at all, in the best of human systems, are here taught clearly and fully. Christ is the Sun; all that move about him become luminous. But withdraw him, and even the light is darkness.

IV. *Power.* The actual practical power of Christ's teaching vindicates his claim to divine honors.

1. It has satisfactorily solved the problems of the soul. All through human history there has run a dark thread of religious doubt. There are certain absorbing questions over which the world has been working, like a school-boy over the puzzling mysteries of mathematics; and these problems every great system of philosophy or theology has tried to explain. These are no minor questions either; they touch life at vital points. What is God? What is man?—whence came he?—whither goes he? How did sin come to be, and how is it to be put away? How was the universe made? What is death, and what is after death?

What answers have been given by even the best and purest schools of human thought? How unsatisfying—how absurd! Think of the shocking and monstrous errors into which mankind have been betrayed in seeking peace with one's self and with God! Idolatry, with human sacrifice and consecrated sensuality; pantheism, atheism, materialism—every form of error in doctrine and evil in practice have been linked with the name of religion.

Now turn to the Christ of God; has he thrown the light of heaven on these dark questions? Think of that cross which is the central and focal point of history, toward which all lines converge from creation; from which all diverge to redemption completed in heaven. Look at Calvary, and in the speechless anguish of the Lamb of God behold every problem forever solved. Do you ask, "What is God?" Here you learn He is love—too just to redeem the sinner without a ransom; too pure to admit him to heaven without holiness; too good to leave him to certain ruin. Do you ask, "What is man?" Look again at Calvary. Man must have been sinful, else why should the sinless One suffer in his stead? Man must have been immortal, for there would be no such sacrifice simply to save him from temporal woe. Man must be free and responsible; otherwise, both guilt and faith would be impossible. Do you ask, "How came sin?" Read the answer in the shadow of that cross; for had not sin come through man, God would not have needed to become man in order to expiate it. The race, which in the first Adam died, in the second Adam may be made alive. Do you inquire,

How is man to be reconciled to God? That cross answers: The God-man is both a sacrifice and example; if we appropriate by faith the merits of his death, and by obedience the merits of his life, both pardon and purity become ours.

The divine Teacher brings the wisdom of God to solve the problems of the soul. Questions over which the brightest and best of men have vainly studied, one solemn hour of dying agony has fully and forever answered. Amid the darkness which might be felt, there is this one spot where light is to be found. The cry that rent in twain the temple's vail opened to view the holy of holies, with its glory everlasting. The smile of peace which shone on his face when he said "It is finished," and gave up the ghost, cleft the darkness of a world's despair with the ray of reconciliation, and to this day no soul needs walk in the gloom. To follow this gleam is to come into the light of life.

2. A still more severe and decisive test of the power of Christ's teaching remains to be applied. How does it actually affect human conduct and character? Is it a reforming, transforming power in the soul and in society? Complete as a philosophy, it meets man's cravings; complete as a revelation, it solves man's problems; does it, complete as a vital force, regenerate human life? Does it prove itself the truth of God by being the power of God? Paul declared that for this reason he was "not ashamed of the gospel of Christ;" not ashamed to preach it as a chained prisoner at Rome, the center and focus of pagan culture, because it was "the power of God unto salvation." His chains clanked as he preached it, but the chains fell from souls as he preached.

Note his word, "power"—δύναμις; the gospel is the divine dynamic force in human history. Practical tests are far more severe than theoretical. Whatever may be said of Epicurus and his philosophy, his followers became, after a time, selfish and sensual; appetite became their idol. And the word "epicure" is a sad witness of the low level of gluttony, intemperance and debauchery to which Epicureanism sank.

The adherents of Stoicism were known as cold, hard men—cold even to cruelty, hard even before want and woe. And the Platonist, purest of all, only dreamed of virtue, and, with a high ideal before him, was practically a cypher!

Now, go back eighteen hundred years and start with Christ's gospel, as it enters on its historic path. It enthrones and enshrines itself in a few humble, unlearned men, and their lives burn with its beauty and end with voluntary martyrdom. Follow the gospel of Christ as it marches down the centuries, and what do you see? Hard hearts, cruel with crime, that no human love could soften, no human power impress, are broken into contrition and love. Weak women, timid and trembling, are fortified by it to dare the scourge, the rack, the stake, the cross, or face without fear the fierce Numidian lion in the arena. Millions of martyrs, under no compulsion but the sweet constraint of love, welcome the agonies of torture, and from all the grades of society come up to the coliseum and soak its sands with their blood, rather than utter one word to disown or dishonor Him whom, not having seen, they love.

The world can furnish no parallel to this! Men have died for a principle, and that principle an error; for a religious faith, and that faith a falsehood; but self-sacrifice so perfect, so pure and so repeated, is peculiar to the followers of Christ, and it has challenged the wonder and applause even of the enemies of Christ!

The teaching of Christ has been for eighteen centuries the leaven and the lever of society—the leaven to pervade, the lever to uplift. At first a handful of disciples in the humble homes of Palestine; then that handful flung by persecution broadcast over the surrounding countries, till from Jerusalem the gospel spread to Antioch and Rome and Alexandria and Constantinople. The cross of a crucified criminal at Calvary is the nucleus of a world's illumination and reformation! The fame of gospel triumphs spread beyond the fields of conflict, and as the lines of influence lengthened, and their circles reached round new centers of power and wickedness, in fear men cried out, "It is turning the world upside down!"

The little army of Jesus, with no badges or banners, no weapon but truth and no force but persuasion, in the face of fearful persecutions, grew mightier year by year. The blood of the martyrs was the seed of new churches; it fell like fertilizing dew on a barren soil. Met with violence, the followers of Christ used no violence; though they kept silence with respect to social sins and vices which had taken the form of institutions, yet they did not tolerate evils with which they forbore. The gospel overcame evil with good. First making the man anew, through each follower it reached out to grapple with corrupt society. Gathering strength, like volcanic fires beneath the surface, it heaved social life like an earthquake, bringing to the dust its palaces of iniquity in high places, and its thrones of regal wrong. Without a loud denunciation of pagan usages, it has gone nowhere except to march over ruins of those nine social evils, polygamy, infanticide, legalized prostitution, capricious divorce, bloody and brutal games, death and punishment by torture, unjust wars, caste and slavery. The pure heart and true conscience of believers were the channels through which Christ undertook to overturn existing wrong. And yet mark the results. Some of these evils ceased to be common practices and became secret sins; some disappeared entirely; some were borne with, as doomed and decaying; and to this day, wherever Christ, the divine Teacher, goes by his gospel, in proportion as that prevails, these corrupt social usages shrink like owls of the night before the growing glory of the day-dawn.

M. Guizot says that he himself was a rationalist in religion until he undertook the preparation for the press of an edition of Gibbon. The investigation necessary to prepare notes for the edition led him to accept Christianity as a system that could not be explained by purely human forces.

Look at English history! About fifty years before Christ's birth, Julius Cæsar landed at Deal only to meet a brood of barbarians living in huts, and half hiding in skins their painted bodies. About 600 years afterward Christianity's golden prow touched the sands of Britain's island beach. And after twelve centuries of conflict and conquest, we see a grand Christian nation, with scarce a remnant of pagan social sins, empress of the seas, mistress of the world, with a band of empire

POWER OF CHRIST'S TEACHING. 313

reaching round the globe, Christianizing India and civilizing the inexpressible Turk; in the wake of her vessels and the very path of her armies carrying a blessing to the nations!

Four hundred years have not passed since this continent was thrown open to civilization; yet to-day sixty millions of freemen are here gathered; from hill and vale Christian churches lift their spires. The gospel of Christ set foot on New England shores and took up its march across the continent, and where in its track do you find these nine social evils? Polygamy hides in a corner, farthest removed from the New England that cradled our American Protestantism; infanticide everywhere a concealed crime; legalized prostitution almost unknown; capricious divorce encouraged, for the most part, only in irreligious communities; bloody and brutal games to be seen only in subterranean holes; death and punishment by torture a relic of antiquity only—we never saw a rack, a cross, a hurdle; cruel wars, all wars, giving place to peaceful arbitration; caste unrecognized, and even slavery now no more existing among us.

For nearly a century the State and the Church seemed half asleep to the fact that human bondage cursed our land; but God, in the late civil conflict, which was the fruit of slavery, marshaled the forces of our nation against this the last of our great national wrongs—this relic of a barbarous and pagan past!

Christ's words are not only vital but vitalizing. We are prone to think there is little power in words without a voice, the magnetism of the man behind the speech. We think the world must be roused as Luther woke Germany, by the trumpet tongue. But the tongue that taught on Judean hills has been silent now for fifty generations, and still the gospel of Christ is the power of God unto salvation to every one that believeth. You read these words, and there is life in them—a soul in them speaks to your soul. You read the words of men, and you feel in rare cases that you are communing with master minds—you read Christ's, and you feel the thrill of the life of God.

Account for this inspiration if you can on any human theory! Who was it solved these problems of the race, brought life and immortality to light, taught man his origin, nature, interest and destiny! Who was he who reformed the soul and transformed society—who by his simple gospel still marches through the centuries with the tread and trophies of a conscious conqueror! Whose words are these that break hard hearts and yet heal broken hearts, that subdue the strong but nerve the weak, and to-day are turning the world upside down! Yes, mere words, with no magnetic voice to lend them power, no personal presence, yet before them vice and wrong, error in doctrine and evil in practice, tremble and totter and fall as before an earthquake.

Once again, what think you of Christ? Consider the teaching of Him who spake as never man spake. Surely the author of the Cosmos and of the Logos must be one and the same: for in both the Works of Creation and the Written Word we find the same inherent symmetry and beauty, grandeur and glory: the same marks of the infinite mind!

Full weight has never been given to the experimental proof, the witness of those who have subjected the gospel of Christ to that most decisive and conclusive of all tests, a personal trial. Somehow the teachings of Christ have found their way into the actual life of the world, to an extent wholly unequalled by those of any other person. The whole fabric of society is interwoven with them: they give shape to our laws and lives, our habits and customs, our ideas and ideals, our feelings and our faith. Our literature is so affected by Christ's teachings that one-half of it revolves about the cross, and two-thirds of it is permeated or modified by the influence of Christianity.

Henry Rogers supposed that suddenly and miraculously, on some given night, every verse and line of Holy Scripture should be blotted or bleached out of human literature, so that every copy of the word of God should become a blank book, and every quotation from it or paraphrase of it, wherever found, should disappear—and it was astonishing to find how vast the number of books that would be rendered worthless! Our poetry, history, oratory, philosophy, science, are all inseparably linked with the truths which Christ taught.

This supposition of Mr. Rogers suggests the kindred question which stirred Sir David Dalrymple to a strange task. At a Scotch dinner where he was present, the inquiry was raised whether if all copies of the New Testament had been burned before the end of the third century their contents could have been recovered from the writings of the first three centuries. Dalrymple's antiquarian mind naturally took up such a task, and in course of two months he found and indexed in the writings of the first three hundred years nearly every verse of the New Testament; and he was satisfied that a new search would discover the rest.

Julian the apostate, and other foes of our faith who tried to burn out from human history all marks of Christianity, tried in vain. God had wrapped the very language of this divine teacher about the thoughts and hearts of men, as the delicate nerves wrap round our veins and arteries; and human literature must be destroyed in order to destroy the Bible—yes, human society must fall into ruins, and human history be blotted out, before Christ and Christianity could be withdrawn from this world. To this grand fact it behooves us to give heed. There must be some divine essence, where you find divine attributes. Here is a gospel first taught by a Nazarene, of thirty years; and it has proved itself practically omniscient, revealing even the thoughts of the heart, practically omnipresent, manifesting its presence everywhere, and practically omnipotent, turning the world upside down. For every effect science and philosophy unite to demand a cause, an efficient and sufficient cause. And for this effect there is but one cause that is sufficient, viz: a divine force must be hidden in this gospel: the secret of its energy is both mysterious and miraculous, and God is in it. Volcanic heavings must be explained by volcanic fires, mountain waves must be traced to those mighty winds that sweep across great seas; the lightning's bolt that shivers and shatters the very pyramids, tells of electric batteries so vast that they can be formed only by masses of cloud that cover the whole sky. And when you see a gospel like this of Jesus, heaving the very world, moving the great souls of society, shattering the giant monuments of superstition and ancient error, you must look for the deep fires, the mighty breathings, the celestial energies of God. Some of us know that in the teaching of Jesus all these are to be found and felt, for we have found and felt them. To the proud, self-righteous pharisee it may still be a stumbling block; to the wise and self-sufficient scientist it may still be foolishness; but in the face of a scorn like that of the Jew and a sneer like that of the Greek, we are not ashamed of the gospel of Christ: for it is the power of God unto salvation.

HOW TO OBTAIN ANY BOOK IN THIS LIST. If your Bookseller does not have these books on hand you can obtain them **Promptly** and **Safely** by sending direct to the publisher, enclosing the price as marked in the list. Send money in postal note (to be had at any post office for 3 cents) or, if preferable, small amounts may be sent in postage stamps.

A CLASSIFIED LIST OF

BOOKS OF PRACTICAL WORTH

SELECTED FROM THE CATALOGUE
— OF —

FLEMING H. REVELL,

Publisher of Evangelical Literature,

148 AND 150 MADISON ST., CHICAGO.

Special Terms are offered on many of our publications when used in quantities for gratuitous circulation.

HELPS IN BIBLE STUDY.

Notes and Suggestions for Bible Readings. Twenty-first thousand. Compiled by S. R. BRIGGS and J. H. ELLIOTT. Large 12mo, 262 pages, with complete index, cloth, fine, $1.00; flexible cloth, traveler's edition, 75 cents; cheap edition, paper covers, 50 cents.

Acknowledged to be the very best help for Bible readings in print. Containing, in addition to twelve introductory chapters on plans and methods of Bible study and Bible Readings, over six hundred outlines of Bible readings by many of the most eminent Bible students of the day.

This is a book which every Bible student should possess. Those who conduct Bible readings will find it most suggestive.—*Christian Progress.*

Symbols and Systems in Bible Readings. By Rev. W. F. CRAFTS. 64 pp., 25 cents.

Giving a plan of Bible reading, with fifty verses definitely assigned for each day, the Bible being arranged with much labor in the order of its events. The entire symbolism of the Bible also explained concisely and clearly. 100 hints upon Bible markings and Bible readings are added.

A year of work upon such a system would yield rich harvests of Bible knowledge and spiritual experience.—*Sunday School World.*

F. H. REVELL, CHICAGO: 148 and 150 Madison Street.
New York: 148 and 150 Nassau Street.

HELPS IN BIBLE STUDY.

The True Tabernacle. A series of lectures on the Jewish Tabernacle and its typical signification. By GEORGE C. NEEDHAM; illustrated, cloth, neat, 75 cents.

C. H. M's Notes. By C. H. MCINTOSH. Genesis, 75 cents; Exodus, 75 cents; Leviticus, 75 cents; Numbers, 75 cents; Deuteronomy, 2 volumes, each, 75 cents. Complete set, in box, $4.50.

> The notes breathe a very sweet and reverential spirit, and the author shows wonderful insight into the heart of truth.—*Evangelist.*
>
> Mr. D. L. Moody says of these books: They have been to me a very key to the Scriptures.
>
> Major D. W. Whittle says: Under God they have blessed me more than any books, outside of the Bible itself, that I have ever read, and have led me to a love of the Bible that is proving an unfailing source of profit.

Life and Times of David, King of Israel; or, The Life of Faith Exemplified. By C. H. M. Third edition, revised, 12mo, 200 pp. Cloth, 60 cents.

The Gospel According to Moses, as seen in the Tabernacle and Its Various Services. By GEORGE ROGERS. New edition, enlarged 16mo, 124 pp. Paper, 50 cents; cloth, 75 cents.

> This work is specially commended as a most striking unfolding of the gospel in the old testament. An absorbingly interesting volume.
> No preacher or teacher should be ignorant of the truth which this small volume very simply but forcibly enunciates.—*The Record.*

Outline of the Books of the Bible. By Rev. J. H. BROOKES, D. D. Invaluable to the young student of the Bible as a First Lessons in the study of the Bible. 180 pp.; cloth, 50 cents; paper covers, 25 cents.

How to Study the Bible. By D. L. MOODY. A valuable little work which should be carefully studied by all who desire to *enjoy* the study of the Book of books. Cloth, flexible, 15 cents; paper, 10 cents.

Ruth, the Moabitess; or, Gleanings in the Book of Ruth. By HENRY MOORHOUSE. A characteristic series of Bible readings, full of suggestions and instruction. Neat 16mo, paper covers, 20 cents; cloth, gilt stamped, 40 cents.

> Contains many fresh and original remarks, all tending to practical usefulness; a capital bit of commenting on a favorite book.—*Spurgeon's Sword and Trowel.*

Bible Readings. By HENRY MOORHOUSE. A series of eleven sermons of comment and exposition, by one pre-eminently the man of one book—an incessant, intense, powerful student of the Bible. Neat 16mo, paper covers, 30 cents; cloth, gilt stamped, 60 cents.

The Date of Our Gospels. A critical argument and examination of evidences, particularly regarding their authenticity and authorship. By SAMUEL IVES CURTISS, D. D., Union Park Theological Seminary, Chicago. Square 16mo, neat, flexible cloth, 50 cents; paper edition, 25 cents.

> The argument is winnowed of superfluous words, and presents a luminous and brief case.—*New York Independent.*

F. H. REVELL, CHICAGO: 148 and 150 Madison Street.
NEW YORK: 146 and 150 Nassau Street.

HELPS IN BIBLE STUDY.

Current Discussions in Theology. By the Professors of Chicago Theological Seminary. Vol. I, cloth, 12mo, 248 pp., $1.00. Vol. II, 328 pp., cloth, $1.50. Vol. III, 360 pp., $1.50.

>There is nothing in our language of this kind. The American student has had to choose between the exhaustive and unremitting labors which are the price of first-hand knowledge, and reviews which rarely fail of being colored with partiality or prejudice. The volume before us is a helpful, fair and trustworthy statement of the present position and recent movements of theology.—*The Independent.*
>
>It may be safely said that from no one book in the English language can ministers gather so much recent information concerning the topics treated.—*Presbyterian Witness.*

A New Catechism. By Rev. J. T. HYDE. A manual of instruction for students and other thoughtful inquirers. Cloth, 12mo, $1.00.

Short Talks to Young Christians on the Evidences of Christianity. By Rev. C. O. BROWN. Cloth, neat, 168 pp., 50 cents; paper, 30 cents.

>Books that are really useful on the evidences of Christianity could almost be counted on one's fingers. One which is singled out from a host of others by its plain straight-forward sense is *Short Talks to Young Christians on the Evidences*, by Rev. C. O. Brown. This little work is systematic without being technical, chatty without being needlessly diffuse, and it is written in a style suitable for the reading of elder youth.—*Sunday School Times.*
>
>Practical and helpful, just the thing to put into the hands of the recent convert. They will richly repay perusal.—*Interior.*

The Life of Christ. By Rev. JAMES STALKER, M. A. *A new edition.* Introduction by Rev. GEORGE C. LORIMER, D. D. 166 pp., neat, cloth, 60 cents.

>This work is in truth a "*Multum in Parvo*," containing within small compass a vast amount of most helpful teaching, so admirably arranged that the reader gathers with remarkable definiteness the whole revealed record of the life-work of our Lord in a nutshell of space and with a minimum of study.

Christ and the Scriptures. By Rev. ADOLPH SAPHIR. Cloth, 16mo, neat, 75 cents.

>To all disciples of Jesus this work commends itself at once by its grasp of truth, its insight, the life in it, and its spiritual force.—*Christian Work.*
>
>In these days of doubt and hypercriticism such a volume breathing a spirit of earnest devotion, lifting the mind to a better conception of the immeasurable worth of the Person and the Word, and written too, by a son of Israel, cannot but be welcome and helpful.

Clifton Springs Bible Readings. Containing the Bible Reading, and addresses given at the Conference of Believers at Clifton Springs, N. Y., by Messrs. Brookes, Erdman, Whittle, Needham, Parsons, Clark, Marvin and others. Square 16mo, 144 pp., cloth, fine, 50 cents; paper covers, 25 cents.

F. H. REVELL, Chicago: 148 and 150 Madison Street. New York: 148 and 150 Nassau Street.

www.ingramcontent.com/pod-product-compliance
Lightning Source LLC
Chambersburg PA
CBHW030017240426
43672CB00007B/992